American Luthier

American Luthier

Carleen Hutchins

the Art and Science of the Violin

Quincy Whitney

ForeEdge

Lisa—
Music teachers
save souls!
Blessings—
Quincy

ForeEdge
An imprint of University Press of New England
www.upne.com

Manufactured in the United States of America
Designed by Eric M. Brooks
Typeset in Garamond Premier Pro by Passumpsic Publishing

Library of Congress Cataloging-in-Publication Data
Whitney, Quincy, 1952– author.
American luthier: Carleen Hutchins — the art
and science of the violin / Quincy Whitney.
pages cm
Includes bibliographical references and index.
ISBN 978-1-61168-592-3 (cloth) —
ISBN 978-1-61168-927-3 (ebook)
1. Hutchins, Carleen Maley. 2. Violin makers —
United States — Biography. I. Title.
ML424.H87W45 2016
787'.19092 — dc23 2015031538

5 4 3 2 1

To Eli

The key, the doorway, the house, and the view—
Such gifts of love, zeal, and patience from you!

Trifles make perfection; perfection is no trifle.

MICHELANGELO

Study the science of art. Study the art of science.
Develop your senses — especially learn how to see.
Realize that everything connects to everything else.

LEONARDO DA VINCI

Luthier

French word for violinmaker; originally,
a "maker of lutes," because he once made a whole
range of stringed instruments, both plucked as
the lute, and bowed as the violin.

—Yehudi Menuhin, *The Violin*, 1996

Fugue

(from the Latin, meaning "to chase")
A complex musical composition for three, six,
or as many as eight voices, in which the *exposition*
introduces a central theme followed by *episodes* in
which each voice enters at a different time, the voices
interweaving and chasing one another as if the
theme is flying around the scale.

The central musical motif is reversed in the
retrograde; overlapped in the *stretto*; suspended
in the *pedal point*; expanded in the *augmentation*;
repeated in a different pitch in the *sequence*;
inverted in the *inversion*. The fugue
ends in the *coda*.

Contents

Prelude: A Piazza in Cremona, xiii

EXPOSITION

1. Naturalist, 3

2. Teacher, 16

Intermezzo: Music — Sound and Sympathy, 20

RETROGRADE

3. Violist, 31

Intermezzo: History — Virtue, Virtuosity, and Strings, 41

4. Luthier, 45

Intermezzo: Anatomy — More Than the Sum of the Parts, 54

STRETTO

5. Scientist, 61

Intermezzo: Science — the Organ, Polyphony, and the Science of Sound, 70

6. Apprentice, 76

Intermezzo: Acoustics — Sound Waves and Sand Patterns, 85

PEDAL POINT

7. Musicmonger, 93

Intermezzo: Lutherie — a Spanish Lute Maker Settles in Cremona, 103

AUGMENTATION

8. Inventor, 111

Intermezzo: Consorts — da Vinci's Dream, 118

9. Author, 124

SEQUENCE

10. Catalyst, 135

Intermezzo: Collections — the Cabinet of Curiosities, 144

11. Editor, 150

12. Lecturer, 156

INVERSION

13. Fiddles and Guitars: Sympathetic Strings, 165

14. Fiddles in the Conservatory: England, Wales, Scotland, 171

15. Fiddles in the Bakery: Sweden, 180

Intermezzo: Innovation — Virtuosos and Inventors, 186

16. Fiddles in the Limelight: Virtuosos on the Vertical, 192

Intermezzo: Market — "Messiah" as Metaphor, 198

17. Fiddles on Exhibit: The Metropolitan Museum of Art, 207

18. Fiddles in the Palace: Russia, 215

19. Fiddling with Time: Cabin Fever, 223

20. Fiddles Live in Concert: The Hutchins Consort, 230

CODA

21. Fiddles on the Marquee: Returning to Ithaca, 239

Finale: Counterpoint, 245

Acknowledgments, 255

Notes, 259

Index, 283

Illustrations following page 108

Prelude ∫ A Piazza in Cremona

CREMONA, ITALY, OCTOBER 1997. Standing in Piazza Lodi, I felt a mixture of excitement and frustration at the realization that my husband Eli and I had clearly reached a dead-end. We had veered off the beaten path of an itinerary we had planned for an anniversary trip to Italy in order to take in the City of Violins, at the suggestion of Carleen Hutchins, whom I had met just a month before. We were now evidently quite lost.

I met Carleen because of a stranger sitting next to me at the New Hampshire Humanities Council annual dinner who, upon hearing that I was a *Boston Globe* arts reporter covering New Hampshire, said I should contact a violinmaker who summered up on Lake Winnipesaukee. Nevertheless, when I took up her lead, the most significant interview I ever conducted was almost the fish that got away. When I phoned Hutchins to ask for an interview, she turned me down flat. In fourteen years, I had never come across an artist, educator, historian, or scholar who did *not* want free publicity. I soon discovered that Carleen Hutchins seldom did the predictable thing. Taken aback by her refusal, I hung on the phone, contemplating my next move. Suddenly, Hutchins blurted out: "What's your angle?" No one had ever asked me about "my angle" before. With no time for a clever comeback, the first thing that came to mind was the truth — I told her I was fascinated by stories where science and art overlap. Bingo. The door opened. "That's exactly what I do," Hutchins said. "When do we talk?"

Two weeks after my feature appeared in the *Globe* in August 1997, Hutchins phoned to ask if I would consider writing her biography. Tired of weekly deadlines and intrigued by the idea of a larger project, I still wondered if everything she had told me could possibly be true, as her story seemed too remarkable to be real. Just a month later in October 1997, a serendipitous trip to Italy cast away all doubt. When Hutchins found out that my husband and I were going to Italy, she asked if we would mind visiting Cremona, "City of Violins" and the birthplace of Antonio Stradivari, as she was bent on tracking down an old friend who had moved his workshop — Maestro Francesco Bissolotti. "Bisso," as Carleen called him, was one of two master luthiers who in 1937 had founded the city's prestigious violinmaking school in honor of the two hundredth anniversary of Stradivari's death. Hutchins wanted to send him *Research Papers in Violin Acoustics 1975–1993*, the definitive collection she had just finished editing.

Now here we stood in Piazza Lodi. After hiking up the stairs to Bisso's abandoned workshop, which held no clue as to a forwarding address, we had reached an impasse. As we sat in our rental car, ready to pull away, two students crossed the piazza, one carrying what looked to be a violin case. I approached the student who had stopped at a pay phone on the edge of the piazza, and in my struggling Italian, I said, "Bissolotti."

"Bisso?" he said suddenly in broken English as he hung up the phone. "We have never met Maestro Bissolotti, but we have come to Cremona today to buy a viola!" The four of us meandered down a cobblestone street as if feeling our way in the dark, until two Japanese gentlemen appeared out of nowhere, asking, "Bisso?" We followed them to an archway leading to a small courtyard, through an open wrought iron gate, into a smaller courtyard, where we found ourselves pulling the knocker on an old door covered with peeling green paint.

We were ushered into the outer room of the workshop of "Bisso," a short man with a mustache and winning smile, who immediately began speaking Italian to the student bent on purchasing a viola. Bisso knew not a word of English, but when I presented a letter signed by Hutchins, his face lit up. He motioned for one of his apprentices, Lorenzo Cassi, to accompany us on a tour of the Palazzo Comunale. When I asked Lorenzo if he knew of Hutchins, he replied: "I have never met her, but we have read every paper she has ever written!"

To find the Collezione Civica in the Palazzo Comunale, one need only look for the tall bell tower in the heart of Cremona. Inside the galleries, glass display cases house the earliest known violin, made in 1566 by Andrea Amati — the undisputed father of the violin — along with a 1615 viola made by Amati's son Girolamo, a 1689 Giuseppe Guarneri violin, and a 1715 Stradivarius violin. On the day we visited, in the corridor just outside the violin galleries, we passed *From Tree to Violin*, a month-long exhibition created by the violinmaking school. Had we visited two weeks later, we would have missed it. The very last exhibit panel was devoted to Carleen Maley Hutchins.

Here in the City of Violins, keeping company with the most celebrated names in the violin world — all of them Italian men — was a living American *female* violinmaker, a woman who had taught herself acoustics by carving violins. I was immediately intrigued. Why had I never heard of this female luthier who had asked me to tell her story? In the midst of our conversations, Hutchins would get phone calls from luthiers in Australia or China, physicists and museum curators in England and Scotland, a dendrochronologist in Paris, a luthier in Belgium, members of the St. Petersburg Philharmonic in Russia, a conductor in California, a faculty member at Juilliard. It became clear Hutchins had developed an international community around violin acoustics and she had created a new family of violins —yet she seemed to be a hidden treasure.

On a personal level, I felt the call to write the story of a violinmaker long before I met Hutchins, owing to my fascination with the violin itself. I took violin lessons in the seventh grade, along with my twin sister. At year's end, she aced the recital, and I left the fiddle and music behind. By seeking out ways to describe music, the violin, and the violinmaker, I have been circling back to music itself, hovering over the same ground my sister knows so well, and thereby connecting with my past and my sister in the unique way that music leads us to places that we can touch in no other way.

As way leads on to way, Carleen, while pregnant with her first child, made her first viola out of curiosity. Shortly thereafter, serendipity in the form of an avid violist introduced Hutchins to the only American physicist experimenting with how to make a better viola. Then one day a composer knocked on her door and asked whether she would make a new violin family. One path led to the next and, once taken, could not be undone. In the process, Carleen Hutchins donned many different hats—naturalist, teacher, violist, luthier, scientist, mother, inventor, author, catalyst, editor, lecturer. Losing herself to her craft, she took on a new, different role every few years, sometimes simultaneously, layering her life with increasing complexity—like weaving new colors into a tapestry, or playing the variegated musical voices of a fugue.

One of the most complex of musical compositions, the fugue is as much a technique as a form characterized by the *introduction* or *exposition* of a central theme (the subject) and its response (the countersubject), which takes the form of various voices entering at different intervals, but in any order, each one treating the central theme in a different way. The *retrograde* reverses the musical motif—just as Hutchins first played the viola and then reversed her path, taking it apart to learn to make one. In the *stretto*, voices overlap, just as science and acoustics overlapped with lutherie. The musical motif is suspended in the *pedal point*, alternating between consonance and dissonance, very much like the tension of balancing a home life with a hobby fast becoming an obsession. The *augmentation* expands the motif, as Hutchins created a new family of eight violins, doubling the size of the string quartet, while sharing her research as an author.

The *sequence* repeats the theme at a different pitch, just as Hutchins contributed three more layers to her field: as the catalyst founding an international organization, as the editor of the definitive research papers in violin acoustics, and as an internationally renowned lecturer. The *inversion* turns the motif upside down, not unlike the way that Hutchins challenged the status quo and dared to introduce a new palette of sound into the classical music field — a theme and variations composed of the variegated stories of six violin octets.

Unlike luthiers before her, Hutchins did not hide or hoard her knowledge or her fiddles in order to build a lucrative violin market based on the shrewd control of supply and demand, as did the violin dealers Tarisio and Vuillaume. Instead she went in the opposite direction, publishing her research and sharing her instruments. As an arts patron, Hutchins sought out ways to make her violins available to players and scientists wherever she found there was interest — on her home turf and in England, Scotland, Wales, Sweden, Russia, and Iceland. The fugue ends in the *coda* — the denouement of the journey of Carleen Hutchins, and the success story of the only professional ensemble in the world performing on Hutchins violins, the group named for her — the Hutchins Consort of San Diego, California, founded in 2000.

In his book *Measure for Measure: A Musical History of Science*, Thomas Levenson deciphers an inner logic in the fugue:

> The lines speak to one another, variation succeeding variation to build an increasingly complex weave of all the elements. The melodies move in and out, until the pattern closes at the end, coming to rest on the original theme. As it unfolds, the piece creates an astoundingly vivid sense of an inevitable logic, combined with an exalting, soaring quality that evokes an older image, the sudden height of a gothic cathedral. It is an artistic effect

> born of the same aesthetic that animates the search for the ideal form in nature; Bach's "Great" fugue [Fantasia and Fugue in G minor, styled "The Great"] matches any of Newton's mathematical arguments in its logic and formal elegance.[1]

Likewise, there was an inevitability and inner logic to the life of one as single-minded as Carleen Hutchins, for whom her work soon became her life on so many levels—and spread her attention and her influence in so many diverse directions within her field.

Right or wrong, whether she could help herself or not, the violin was the central theme of Carleen's life. Her life fit inside the violin world, despite the fact that she was an unlikely outsider. Luthiers criticized her for "demystifying" their craft by bringing science into the workshop and giving away centuries-old secrets. Dealers objected to her public comparison of old and new violins and to her emphasis on acoustics rather than age, provenance, or labels. Some players loved the violin octet, but many more were confounded by anything outside the traditional stringed instrument or anything that might compete with the string quartet.

Conversely, Carleen Hutchins touched every corner of the violin world—the study of sound, music, and violinmaking; history and anatomy; science and violin acoustics; consorts; musicology; museum collections; virtuosos; and the violin market. Like the immutable parts of a fiddle working together to produce one marvelous sound, all these worlds connected to one another as the interlocking themes of the fugue played out in the life of Carleen Maley Hutchins.

On June 24, 1998, Carleen Hutchins was awarded the Honorary Fellowship of the Acoustical Society of America—its highest honor and the same commendation that had been conferred on her mentor, Frederick A. Saunders, in 1954. The ASA Citation credited Hutchins "for her unique role in combining the art of violin making with the science of acoustics." The physicist Gabriel Weinrich highlighted the characteristics that made this work possible.

> An undergraduate biology degree, followed by fifteen years of teaching at public and private schools in Manhattan and then staying home to raise small children, is surely not what most experts would recommend as

preparation for a brilliant career in acoustics and violin making. Yet that is exactly how Carleen Hutchins began, deciding in 1947 . . . to learn to make a viola as a hobby [then] offering her services to Saunders to make violins for his experiments, a collaboration that lasted fourteen years, and changed the face of violin acoustics.

Of the various requirements that define the essence of a scientist, the very first one may well be having no respect for authority. Indeed, this is nowhere more crucial than in the area of violin studies, dominated as it is by the major authority of deities such as Stradivarius, Guarnerius, Amati —all dead for more than 250 years; and of the minor authority of violin-making priests who lead the people in the adoration of those deities, scorning all attempts to inform this wonderful art . . . with any infusion of science. Only someone with Carleen's personality and talent could have invaded such a field with a true scientist's "show-me" attitude, and persisted in her efforts with incredible energy and scrupulous honesty for what is now the major part of a century.

Of course scientists do not exist in isolation. They need a community to provide the means to share results, hear criticism, see their labors repeated and their conclusions verified or disputed. Only someone with Carleen's personality and talent, finding . . . such a community was lacking, would have undertaken to create one. . . .

Another requirement for a true scientist is surely a willingness to do something that she does not know how to do. The story of the Violin Octet has been told . . . in articles in *Physics Today* and *Scientific American*. . . . The early articles made her famous in the scientific community far beyond acoustics. . . .

The idea of scaling is an old one. . . . Carleen's Violin Octet represents the first attempt to scale a family of instruments scientifically, by endowing them with the same acoustical properties, relative to their tuning, as the violin[,] . . . an abstract scientific concept formulated to satisfy a requirement that was first expressed to Carleen as a musical one.

It is possible that her most enduring technical legacy will be the quantification of plate tuning . . . introducing the old technique of Chladni patterns[,] . . . a technique that is both teachable and verifiable.

Like the old army recruiting poster of Uncle Sam pointing his finger straight at us, there she has . . . been, lovable and supremely command-

> ing, her sharp eyes drilling into our scientific souls with the message that "Violin acoustics needs YOU!" The response to that call has always been irresistible. Carleen Hutchins, we salute you.[2]

Carleen Hutchins died on August 7, 2009, at the age of ninety-eight. The next day the *New York Times* ran a half-page obituary with two photos. The *Strad* magazine featured articles on Hutchins in its November 2009 and 2010 issues.

Exposition

Portion of the fugue
that introduces a central
theme — the subject,
followed by episodes,
each voice entering at a
different time

Timothy A. Smith, "Anatomy of a Fugue"

1 ∫ *Naturalist*

Perhaps from birth, Carleen Maley Hutchins was destined to be a displaced rebel, influenced by the constellation of events and circumstances that happened more than a decade before she was born—the bittersweet story of true love betrayed. Given the fact that a child absorbs the energy around her, Carleen became a rebel long before she could talk, thanks to her father, Thomas Maley.

It may be far worse to inherit the wounds of our fathers than their sins. When his mother died from childbirth fever delivering her eleventh child, Thomas Maley was just fourteen. The task of providing for the family in Brooklyn, New York, suddenly fell to Thomas, the only surviving boy of three sons and the brother of seven sisters. Consequently, he never finished school and went to work in the stock market at age fourteen just to support the family. The loneliness and weight of responsibility bored a hole so deep, a wound so profound, in young Maley that he would not simply project the blame onto his closest family members; rather, he held it over them for a lifetime.

Thomas William Maley Jr. was born October 13, 1868, in Brooklyn. Grace Isabel Fletcher was born two years later on August 16, 1870, also in Brooklyn. Thomas and Grace fell in love in high school and planned to be married. But then around 1899, Thomas suddenly changed course, met another woman by the name of Nellie Reeves, and married her—leaving Grace shocked and stranded. Grace went off to Chicopee Falls, Massachusetts, to get secretarial training in order to earn a living, expecting to never see her old lover again. But Thomas Maley was full of surprises.

On May 29, 1902, Nellie Maley and her baby died in childbirth, perhaps of typhoid fever contracted via the extra milk given to her while she was pregnant, though the true cause of death was never known. Thomas went completely to pieces and moved in with his in-laws in Brooklyn, where he lived for seven years—in essence, adopting Mrs. Reeves as his own mother. Forever bereaved by Nellie's death and the loss of his education, Thomas would take himself off to Prospect Park with a set of Shakespeare and a Bible because someone had advised him that if he could read those two things, he would get a good education. Thomas had a good brain, was brilliant with figures, but was not so adept at managing his own life.

Perhaps it was the emotional displacement that Maley felt that inexplicably sent him back to his old sweetheart early in 1909. On May 10 of that year, Grace Fletcher married Thomas Maley in Brooklyn. Carleen never made sense of this turn of events and always wondered why her mother would take Thomas back after his betrayal so many years before. Though Carleen never fully understood it, she came to terms with it in the only way she knew how, by accepting an irreconcilable truth as fact, often explaining the puzzling circumstances of Thomas and Grace by concluding simply: "Somehow they were meant to be together. I don't know how or why."[1]

The newlyweds had lived in Brooklyn for less than a year when Thomas, ever the social climber, decided he wanted to move to Montclair, New Jersey, so he could play golf at the Montclair Golf Club. Thomas and Grace moved to 22 St. Luke's Place in Montclair, a dark, second-floor apartment opposite Hillside School and within walking distance of the trolley car that would take Thomas to the golf club. Carleen described her father as one who loved attention — "a darn good-looking ladies man." Into this state of affairs, just a year after the Maleys moved to Montclair, an only child was born on May 24, 1911, in Springfield, Massachusetts. When Grace discovered her baby was upside down in the womb and that a cesarean section might be necessary, a procedure that at that time often proved fatal, Grace returned to Springfield to give birth, in order to be attended by a surgeon she had met years before.

Though Grace stayed ten days in the Springfield hospital, her baby was never officially named. Years later, when Carleen tracked down her birth certificate, it read: "Blank Maley, female." Thomas had insisted that his daughter be named Carolyn, after the first girl born in the Maley family following their arrival on this side of the Atlantic — on a clipper ship that had been frozen in the St. Lawrence River. Grace insisted that her only daughter be named Carleen. The baby was never officially christened. Eventually, Carleen took the matter in hand, went to the Church of the Ascension, most likely in Springfield, and "got [her]self a birth certificate, a proper one, and baptized *Carleen*." The fact that Grace won the name battle is indicative of how important she was to Carleen and, in contrast, how dispassionately Carleen viewed her father. Even in the instance of her birth, displaced from her name and baptism, Carleen Maley was forever caught in the fray between disputing parents.

When the family first moved to Montclair, Thomas Maley was doing well economically, as he owned a successful hand-rolled cigar factory. He loved socializing with "high-class muckety-mucks" like the minister of Montclair's First Baptist Church, Harry Emerson Fosdick. In fact, Carleen did not remember seeing much of her father during this time, as he spent every weekend playing golf and socializing at the Montclair Golf Club. Occasionally, on weekends, Grace would take Carleen on the long trek to see her father—a half-mile walk to the trolley up Bloomfield Avenue to Verona, followed by another long walk uphill to get from the trolley to the golf course. In 1912, Thomas and Grace bought a newly built house on a corner lot near the edge of the woods, a four-story, brown stucco Dutch colonial at 112 Essex Avenue, on the corner of Frederick Street with a large empty lot next to it. For recreation, Thomas would practice driving golf balls across the fields and then get his daughter to chase them down and pick them up.

At this point, Thomas shocked Grace once again in a way that stung almost as much as his first betrayal. Still desperately in need of a mother figure, he persuaded Grace that it was their moral obligation to take in Nellie's parents indefinitely. Fifty years later, when placing markers on the Reeveses' graves, Thomas Maley described to the director of the Evergreen Cemetery the bizarre set of circumstances he had created with a matter-of-fact tone of normalcy: "I re-married and with my present wife we moved to Montclair where we maintained the old couple until their death."[2]

And so, in this way, Thomas passed his own sense of displacement on to Grace, demanding she live with the constant memory of his betrayal by asking her to accommodate Nellie's parents as if they were family. So Grace—and eventually Carleen—paid dearly for the void Thomas Maley felt all his life, a void that, at least in his daughter's eyes, he expressed in social insecurities, in sporadic bouts of being in and out of work, in the ways he pursued women, and in the ways he pushed his only child. "Father was always somewhat depressed and always groaning about the whole situation. I think Nellie's baby was a boy. My sense is father always wanted me to be a boy, was sure I should have been a boy, and always treated me like a boy."

Thomas Maley would dress Carleen in boy's clothes and then complain about her "play-acting." In addition, he discouraged his only daughter's insatiable curiosity, because it tended to shatter his sense of the order of things. Meanwhile Grace tried to make a lady of Carleen, brushing her long hair and letting it hang down the back of her white dress, adding a pink bow on Sundays. But the tomboy would run home, climb into her Indian costume and play in the tepee she had made of corn shucks, where she loved banging meat skewers into knives. At one point, Carleen had two chests of drawers — one full of boy's clothes and one full of girls' clothes.

With neither a brother nor a sister to occupy her days, Carleen befriended the outdoors. Across the street, in all directions, there was nothing but fields and woods. The yard at 112 Essex and the adjoining empty lot surrounded by woods became Carleen's oasis. In nature, she could escape the tension she felt for all her life between her mother and the Reeveses and distance herself from the constant directives of her father, who was always trying to get her to conform to his way of thinking.

Grace was on her own much of the time raising Carleen. On winter mornings, Thomas Maley would shake down the furnace and then fill it up again with coal before taking the train to New York, leaving Grace and Carleen to deal with Mr. and Mrs. Reeves. Eventually, Grandpa Reeves suffered dementia and went to a nursing home, but Grandma Reeves lived with the Maleys for the rest of her life, until Carleen was an adult making her own way in the world. Mrs. Reeves had a room on the second floor next to the bathroom, just down the hall from Carleen's room. Despite the fact that Grandma Reeves wanted to go to an old people's home, Thomas Maley insisted she stay in the house. Carleen recalled: "I never knew how my mother stood it. She and Mrs. Reeves hated each other. But father wanted her there in the house with us. He wouldn't let her go. My father was very self-centered — he just never grew beyond the age of fourteen, when his mother died."

Carleen played mostly with boys, often pretending to be soldiers. By the time she was four, she had put together her own soldier's uniform with wraparound leggings, a soldier's jacket, and a cavalry hat. Grace would "fix it" so Carleen and the boys could dig trenches in yard, so they could play soldiers and throw mud slugs at each other. Thomas had a fit about the grass being torn up. When Carleen was five or six, she met real soldiers returning from World War I who had been invited by her parents to come for Sunday dinner. The soldiers would give the soldier-girl the buttons off their collars, and Carleen collected them with enthusiasm. One soldier gave the five-year-old a toy bugle, a tin horn hitched with a button to the front of her uniform. Carleen loved that bugle with a passion and learned from one of the soldiers how to play it, until the day a wagon accident that almost killed Carleen smashed her prize possession.

Carleen failed at piano lessons, and piano lessons failed her; her teacher told her she had "wronged-shaped fingers." But Carleen loved music. Thomas Maley bought a special player piano with lots of classical music rolls. Upon returning home each day, he would put a new roll in the piano. Between his passion for music and the family singalongs with Thomas's five sisters who lived together nearby, Carleen heard music all the time.

The corner lot at Essex Avenue and Frederick Street offered an expansive vantage point from which to view everything. Carleen watched spellbound as builders constructed new houses all around and the surrounding woods and meadows disappeared. In 1917, at age six, she taught herself to whittle with a Boy Scout knife. She played on her own outdoors, pursuing her passion for making things or learning to play army bugle calls on a "real" bugle, given to her by the same neighbor who had given her a "good" tool set. "Oh, how I loved that bugle! I would stand at the kitchen door and blow that horn as loud as I could just so the neighbors would know I was around!"

By the time she turned eight years old, Carleen was eyeing nice scraps of wood in the building lots around her and then returning to pick them up once the workmen went home. She was either building things or taking them apart. When her parents gave her a Victrola, it proved to be too great a temptation. Carleen took apart the record player to see how it worked, then fixed the turntable as a wheel on the ground and made herself a little wagon out of the Victrola. "It couldn't carry my weight and still run but I made it go for a little while, but my family was upset because I tore up the Victrola!"

By age nine, encouraged by Grace in her love of animals and nature, Carleen began collecting things—moths and butterflies, rocks, leaves, pressed flowers, frogs, toads, and turtles. When the side yard turned from garden to baseball field, the backstop was set up against the house. When the balls would fly up and break the kitchen windows, Grace never objected, bent on encouraging Carleen to have her friends over to play. Thomas, on the other hand, became more possessive and controlling, wanting Carleen to play golf instead and forbidding her to have a pet because he did not want to be bothered with the mess. Carleen loved camping and doing things on her own. Grace got Carleen a "real" tent and helped her set up her own campsite in the side yard with a flagpole and a stone fireplace. "My father didn't think too much of that. I learned to make one-pot meals over a fire outdoors. I didn't know how lucky I was!"

In the third grade, because of overcrowding, Carleen was pushed ahead a grade. As a result, she was often at least a year younger than her peers. She soon found that golf could not hold a candle to the Girl Scouts. Even though Carleen was too young to join Girl Scouts, Grace went to bat for her daughter by inviting the local troop leader to host a meeting in their side yard. "They let me get in on some meetings when I was nine, and the older girls didn't like that. Then I got hold of a GS Handbook and looked at all the pictures of the badges, and that seemed like an exciting world!"

By the time she turned ten, in May 1921, Carleen was ripe for summer camp, and Grace allowed her to go to her first Girl Scout camp at Bear Mountain—a life-changing event for Carleen. "We had to go up the Hudson River on the Bear Mountain boat, then take a bus into the hills, to get to the back of Bear Mountain and Upper Twin Lake, a lake surrounded by hills. I just loved it there. After three weeks, I cried all the way home. Then I cried for another two weeks, and mother let me go back for another three!" Carleen was hooked on the Girl Scouts—and so was Grace. The next year, in the summer of 1922, when Camp Watchung was opened in the New York Palisades, a relief nurse was needed. Grace found a way to join her daughter at camp, by first volunteering as camp nurse, then later as camp dietician. With Mrs. Reeves home to care for Thomas, Grace was free to get away, and she joined her daughter each summer for the next seven years.

In the summer of 1923, Carleen was asked to be camp bugler. This was especially lucky, because things were not going well financially for her father. With the manufacture of machine-made cigars, the bottom fell out of the cigar business, and Thomas Maley had to declare bankruptcy. "We nearly lost the house and everything else. If the house hadn't been in my mother's name, we wouldn't have had it at all." For the next six years, Carleen paid for camp by bugling "Reveille," "Get the Flag up the Pole," all the meals, and "Rest Hour," but she kept forgetting the time. She struck a deal: if her friends would help her keep track of bugling, Carleen would cut their hair for free.

At this time, as Carleen was building things on her own, Grace marched up to school carrying bookcases and a birdhouse Carleen had made to argue the unlikely case that a girl could study woodworking in the 1920s. As a result, Carleen was enrolled in woodshop in the sixth grade. Carleen had little patience when things got in the way of chasing moths or climbing trees. At age twelve, when her long braids got tangled in the apple tree, she just cut them off. When Grace, as camp nurse, drove a truck into town and ran over a rattlesnake, Carleen took notice. "I skinned it and we ate it!"

In 1926, a new Girl Scout camp, Camp Madeleine Mulford, came into being when the state of New Jersey donated five thousand acres to save forests on Kittatinny Mountain, creating Stokes State Forest. This was a dream come true for a curious tomboy. By now, Girl Scout Director Mary Littlefield was well acquainted with the tomboy scout from Montclair. During the winter of 1926, Littlefield invited Carleen to accompany her on several occasions to visit the campsite to watch loggers from Bangor, Maine, fell massive hemlocks to build a woodsmen-type camp. Spellbound by this activity, Carleen wedged her way into the process until the loggers showed her how to cut and mark logs, eventually allowing her to take an ax and mark logs. After the camp was built the following summer, one logger stayed on — Old Man Williams, but campers called him Dutch.

Dutch taught Carleen primitive woodcraft: how to use an Indian crooked knife and a one-handled draw knife to carve ax handles; how to carve a canoe paddle from poplar; how to make snowshoes from an eight-foot strip of steam-bent hickory; and how to split brown ash to make baskets. When the damming of the man-made lake left a huge gum tree stump on shore, Carleen spent hours chipping away at it with an ax and chisel to make a gum tree drum that she cherished for the rest of her life. Before long, she was sharing her knowledge of the woods and woodcraft with campers and eventually became a camp counselor, leading nature hikes and teaching wilderness skills, including showing leaders how to make a pack basket.

By the time Carleen reached high school, woodshop had become a highlight of her school day; there she learned how to use lathes and all kinds of woodworking power tools — a band saw and a planer. From 1922 to 1929, she was always in the middle of one or two projects. She made a breadboard and breadbox, bookcases and bookends, and hollowed out a two-foot-long chunk of mahogany to make a model sailboat she named *The Stormy*

Peckerel. She made a twelve-foot canoe out of barrel staves, wood strips, and canvas, added a sail, and then took it on excursions up and down the lake at Camp Madeleine Mulford. Carleen learned skilled carpentry and cabinetwork, and eventually landed the job to do the finish work on two big trophy cases for Montclair High School.

In high school, Carleen traded her bugle for a trumpet, using her first bank account to buy a secondhand Conn trumpet for $50. She began taking lessons from the local piano tuner, who happened to play trumpet. Carleen loved to practice, soon outplayed all the boys, and became the solo trumpeter in both band and orchestra. "The boys hated me for it. I was never very popular with the gentlemen around me because I could usually do what they were doing only do it a little bit better, which has been a problem, I might add!"

Carleen gravitated to and excelled in science and technical courses. Her high school physics teacher decided she needed an extra project—her first introduction to acoustics. Carleen placed tuning forks over glass tubes of different lengths in order to demonstrate how the tuning forks would resonate with different-sized columns of air inside the glass tubes, thereby producing correspondingly different musical tones. By noticing which forks "fancied" which columns of air, Carleen learned about resonance and pitch. Carleen recalled: "This was my first introduction to air modes, which I didn't know at the time."

By the spring of 1927, Carleen was still just sixteen, but she had already worked two years as a camp counselor, getting paid as much as $50 for a summer. Mary Littlefield recommended that Carleen interview in New York City with the National Girl Scouts for a job at Camp Edith Macy, the National Girl Scout Training Camp in Briarcliff Manor, New York, teaching two- or three-week courses for Girl Scout leaders. Carleen was accepted, despite the fact that she was two years younger than most instructors.

In high school, Carleen's primary social outlet for interacting with her peers was sports. She played basketball, soccer, ice hockey, and field hockey. But when Carleen tried to bring friends home, Thomas Maley consistently sabotaged his daughter's efforts at making friends. Carleen recalled: "My father would make it impossible for them to come back by saying or doing something they didn't want him to do again. He was possessive and made it uncomfortable for anybody who got in the way. He did this every time."

More often than not, Carleen's memories of her father involved his attempts to get his own way. "My father did not like talking to me when my mother was there because she would interrupt him. So he would take me on nice long walks and talk my ears off about what he wanted to do, and what he wanted me to do. I let him pretty much do what he wanted and tell me what he wanted, and then I would pay no mind to it." Carleen rarely confronted her father about his past actions, largely out of deference to her mother. "I never talked to him about it. I just accepted what happened. My mother wouldn't let me talk to him. She was afraid we would fight and never speak to each other again, and that pretty near happened. Things never changed." Her intense loyalty to her mother sharpened over the years, especially as Carleen observed how Thomas treated Grace. "My father did not treat my mother well. If she hadn't cared about him, they would not have stayed together. He had a couple of ladies up the street, and that really infuriated me. My mother never let on she knew anything. There was never anything said, but I knew what was going on; you can't help it."

By the spring of 1928, Carleen had just turned seventeen and had finished high school, but Grace felt that her daughter was too young for college, so Carleen repeated her senior year at Montclair High. No longer displaced from her grade, Carleen now returned to old friends and felt more relaxed socially. "I got back into my second senior year with students I knew in the second grade and was really content." That summer, Carleen got a job working for the season as a food lieutenant at Camp Edith Macy. The experience further widened her horizons: "In the Girl Scouts, I met people who were passionate about what they did — folk dancing, arts and crafts, nature specialists, theater and dance specialists, plant ecology, and the geology of the Westchester fold. I got excited because these were experts teaching us."

In the process, Carleen met strong, independent women like Harriet Bartlett, Alice Wagener, and Edith Conant, director of Camp Edith Macy. It did not take Conant long to see that Carleen Maley had many skills and talents beyond that of a food lieutenant. When Conant spotted a copy of *The Life and Times of Leonardo da Vinci* on Carleen's shelf, she took an interest in the young woman and their conversations grew. Eventually, Edith asked Carleen to be her assistant. During that summer, on a two-week break between courses, Conant ventured north to Wolfeboro, New Hampshire, to her family home located on Lake Winnipesaukee, and invited Carleen to come along. Carleen would never forget the twelve-hour ride on rough back roads, bouncing wildly in the rumble seat of a Model T Ford roadster seated next to Girl Scout chum Julia Landis and freezing in the cold wind, with Edith Conant and Alice Wagener sitting up front. After such a jarring trip, arriving at a lake house in the New Hampshire woods was nirvana to Carleen. "I walked into the great big living room, sat down by the wood stove fireplace, was handed a bourbon and ginger and just melted. The next morning I got out and looked at the woods in this place. I'd never seen anything so beautiful in my life. I knew I belonged there."

Bereft of a good relationship with her father, Carleen was ripe to meet her first mentor, and it was logical that it would be a naturalist—Frank Lutz, curator of entomology at the Museum of Natural History. Lutz was an innovator in his field. He set up the first nature trail in America, studied insects in their natural habitats, and devised museum exhibits in natural outdoor settings.[3] When Carleen met Lutz in the spring or summer of 1928, he took a real interest in her work (raising, categorizing, and mounting moths) and invited Carleen to visit the museum so she could help him classify things, thus introducing her to its back rooms and galleries. Lutz urged Carleen to attend Cornell because of the exciting work of the legendary Cornell entomologists John Henry Comstock and Anna Botsford Comstock. Anna Botsford Comstock was most famous for being one of the first professors to take her students outdoors to study nature. Nevertheless, though she had begun teaching nature study at Cornell in 1897, she was still denied full professorship for two decades before she became the first female professor at Cornell in 1920.

In June 1929, when Carleen graduated from high school, she finished with A's in science and shop, and a string of B's and C's in language courses. As her father had never thought much of her study habits, Carleen, seated between her parents in a her white graduation dress, was as surprised as her father when she received the $500 Marjorie Bethel scholarship awarded to a well-rounded student. Hutchins recalled: "I was just doing things I wanted to do. When that scholarship came along, it kind of set me up."

Though Grace had assumed that Carleen would attend Wellesley and had already registered her there, Lutz had made an impression, and the die was cast. Carleen recalled many years later: "I still have a beautiful early book he gave me on butterflies and moths." In it, Lutz wrote a dedication that Carleen always cherished: "For Carleen, for her live interest in living things." In the fall of 1929, Carleen enrolled at Cornell. It seems somehow fitting that a pioneer like Carleen Hutchins took her formal education at the university known for its "great experiment," that of coeducation. In 1870, Jennie Spencer hoisted up her skirts and trudged up the hill to the college as the first woman to matriculate at Cornell. Three years later, Emma Sheffield Eastman became the first female graduate. At the time, many embraced the idea of "sex-sectarianism." Many Americans vehemently opposed coeducation out of fears that it would "feminize men, lead women astray from the path of 'true womanhood,' and create 'hard-minded' women."[4] Though Ezra Cornell and Andrew Dickson White opened Cornell University in 1868, it was not until 1872 that it became the first major eastern institution to admit women with men. In 1875, when the first women's dormitory, Sage College, was completed, it was an elegant building housing 120 women but remained the university's white elephant, because, despite the best of intentions toward inclusion, women students remained socially marginalized. Soon all women were required to live in Sage Hall. But, practically speaking, on campus, the sexes remained socially separate.

Carleen eventually became president of Sage Hall during her senior year. She described the clear "sex-sectarianism" she encountered as a freshman in 1929. "We got whistled at going across campus, yet no coeds were ever invited to the big house parties. It was considered a disgrace for a man in a fancy fraternity to be seen with a coed. Never mind, we had a beautiful time; we did all sorts of athletics instead!" Freshman year, Carleen took archery, crew, fencing, soccer, and was part of the rifle team. In her sophomore year, she dropped archery, picked up field hockey, and resumed fencing. She played field hockey for three years and fenced for four. The highlight of Carleen's collegiate athletic career was finishing as a fencing intercollegiate runner-up two years running, culminating in two matches played against the same New York City fencer who beat her twice "by a whisker—five touches to win and I took her 4–4 each time."

Cornell academics were not overwhelming for Carleen. But she quickly became restless when she discovered that entomologists could spend three months studying the insides of a grasshopper under a microscope, while biology majors were taking field trips. Meanwhile, in the spring of 1931, at the end of her sophomore year, Carleen was called in to see her adviser, a psychology professor concerned about her poor freshman aptitude tests. When he admitted he had not even looked at Carleen's academic record —all A's and B's—the discussion ended, and Carleen promptly switched advisers. Carleen switched her major to botany and zoology, returned to her passion for the natural classroom outdoors, and immediately signed up for every course in ornithology.

At this point, the academic field of ornithology did not yet exist—but it began in the 1930s at Cornell with Dr. Arthur A. Allen, a renowned birder who, after teaching ornithology in the Department of Zoology for four years, was appointed assistant professor of ornithology in the Department of Entomology. Thus, Allen became a one-person department that was called the Laboratory of Ornithology, a term assigned to Allen's endeavors to justify the space given to an ornithologist within a department devoted to the study of insects. Allen often took students out to Sapsucker Woods to make some of the first recordings of birdsong. By 1931, the department had purchased its newest recorder and recorded forty-one species of birds —the largest collection of birdsong in the world.

During the winter of 1931–32, ornithology lab researchers Allen and his associates Albert Brand and Paul Kellogg had been working to improve recording electronics. In the spring of 1932, their new parabolic recording system was ready—at the same time Carleen Hutchins began following Allen into the field, where they would set up a microphone in the woods. Hutchins recalled: "I was privileged to be one of the first students to work with Dr. Allen, who would just whistle and up would come a chickadee and sit on his nose."

Carleen gained much more from her field trips with Arthur Allen than a love of birding. She absorbed the way he taught, how he lectured and drew people in regardless of how much or how little they knew about his subject. Olin Sewall Pettingill, one of Allen's graduate students, described his mentor: "In his calm, unassuming yet persuasive way, he generated enthusiasm and encouragement. He was an unswerving optimist. His personal warmth made him easily approachable. He was never too busy or too tired to give me his undivided attention."[5]

During her junior and senior years, Carleen assumed several leadership roles in the Women's Student Government Association and the Women's Athletic Association Council. As a junior, she was elected to the Raven and Serpent, the junior honorary society. Carleen wanted to go to medical school and was conditionally accepted to Duke Medical School pending taking a few courses in chemistry and physics. But ultimately she decided against it, discouraged by those closest to her, who could see no reason why a woman would want to become a doctor. Carleen recalled: "I didn't have the courage to fight the whole system, and there wasn't any money in 1933 so that was that."

Carleen shifted to taking courses in education, with the idea that she could teach science. In her senior year, Carleen was one of twelve women elected to Mortar Board (senior honor society) and one of nine women elected to Penthama (senior honor athletic society). She narrowly missed making the Olympic fencing team. She was a member of Dot and Circle, the rifle team, and The Foil, the fencing society. Carleen was awarded the Women's Athletic Association "C," which was bestowed only on rising seniors who had been on eight athletic teams at Cornell. She also belonged to Alpha Xi Delta sorority and was a member of the Cornell Women's Musical Clubs, where she was one of two women who played trumpet in the small orchestra at Cornell; she also played in the band. By her senior year, Carleen would recall that not much had changed with respect to social relations between the sexes. The Cornell yearbook gives a sense of the solitary existence of a Cornell coed. The yearbook contains sixty pages featuring members of fraternity houses, while just one page is devoted to the Alpha Xi Delta sorority.

Carleen Maley graduated on Monday, June 19, 1933, in Cornell University's sixty-fifth annual commencement.

2 Teacher

Nature had always been Carleen's oasis and her buffer. Now, upon her graduation from Cornell, it provided her with a summer job that brought her to New Hampshire once again, followed by a fall internship at the Brooklyn Botanic Garden. In both contexts, Carleen was called upon to perform menial tasks that nonetheless, she knew, served a larger purpose. But in those tasks, she was grateful to find a sense of belonging as well.

In Wolfeboro, New Hampshire, by the summer of 1933, Edith Conant had determined that the only way to save her family's house on the shores of Winnipesaukee from being sold was to open it to guests — but who would help her make it go? Conant did not know another person as qualified in the skills of outdoor living, woodworking, and general self-reliance as Carleen Maley. As such, Carleen, with her can-do, "fix-it" mentality, quickly became the jack-of-all-trades manager of the "Inn." The first "official" year of the Conant guesthouse was 1933, as evidenced by the first page of the Conant "Inn" log book.[1] From June 29 to September 2, twenty-seven people stayed as guests at the Conant "Inn." Carleen recalled those days of keeping the Conant home afloat through hospitality and a lot of hard work: "I was the handyman; Julia was the dietician/supervisor. We had two cooks in the kitchen and used kerosene almost entirely for lamps, lighting, and cooking. We had a pump that I had to run every day to keep the water tank filled with water from the lake."[2] As hard as she worked, Carleen loved every minute, because she felt she was needed and she enjoyed her friendships with Edith and Julia.

After inn-keeping that summer, Carleen returned home to Montclair to live with her parents — and Grandma Reeves. When her Cornell adviser recommended Carleen to Stuart Gager, director of the Brooklyn Botanic Garden, even though there was no money for the job, Carleen jumped at the chance to work for the love of it. Each morning Carleen would take a train from Montclair to Brooklyn with her brown bag lunch in hand, a journey that took her two hours each way. "I was paying my own expenses and my own way to get there and back. But this was something to do because there were no jobs in 1933."

Carleen found herself doing the dirty work no one else wanted to do — tasks like washing scale bugs off of palm trees with a toothbrush while standing atop a twenty-foot ladder poised under a skylight. Still, her enthusiasm about nature was contagious. Whether she was gardening, working in the greenhouse propagating different kinds of cactus plants, filling packets with seeds for inner-city schoolchildren to plant in a community garden, spreading volcanic ash in the rock garden, or learning how to talk to large groups of students in the Japanese Garden, Carleen loved it all and communicated her fervor.

In the spring of 1934, Carol Preston, a Girl Scout chum teaching at a private school in Brooklyn, mentioned to Carleen that there was an opening for a science teacher. On Preston's recommendation, Carleen got her first paying job, teaching science at the Woodward School. With her first teaching job came the opportunity for Carleen to leave home. Jesse Dotterer, who had known Carleen through Alice Wagener and the Girl Scouts, lived on 10th Street in Manhattan with her mother and brother. They were glad to rent a room to Carleen.

The Woodward School was a progressive school. Consequently, when Carleen began as a teacher, she also returned to school and began taking education courses at Bank Street College of Education, working in a hands-on "laboratory" nursery school. She immediately identified with a progressive education because she had lived it. "My mother gave me the best progressive education I could have had — I was allowed to grow and learn on my own."

The Woodward School stood on high ground — a big, old brownstone complete with a widow's walk and a big yard perched high on a rise on Clinton Avenue in a fancy section of Brooklyn. True to form, almost the first thing Carleen did was to cause a commotion by encouraging the children to dig up the yard to plant lily and daffodil bulbs so they would come up in the spring — the way they did in the Botanic Garden. Even though she had to create nearly everything from scratch, Carleen could not have been happier. "I was teaching science in the corner of the skylight of the attic with almost no equipment. I had to improvise practically everything. I had all this experience at the Brooklyn Botanic Garden raising things, so I created a roof garden — a greenhouse up on the skylight by the roof. I felt completely at home there. I loved it."

Carleen applied the same principles of experiential learning to building a science and woodworking program at Woodward. When she eyed a room in the cellar that had a great big bench that filled the whole room, she asked the custodian if she could cut it in half to make room for a workshop. When he declined, Carleen appealed to and received approval from the head of the school and cut the bench in half, infuriating the custodian. "He didn't speak to me for quite a while, but when he saw the kids starting to use tools and make things, he was all for it." Eventually, Carleen ended up with the full endorsement of Miss Woodward, the director of the school, to build a science lab and a woodshop in the cellar.

In the summer of 1935, after her first year of teaching at the Woodward School, Carleen returned to innkeeping in New Hampshire. The guest list had risen to fifty-nine. Later that summer, as she got ready to return to teaching at Woodward, Carleen found her two friends urging her to join their ranks in renting an apartment. By the end of the season, Carleen had decided to move into an apartment with Edith Conant and Alice Wagener in a house at 43 West 9th Street. A bit cramped but comfortable, the three paid $50 a month for a small, first-floor apartment rented to them by Frank and Essie, a couple who lived downstairs in a basement apartment with their three grandchildren. Frank and Essie would do the cleaning, and Essie would cook dinner two to three times a week. Carleen recalled: "Essie was a good cook so we had a lot of help and it cost very little for the three of us to live there."

Carleen taught at the Woodward School for four years. Each summer, she returned to New Hampshire to run the Conant "Inn." The chores at the Inn gave rise to Carleen's reflections about teaching, the nature of motivation, and how to instill it in children who seem to lack imagination. The lessons she learned from innkeeping informed Carleen as she wrestled with how to express her own authority in the classroom. Despite long hours of lesson-planning for so many different grades, Carleen loved teaching at Woodward and wrote in a journal she kept from 1938 to 1939: "But I get such a thrill out of it all. I guess I was born to be a teacher and I love the children."[3] But, as time went on, logistics for running the Inn in Wolfeboro seemed to be getting more and more complicated and less enjoyable — not because of the surroundings but because of the social dance of figuring out relationships. The more she sensed difficulties with her friends at the "Inn," the more Carleen began to realize the importance of widening her social circle, but often she had to talk herself into taking initiative.

By the summer of 1939, her seventh summer in Wolfeboro, Carleen's frustration with Edith Conant seemed to escalate daily. "It is unbelievable to me what a fool I have been all these summers—to be taken in by the noble conception of sharing in a joint enterprise. The hardest part is that I was fooled because I cared and learned to love this place almost as if I too had grown up here." Occasionally, when Carleen's lapses might result in letting the water run out or in the clogging of the pipes, Edith would generally treat Carleen with kindness and a firm hand but sometimes with a sting Carleen did not understand. "That sting is foremost now the rosy cloud is vanishing. It has taken a long and painful time to finally realize that my only reason for being needed here is what can be gotten out of me."

Carleen began to ponder how to deal with hurt and to seek out other relationships. "Somehow no matter how many things I do, I can't shake off the hurt. That point of view has in it more real freedom than I ever had before—if I can take it. Will it be possible for me to throw off the mantle of wanting approval? Long enough to find someone to live with the rest of my life?" She needed to find new ways of working out her feelings. "Chopping wood used to take care of working out my excess feelings. But . . . resentment and hate don't work that way. I used to thrive on kindness and the almost suffocating love of my family. I used to think naively that I wasn't capable of jealousy or hatred, but that was only because I was never given cause to feel that way."

By late August, Carleen began to look within herself to manage her own emotions. She wrote in her journal: "When I haven't the sense to let well enough alone and say nothing—realizing that anything I would say only makes matters worse—I get so mad and smolder that anything said is taken in the wrong way. Someday maybe I'll learn who is boss around here."

Intermezzo

Music – Sound and Sympathy

Music occupies more areas of our brain than
language does — humans are a musical species.
— Oliver Sacks, *Musicophilia*

Imagine taking a Lilliputian journey that begins when you enter a cavernous arena. At one end you see undulating hills; the other end narrows to a tunnel. You enter the tunnel, overwhelmed by deepening darkness accompanied by a persistent wind. At the far end of the tunnel is an opening covered up by a membrane that is bulging back and forth like a billowing sail, moving in response to the wind at your back. It looks like a vibrating drum. When you dematerialize and pass through this membrane, you find a hammer pushing an anvil that pushes a stirrup. The stirrup rocks back and forth, revealing a small oval window behind which you hear liquid sloshing. Entering behind this window, you see a river running uphill through a canal that seems to defy gravity as it climbs upward. The wind at your back has now transformed into waves on the river passing over thousands of grassy reeds, vertical shoots popping up above the surface of the river, waving, vibrating, like some grand musical instrument composed of wind, river, and vibrating strings.

You have just followed the path of a sound wave as it enters an intricate and powerful "musical" instrument — the human ear — the mechanism that, in combination with the brain and the nervous system, determines how we hear sound and experience music. Actually, the reeds amount to 3,500 inner hair cells and the 12,000 outer hair cells that compose the *organ of Corti*, named for the scientist who discovered these tiny stringlike cells that sound waves play like the strings of a piano. But the human auditory mystery does not stop with the physics of motion — of vibrating air, strings, and liquid. Auditory perception is even more complicated than originally thought, for it involves the improvisational capabilities of the brain.[1]

Dutch artist M. C. Escher made famous the endless staircase — a classical visual paradox that tricks the eye into embarking on a geometrically impossible journey. In the 1960s, Roger N. Shepard of Bell Laboratories produced a rather remarkable acoustical counterpoint for this visual puzzle. When Shepard played a repeating sequence of computer-generated tones that moved up in an octave, listeners did not hear the pattern stop and start, but rather perceived that the pattern ascended endlessly in pitch. The reverse observation regarding descending pitch was also true. In fact, the latest research suggests that musical perception is related to the processing of speech, even the peculiarities of language and dialect, so that a native of England may perceive patterns differently from a native of Texas.[2] Further research has overturned long-held assumptions, like the idea that a musical passage has a universal identifiable quality regardless of the key in which it is played. Evidently, melody is not quite melody anymore. It turns out that the brain may actually reinterpret relations between tones transposed in another key, an idea as revolutionary as a visual shape changing when it shifts to a new location.[3]

There are sounds all around us. Seldom do we experience complete silence. Hearing is unique in that it involves at least two senses simultaneously. We can feel vibrations that we can neither see nor hear. We can also hear vibrations that we can neither see nor feel.

The pace at which something is moving back and forth is called the *speed of vibration*, otherwise known as *frequency*. The measure common in working with the speed of vibration is usually the number of times in one second that a moving object takes to move back and forth once or to complete one cycle. A pendulum that completes three cycles in one second is said to possess a frequency of 3 cycles per second—a very slow vibration, or frequency, slow enough for us to see and feel the vibration but not to hear it. How fast does a vibration have to be for us to hear it? Most people *feel* vibrations as slow as 1 cycle per second up to 300 cycles per second. We can *see* vibrations between 1 and about 8 or 10 cycles per second, a phenomenon that forms the basis for the invention of moving pictures.[4] We *hear* vibrations from about 16 to 20 cycles per second up to nearly 20,000 cycles per second. As animal life evolved over millions of years, the auditory window of human hearing became focused on those frequencies that enhanced survival, enabling early humans to hear low, soft footsteps or the breathing of predators and the high frequency of an advancing windstorm or the loud scream of a bird.[5]

Sound waves travel in all directions from a source, like the circular ripples on a pond when a stone is dropped or the way a candle flame lights up a room. When a pendulum moves back and forth, however, it possesses only one wave motion or frequency at a time, which are called *simple waves*. A tuning fork sends out simple waves. Practically all other sound sources, especially the human voice and musical instruments, send out multiple waves simultaneously and so are called *complex waves*.

The different frequencies composing complex waves come from the different ways that a string, bar, or the air inside a tube vibrate at the same time. These different ways of vibrating are referred to as *modes*.

If you tied one end of a clothesline to a post and held the other end in your hand and then swung it for a game of jump rope, you would create one moving loop with a still point at each end. These still points of no motion—the post and your hand—are referred to as *nodal points* or *nodes*. If you turned your hand faster and pulled tighter on the rope, you could create two sections instead of one, with three still points, one at each end and one in the middle. By moving your hand even faster—three or four times as fast—you could make the rope move in three or four sections. Each section is a *mode of vibration*. The jump rope is an easy way to visualize different modes of vibration of a sound wave referred to as *overtones*. The rope going around in one, undivided piece demonstrates the *fundamental vibration* or *mode*—a specific sound at a specific frequency. The rope in two sections illustrates the *second mode*, or a vibration that is moving twice as fast as that of the fundamental. The rope in three sections is moving three times as fast as the fundamental, representing the *third mode*.

In a musical sound, many modes are vibrating at the same time. The quality of a musical instrument depends on the presence or absence of certain modes of vibration. The strength of each mode, combined with the time it starts and stops producing a particular sound composes the *tone color* of an instrument. Though there are actually hundreds of modes that make up a given sound, useful measurement of them does not go beyond the first ten or so. The study of modes and how they are produced in different musical instruments constitutes the field of musical acoustics.

As the human ear is sensitive to even small changes in the quality of sound, we are just beginning to understand why some people like some sounds and not others. Many eons ago humans discovered the pleasure of music, perhaps because they needed it as much as wanted it. Documentation of the earliest known flute, found in a cave near the town of Nova Gorcia,

Slovenia, in southeastern Europe, dates to being made forty-five thousand years ago by Neanderthals. Paleontologists have found some painted caves in southern France, dated to fifteen thousand years ago, in which markings on the walls correspond to distinct pitch and resonance patterns, suggesting that the cave itself was a resonating chamber — a musical cave. Much of the auditory mystery and the magic of the musical instrument lies in the fact that we cannot visualize these separate modes of vibration occurring simultaneously. Unlike light that offers us visual patterns of sunlight and shadow on a sunny day, sound waves are like the wind, leaving no visual trace for us to follow — just the evidence of invisible but audible sound.

A small figurine "Marble Seated Harp Player" on display on the main floor of the Metropolitan Museum of Art, dated circa 2800–2700 BC, is one of the earliest representations of a musician.[6] It reminds us of the link between stringed instruments and antiquity and the common use among ancient and contemporary cultures of the secular musical instrument for a sacred purpose. This dual purpose of music as both secular and sacred has its roots in the very nature of sound in that it is both physical and metaphysical — or beyond the physical. The Greeks referred to both *musica practica* (music as physical sound) and *musica teorica* or *ars musica* (the philosophical, imaginative, and historical concept that music means more than itself). The harp player represents both types of music. In ancient cultures, the harp produced physical sound that was used for a metaphysical purpose.

Perhaps the earliest use of musical instruments across cultures was to create mood — a confluence of sensations related to the connections between mind, body, and spirit — for sacred ceremonies and rituals. In 1929, archaeologist Sir Leonard Woolley uncovered Sumerian harps judged to be circa 2600–2300 BC. In another instance, excavators uncovered a massive pyramidal temple circa 2100 BC and then dug through an eleven-foot-deep silt deposit and found evidence of the Great Flood from the times of Noah, circa 4000–3000 BC. They uncovered a mass grave of one queen — identified by the inscribed lapis lazuli seal laid upon her shoulder. A large number of skeletons laid in rows, side by side, as if asleep — musicians, soldiers, ladies-in-waiting following their divine master to her grave — suggests mass suicide caused by despair or a ritual sacrifice or a ceremonial drinking of poison. Remnants of two wooden harps indicated that two harpists had performed in the corner of the grave, accompanying their queen in death.[7]

Sacred and secular music have been intertwined throughout history. Over the centuries, perception of Western European music was influenced by two diametrically opposed viewpoints — Greek mythology and early Christendom, causing music to be perceived as many different — and sometimes contradictory — things. Embedded in the concept of music are the ideas of solace and comfort, dance, science, mathematics (number, interval, and ratio), nature, civilization and culture, virtue, harmony (celestial, bodily, and natural), beauty and aesthetics, allegory, symbol, metaphor, ideology, language, politics, and style.

One of the earliest perceptions of Western music was simultaneously scientific, mathematical, and spiritual, as expounded by the mystic mathematician Pythagoras (570 BC), the first known scientist and instrument maker. Some scholars say Pythagoras made major acoustical errors in his observation of blacksmith's hammers or weights hung from a string. But the spirit of his legend is true. His most important contribution may have been the use of the monochord to investigate musical ratios, thereby discovering the arithmetical nature of the musical scale — the numerical basis for acoustics.[8] The monochord is an instrument with just one string. When plucked, the open string vibrates at a particular frequency and produces a specific pitch. By holding the string down at the halfway point, the length of the string is halved, and, when plucked, produces a pitch an octave higher, as the string is then vibrating at twice the frequency of the original. This string can be halved again, and so on. In this way, the monochord served as both musical and scientific laboratory instrument to illustrate the mathematical properties of musical pitch. In a sense, a particular pitch could be "seen" by observing how the changing length of the string, when plucked, produced different musical pitches. But, philosophically, the monochord soon became much more than the simplest of stringed instruments; it became a metaphor for humankind to contemplate the universe. The fact that all simple numerical ratios could be visualized as sounds meant that proportion itself became visible whether it was expressed in the harmony of the spheres or in a "golden section" in architecture.[9] Because music lay at the center of this set of ratios, music remained of central importance.

The story of Orpheus reinforced the concept of music as physical sound with metaphysical power. Orpheus is most often depicted holding a *lira da braccio* or a lyre — the mythical instrument most like the modern violin. Legend had it that the music Orpheus played on this instrument was so sweet and powerful that it launched a ship; drew its crew away from the charms of the women of Lemnos, who had killed their husbands; fixed clashing rocks in their places; diminished the power of the Sirens; and lulled to sleep the dragon guarding the golden fleece.[10]

As musical concepts of science, number, and celestial harmony emerged simultaneously, stories of legendary musical figures, both secular and sacred, merged in the medieval narrative—tales of Isis, Apollo, Pythagoras, and Plato woven together with those of Adam, Moses, and David—so that each was a tale of music and music that was more than itself.[11] However, during the Dark Ages, musical practice remained distinctly separate from the idea of music. Under the auspices of Pope Gregory I, known as Saint Gregory (540–604), the only music in the early church was unaccompanied plainchant sung by the monks.

Nevertheless, musical curiosity proved resilient. Despite the fact that Augustine specifically condemned all music except voice, and no organ "officially" appeared in churches before the ninth century, organs were known in Byzantium and among the Moors.[12] In fact, in 757, the first organ arrived in Western Europe as a gift from the Byzantine emperor Constantine V to the Frankish king Pepin, described in various monastic chronicles as "an instrument never before seen in France."[13] All who saw this organ, including Pepin's son, Charlemagne, and his son Louis—viewed it as a mechanical marvel worth possessing. So in 826, when a Venetian priest named Georgius came to the court of King Louis, offering to manufacture an organ, records show there was great haste to build the first organ at a barbarian court "in the Byzantine style."[14] Beyond its musicality, the Byzantine organ demonstrated power and technological mastery. To possess an organ that could give forth a magnificent roar no man could create by himself was synonymous with displaying power and legitimacy.[15]

In 910, sacred and secular realms came together again when William the Pious, Duke of Aquitaine (875–918) surrendered his family monastery at the request of Abbot Berno, to found the first Benedictine Abbey of Cluny in Saône-et-Loire in Burgundy. Consecrated in 915, the monastery Cluny I housed twelve monks.[16] By 932, Odo, successor to Berno, received permission from Rome to spread Cluniac tradition.[17] Under the leadership of Odo of Cluny, this single monastery became a liturgical and political empire.

Austere Cluny edicts required the largest monastic community in Christendom to practice the liturgy with great uniformity—yet the church still banned musical instruments, as they were associated with pagan worship.[18] Eventually, however, Clement of Alexandria, among others, suggested that using a zither or lyre to accompany plainchant was acceptable because it was associated with King David the Psalmist, depicted in medieval and Renaissance art as a shepherd boy, warrior, or triumphant king, known by the harp or lyre he plays.[19]

Though the common assumption among scholars regarding the advent of stringed instruments in medieval Europe is that they arrived via the Moors in Spain, there may possibly have been one exception. The *organistrum*, or *symphonia*, later referred to as a *hurdy-gurdy*, may actually have developed directly from monastic life, as an improved monochord enabling a cantor or monk to learn to sing the liturgy *sine magistro*—without the help of a teacher.[20] In fact, around 942, Odo of Cluny wrote a Latin dissertation titled *Quomodo Organistrum Construatur* (Instructions for building an organistrum).[21]

In 1088, Cluny III was built on a twenty-five-acre campus. It had a massive basilica with two naves and a dozen chapels, six lantern belfries, and an interior measuring more than six hundred feet with a sanctuary bathed in the light from three hundred windows and choir stalls for more than three hundred monks. This one monastery spawned many others. At the height of its influence, the Cluniac order included more than 1,500 monasteries. The abbot of Cluny was second in power only to the pope himself.[22] Eventually, the organ gained favor with the Church and soon became a symbol of spiritual transcendence. From the tenth to the fifteenth centuries, the organ belonged to God.[23]

While musical instruments did not fare well within the Church at this time, they managed to survive in the secular realm outside the church—in the possession of minstrels and singing bards—the troubadours. The Moors are also credited with bringing the "Minnesang," the medieval courtly love-chant to Western Europe. Sacred and secular merged again in William IX, Duke of Aquitaine (1071–1126), troubadour, vernacular poet, composer, and knight who lead the Crusades of 1101.[24]

But by 1200, Cluniac religious fervor threatened not only the way of life but the very lives of the troubadours. The Church declared troubadour poetry subversive and offensive. Under the Inquisition, created in Toulouse to interrogate Cathars, courtly love—along with its lyrics and music—was found to be heresy. In fact, in 1209, Gui d'Ussel was coerced to promise an emissary of the pope that he would stop composing. The Church condemned the music of the troubadours and sent them packing along with their instruments. Though actual fighting occurred west of the Rhone, the antimusical tremor had a ripple effect across the south, forcing many troubadours into exile in Italy or Spain. Those who stayed sang no more or were forced to change their songs.[25]

Retrograde

Statement of
the motive's pitches
in reverse order

Timothy A. Smith, "Anatomy of a Fugue"

3 ∫ *Violist*

Although Carleen had enjoyed the pioneering aspect of the Woodward School, she was making just $1,200 a year. When Mary Gibson, a friend and teacher at Woodward, got in touch with the Brearley School and told Carleen about an opening for a science teacher, Carleen had to take it seriously, despite her loyalty to Woodward. When Brearley, a posh private school located in the Upper East Side of Manhattan, offered her $1,500 a year, she decided to take the job of teaching science to the first four grades.

Just a week later, Carleen's thoughts suddenly turned away from Brearley to the shores of Lake Winnipesaukee, as New England turned upside down. On September 21, on a most unlikely sunny day boasting magnificent blue skies, the massive hurricane of 1938—undetected and unnamed—traveled six hundred miles up the Eastern Seaboard in just seven hours without forecasters ever mentioning the word *hurricane*. The next morning, seven hundred homes perched on the Rhode Island shoreline were swept out to sea. New Hampshire was said to have lost half of its white pines, as the entire region was carved anew and remapped. Carleen later learned that the pine forest surrounding the Conant estate had been overturned, tree trunks broken like matchsticks.

Meanwhile, timing could not have been better for Carleen Maley to step into the Brearley School—at a time when the legendary Millicent Carey McIntosh commanded the post of head of the school. Though a daughter of privilege, "Mrs. Mac" took on the values of her own mother, who had been a member of the first class of Bryn Mawr in 1885, a Baltimore Friends Meeting minister, and a suffragette fighting for prison reform and racial equality.

Since opening its doors in 1884, Brearley—an inconspicuous twelve-story building located at East 83rd Street in Manhattan overlooking the East River—had garnered the reputation of serving the most advantaged students and daughters of celebrities.[1] The class of 1938 went on to study at Barnard, Bennington, Goucher, Radcliffe, Smith, Wellesley, Bryn Mawr, and Vassar. Regardless of such clientele, Mrs. Mac challenged assumptions, broke down barriers, and often did the unexpected, forging her own style of open-ended leadership based on Quaker sensibilities of tolerance and moderation, common sense, and building a community that discounted issues of class or status.[2]

Mrs. Mac had a gift for demonstrating in her life and her work the fact that common sense and compassion were to be valued and that confidence came from breaking down big tasks into smaller ones. Into this mix walked a young Carleen Maley, wary of traditions set in a more structured environment but eager and excited to set up her own science laboratory for the first four grades in her Lower School science room — room 2D, a small classroom with two windows and a partial view of the East River. Using skills she had already mastered as a Girl Scout, Carleen designed and built a hands-on laboratory for fifteen young people working at benches with access to a soapstone sink, regular tools, and a sand table for lessons in geography and the formation of deltas and rivers. She built a three-tiered cage to keep chickens and placed it on a shelf over the windowsill, where she also kept cages for mice and guinea pigs. Her incubator held eighty-five eggs each spring. "We'd cut open an egg at every stage to see what was happening and they could watch the heartbeat and watch the whole chick develop."[3]

Amidst all the commotion of creating the science world at Brearley, it did not take Carleen long to realize that Brearley had a very active cross-curriculum music program. All third graders took piano lessons. A "musical rest" became central to the daily routine, and advanced students were given extra practice time. In addition, the entire music faculty was made available for lessons and practice sessions after lunch on Fridays. Under these fortuitous conditions, Carleen was not surprised to learn that several of her colleagues loved to play chamber music. One day Carleen opted to bring her trumpet along to a friend's apartment. It did not take long for her friends to point Carleen in another direction. "The trumpet is fine outdoors on the street but not in a New York apartment. How about trying a viola? We always need a viola!"

Baffled as she studied the parts for unfingered trumpet in her first glance at a Brandenburg Concerto, Carleen knew the music was beyond her. But she plowed ahead, borrowing a big eighteen-inch viola from the school closet. Marie Bond, a student at Juilliard who was teaching violin at Brearley first taught Carleen how to play the viola. Within a month or so, Carleen could hold at least one note per measure in an "easy Mozart quartet." This was Carleen's first chamber music experience. The group played at the home of Bernice Hess, on St. Mark's Place, near the Bowery, with Hess playing cello; Dee Smith, second violin; and Carleen on viola, led by Marie Bond, first violin. Carleen recalled: "Those were lovely experiences together because we were all struggling and being patient with each other. They were particularly patient with me as I started to try and play the viola."

Eventually, Carleen found the school's big viola too much to handle and got up the courage to go to Wurlitzer's, where she purchased a smaller, factory-built Hornsteiner viola for $75. Though she was delighted with it at the time, she later realized that it had a very poor tone quality and was quite hard to play. However, she kept at it for a few years, thanks to the efforts of Marie Bond. When asked about the challenge of switching from trumpet to a stringed instrument, Carleen's response was classically simple: "The viola is the same pitch as the trumpet and I wanted to play music. The *sound* is everything!"

At the end of her first year at Brearley, Carleen was still seeking the approval of authority figures, baffled by her own self-doubt. On July 9, 1939, Carleen recorded in her journal: "Somehow I have a childish feeling about the person I work for — expecting her to be interested in my problems, wanting her to listen to my critical evaluation of what is going on as I see it, wanting her to like me."[4]

The summer of 1939, Carleen returned to Wolfeboro to help with the Conant guesthouse. But by late August, she had also grown muddled and frustrated about innkeeping, because her friendship with Edith Conant was wearing thin. With the added concern of her mother's health problems, Carleen pulled away from the Conant place, and returned home to live — only to discover that it was not easy to go home again. In early September, Carleen wrote in her journal: "My desire to get home started to turn to its usual channels of bewilderment and dissatisfaction at having to fit back again into the place fixed for me. . . . Mother looks tired and worried but full of life. . . . Dad is the same — golf and business and his mind full of jobs around the house that he has saved up for me to do!"

As she returned for her second year at Brearley, personal frustrations about the summer dissipated as Carleen took to teaching with growing confidence. On October 14, 1939, she wrote: "School is amazingly pleasant. After a few bits of the old feeling left over from last June I have somehow gotten into the swing of things. Being left alone to work as I see fit seems now to be in the nature of a compliment rather than stony isolation because nobody was interested in what I was doing. Whether they are interested or not doesn't seem to matter."

Carleen soon put her hands-on learning philosophy to work. Grade 1 cared for the two ducks that Carleen kept in the classroom. Grade 2 planted different bulbs and experimented with plants. In one six-week unit, Carleen created a saltwater aquarium housing starfish, a hermit crab, sea urchins, sea anemones, mussels, snails, a sea cucumber and lots of sea lettuce, a place where students observed how a starfish eats an oyster! Grade 3 made dye from bark and leaves; grew food plants like corn, beans, oats, and rye; experimented with water and sand to see how a river valley is made; and made candles from bayberries. Grade 4 experimented with magnets and learned how to make electromagnets, compasses, and thermometers. Carleen also created an observational beehive.[5] Mrs. Mac later fondly recalled how Carleen Maley dramatically changed science instruction at Brearley: "Sex instruction went into high gear. Grades 1 and 2 increased the scope of their animal husbandry. Baby rabbits, mice and hamsters were born in homerooms, tended with loving care by rapturous children."[6]

Carleen's teaching experiments often spilled out into the hallways and the rest of the school and carried with them their own kind of celebrity. During a unit on Indians, Carleen brought the wild into the classroom, taking third graders to buy buffalo meat at Fulton Market downtown, then roasting it on sticks over a fire built in the sand table—setting off the smoke alarm and causing another kind of alarm from the administration.[7] She and her students studying Holland tromped around the halls in wooden shoes. For a New York City unit, she and her students painted the East River on the floor—until some pupils, including the Rockefeller kids, discovered that the blue paint was nice and slippery so began sliding in it. Carleen soon got an urgent message from one nanny saying, "Stop that!"

The summer of 1939 was the last summer of the Conant "Inn." Meanwhile, Billy Conant, one of Edith's brothers who had been in the air force and stationed in Paris, had retired and came often to stay at the family home in Mirror Lake. In that proximity, he became acutely aware of the central role Carleen had played in keeping the guesthouse afloat. Nevertheless, most of the Conant family had not appreciated the innkeeping efforts. When Edith found herself at odds with her family over this issue, she placed Carleen squarely in the middle by asking her friend to go to the house to claim some of Edith's possessions. Carleen recalled: "The fuss with the Conants over possessions was the worst — the way Edith let me down when she found herself at cross-purposes with her family. Somehow it was all a situation that was a bit too much for all of us."

Shortly thereafter, at the time of Edith's premature death, Billy inherited the whole camp — minus liens on the property that had helped another brother keep his job. Meanwhile, the 1938 hurricane had covered the Conant land with a messy conglomeration of uprooted pines spewed around like giant broken matchsticks. Carleen recalled: "I can't remember if I spoke to Billy or if Billy came to me, but I don't think he wanted all that land because all the trees were down. He knew how much work I had put in to run the place during hard times — lugging coal, and ice, and keeping the kerosene lights lit." In 1940, Billy Conant offered Carleen the chance to buy 150 feet of shorefront at $7 a foot. "A thousand dollars!" she later remembered. "It was all I had to my name."

But she took the gamble. During her summers in New Hampshire, Carleen had become good friends with Harriet Bartlett. They had climbed mountains and talked about the idea of buying a piece of land together, so at first they jointly shared a small house on the southern acre of the Conant's property that Billy had sold to Carleen. In the summer of 1941, Carleen met a lumberman, Eric Correau, who agreed to come and help get the land cleared up. Correau showed Carleen how to pull a two-person cross-saw. For two weeks he and Carleen worked on cutting up the big trees, some of them as large as two feet in diameter with trunks thirty to forty feet long, then transporting them to a sawmill to be cut into sizes for framing a house. To build the house, Carleen hired Fred Varney. When Varney gave Carleen the job of cutting and squaring forty-eight pieces of 2 x 6's with a cross-cut band saw, she completed the task in one morning, thereby earning her a spot on the crew.[8] Carleen worked all summer on her new house.

It was also during the summer of 1941 that Carleen met Morton Hutchins. Clarence Joyce had married the oldest Conant daughter — Ruth Conant, Edith's only sister. Joyce wanted to take trips north to places in New England, as well as stay at his family's lake house, and he did not like to drive. Because Mort worked for Joyce as a chemist at a color laboratory in Cambridge, Massachusetts, Joyce asked him to be his driver. At the camp, which still had no electricity, Mort would spend most of the time in the living room while Carleen was in and out of the kitchen, cleaning and filling the kerosene lamps, or was outside with the wheelbarrow, shovel, hoe, and rake, hauling sawdust-covered blocks of ice to fill the iceboxes. "One day I was sitting beside the pump trying to get things going and Mort came and helped me. We got to talking and found we enjoyed each other and things went on from there."[9]

Once the summer came to an end, Carleen and Mort did not see much of each other at first. Mort was working for Dupont in Leominster, Massachusetts, and Carleen returned to Brearley. Then Mort got transferred to a plant in Arlington, New Jersey — the last stop on the train from Montclair to New York. As he had a car and could drive around, he and Carleen began doing things together. Carleen recalled: "One winter we went outdoor camping and cooked ourselves a very fine meal over a fireplace in the snow which was kind of fun."

The summer of 1942, the cabin was just barely livable, and Carleen spent her first full season there with Harriet Bartlett. Mort helped Carleen with a good deal of the finish work on the house over the next few years. Carleen hand-planed all the pine floor boards and took great pride in the sheer joy of owning her own lake cabin in the New Hampshire woods. At the same time, she also began to realize that, at age thirty-one, she wanted more than a job and a house. But even though building the lake cabin had empowered her, Carleen floundered about a new job offer and the most important relationship in her life. In March 1943, she wrote:

> Several crossroads have been reached and I'm all of a piece confused about which way to turn.
>
> Mort has asked me to marry him — at long last — and I've wanted it. Facing all the changes it will mean — especially with the family — is another matter. Mom and Dad say all right if I am sure it is what I want. But they are both concerned over the stuttering and what it may indicate for our children. Also I'm sure they secretly would want someone more outstanding as a person than Mort seems to be. Maybe that is what is weighing me down, too. But there is so much about Mort that I love — and I know he loves me. I have never yet seen him in a situation that he couldn't cope with. Somehow whenever we start to work things out together we

both get a lift from it. Even cutting down the old pear tree yesterday was exciting although there were several low spots. We each work at a different tempo—and therein will lie our greatest adjustments.

Mort has just called to say he has his grandmother's ring. We'll go to Jensen's Friday to see about having it reset.

I'm sure we have something together that will carry us over the inevitable bumps or adjustments and all.[10]

On June 6, 1943, two years after they had met, Carleen Maley married Morton Hutchins in the yard at 112 Essex. Carleen shared two memories about that day—her fancy, white satin wedding dress and the delays before the ceremony. While staring at the classic professional wedding portrait sitting on her bureau, Carleen explained: "My mother had always wanted me to go to Wellesley because she wanted me to be a lady. That lady tried so hard to make me a pretty girl. I remember she took me to Bachrach's in New York. That picture of me in my wedding dress—she really did it that time!" Carleen and her mother had planned a wedding ceremony at home and a party in the yard with twenty-five to thirty people. Memories not only embellish events, they sometimes winnow things down to their essence. Carleen recalled: "The morning of my wedding, it was muddy and I remember I was weeding the radishes. Mort was an hour late; the minister was an hour late; mother was miserable. Everyone was late due to the train. Lots of Brearley friends in the yard, where the radishes looked great!"[11] Carleen and Mort found an apartment on the top floor of an old brownstone in Manhattan on West 12th Street, nearby St. Vincent's Hospital.

During the summer of 1943, Carleen debated whether to leave Brearley for a new opportunity as assistant director of New York Public School 33, a referral from a Cornell crony, Adele Franklin. Brearley meant security, friends, a pension, music, and long vacations. The city school job offered little security beyond salary, no pension, and new challenges in an executive job. As she debated with herself in her journal, Carleen wrote: "Father says to take it. Mother hates to commit herself. . . . In the meantime the viola is wonderful—even if poor Johnnie howls when I play!"[12]

In the end, the challenge to craft her own version of John Dewey's philosophy of interactive education in an entire school proved alluring, so Carleen asked for a leave of absence from Brearley. Located on 9th Avenue at 28th Street in the Chelsea section of Manhattan, P.S. 33, a brownstone originally built in 1856, and added on to in 1874, housed nearly eight hundred students, kindergarten through junior high, with thirty to forty to a classroom. When the two sections of the building were joined, the roof was never properly aligned, so it leaked. "They never quite fixed the roof, so we had buckets all over the floor."[13] But that was just the tip of iceberg. Carleen found herself in the middle of a two-tiered system of management. Though Ruth Harding was the principal of the school, she had not hired Carleen. Adele Franklin, director of the all-day neighborhood school program, had hired Carleen as assistant director. Carleen was commissioned to reduce classroom size by hiring part-time teachers to take a partial class each day and give them a hands-on, out-of-classroom experience.

Carleen recalled that while the assistant principal seemed excited about the idea of hands-on learning, she "didn't know a darn thing about it. I did a lot of training of her as well as some students. Teachers hated me because I was interfering with what they were doing—they were upset to learn something new."[14] In one instance, on a field trip to the Museum of Natural History, one student brought along a hand-held xylophone Carleen had helped them build out of redwood scales. Carleen recalled: "He was one of the boys who was always in trouble—you know the one with imagination. He gets up in the middle of a discussion about sound and the motion of the spheres and says: 'I want to show you something we did with Miss Maley.' The discussion leader nearly dropped on the floor. She said: 'You mean, you made this?'"

Just as Carleen found herself ruffling the feathers of classroom teachers, she inevitably upset the apple cart of administration. When the principal suggested forming a committee to address the problem of first graders who could not read, Carleen, in the absence of her boss, took the bull by the horns. "I said, 'If you form another committee, you are just going around in circles.' I could hear the other teachers gasp. I said, 'You need someone to deal one-on-one with these kids to find out why they can't read and then give them a specialized program.'" The principal took her suggestion and eventually found funding from the Mental Hygiene Association to pay someone to do the job.[15]

The program proved successful and took the load off the teachers in the fourth and fifth grades. In fact, Carleen, in learning to lead by her own instincts, wrote with some pride at the end of the school year about the successes she had helped to institute at P.S. 33. In the *Brearley Bulletin*, April 1944, she described the unusual atmosphere of this public school, where the learning units were linked directly to the administration of the school itself.

> There is a teacher in charge of each Service Class, but the work is done by the children themselves. The Milk Service is run by the third grade who study milk in all its processes and get practice in arithmetic, bookkeeping and counting money, as well as assuming responsibility for delivering hundreds of bottles daily.
>
> The Post Office is usually managed by the fourth grade studying the westward expansion of this country based on the development of our postal system from the days of the Pony Express. . . . A fifth grade runs the Supply Service. Their studies take them to the origin and manufacture of articles from all over the world, which the school uses. A sixth grade is running the Library, studying . . . early peoples of the world, and the gradual growth of language and the printed word. . . . The Visual Instruction Service is managed by the sixth grade who learn to run and care for the machines. . . . With this goes a science program based on the study of light waves, lenses, projection machines and electricity.

Carleen ended her description by thanking Mrs. Mac for the leave of absence from Brearley and "supplying the extra push and courage that I needed to leave the good life at Brearley for these stimulating . . . somewhat hectic, waters."[16]

The next summer, Carleen and Mort returned to their cabin in New Hampshire, still sharing it with Harriet Bartlett. A few years later, Harriet bought some land next door.[17] Despite her feelings of success at P.S. 33, Carleen was still adjusting to her own passions as a newlywed learning to be a wife. During this time, summer days at the cabin consoled her spirit, while during the winter she continued to find a welcome escape in ensemble sessions, playing viola in quartets with her Brearley friends. Carleen's musical activities inevitably left her husband behind, because Mort was tone-deaf and unable to actively enjoy music. The cabin and music became increasingly important to Carleen as she tried to reconcile the contradictory feelings she had about how professional opportunities often clashed with personal challenges.

Upon leaving P.S. 33, several job possibilities opened up for Carleen—the directorship of the Mental Hygiene Association; a position as assistant principal in the New York City school system; and a job with the city and country school that would have led to being its director. Hutchins recalled: "There were at least five jobs that I would have loved to have taken. But I realized that I couldn't take any one of those jobs and stay married to Mort. He wasn't that kind of guy that would put up with that stuff. It would mean being away a lot, and it just wouldn't have worked out at all." Carleen recalled the vivid realization she had about Mort and marriage at the end of her first year at Chelsea: "I realized his way of thinking and mine were utterly different. Always have been. He's always thought in straight lines, and I think in circles—overlapping circles, endless ones—and it upsets him completely. I mean this is what we wanted to do. We just got married, and I had to fix my schedule so we could do it."[18]

Intermezzo

History – Virtue, Virtuosity, and Strings

I'm rich in gold and rich in tone;
if you lack virtue, leave me alone.
— Anonymous

These words inscribed above the keys of a 1540 spinetta equate personal virtue with musical virtuosity, a Renaissance ideal that has its roots centuries earlier — in the twelfth-century tradition of troubadours and aristocratic women who valued the ideals of Greek antiquity, chamber music, and especially stringed instruments. The delicate craftsmanship of this pentagon-shaped spinetta, which sits in the galleries of the Metropolitan Museum of Art, has its own story with its inlaid wood and mother-of-pearl, pierced-paper Gothic rose sound hole; inlaid dolphins; and carved figures of grotesques bracketing the keyboard.[1] Its delicate sound of vibrating strings echoed and paralleled the sound of a noblewoman singing. Though its maker remains anonymous, the spinet was commissioned for Eleanora delle Rovere, daughter of Isabella D'Este, "First Lady of the Renaissance."

One treatise from around 1200 recommends that women not only sing and recite poetry but welcome troubadours. Another urges women to play the psaltery, the *guiterne*, and the *citole*. A third recommends that a woman know how to play the psaltery, the *lire*, the *gigue*, the *rote*, and the *vielle*.[2] Though the core of their art form was poetry and song, the troubadours also often accompanied song with stringed instruments, beginning with the *vielle* and *lira da braccio*. But by 1200, exiled by the Church as pagans, the troubadours headed west to Spain, taking their plucked stringed instruments with them, falling in step alongside pilgrims venturing to the Santiago de Compostella — "St. James in the Field of Stars," the supposed resting place of the bones of St. James, brother of John.

In 1252, with the coronation of King Alphonse X, both pilgrims and troubadours found a haven in the realm of the benevolent king who ruled Castile and Leon until his death in 1284, merging sacred and secular in a way no one has done since. The king's cultural openness had a significant direct and indirect influence on medieval music and science, and fostered a cross-fertilization of cultures that eventually spurred the arrival of bowed stringed instruments in Western Europe. A devout Christian, Alfonso openly fostered the music of the troubadours. In fact, to express his own zeal as a Christian, Alfonso merged the secular songs of the troubadours known as *cantigas* with devout religious texts, the greatest example of which is the *Cantigas de Santa Maria*—one of the largest collections of secular music from the Middle Ages.[3] The elaborate illustrations of the *Cantigas* offer valuable clues about medieval instruments played in the court of Alfonso.

From his extensive studies in iconography, Roger Edward Blumberg concluded that *bowed* stringed instruments most likely originated from the *plucked* stringed instruments troubadours brought with them when they fled to Spain from southern France. Hundreds of images of musical instruments of the time, collected by Blumberg, reveal a stark and striking correspondence between the viols—and eventually, the violin, viola, and cello—and their bowless strummed counterparts. These images suggest the idea that one anonymous musician might have simply put a bow to a lute, mandolin, or guitar and inadvertently started the evolution to the violin, viola, and cello.[4]

Meanwhile, on a practical level, another major innovation transformed music—both sacred and secular—when French philosopher and mathematician Jean de Muris (1290–1351), invented a method of precise two-color musical notation in which black notes connoted time divided by three, and red notes connoted time divided by two. For the first time, a single note could indicate pitch, duration, and meter, allowing a composer an infinite range of possible note patterns to create an endless variety of multipart polyphonic musical compositions.[5] Composers now were able not only to experiment with sound; they could also manipulate time. De Muris was clear about the implications of his discovery: "What can be sung can also be written down. Moreover, there are many other new things latent in music which will appear altogether plausible to posterity."[6] The newfound ability to manipulate sound in time brought music out of the monastery and into the parlor, literally, personalizing musical performance and composition. Originality naturally spawned the development of new musical instruments.

The timing was right for a new musical instrument that superbly answered the desire for parlor music and personal musical expression—the portable organ developed by Henri Arnaut (1400–1466), a Dutch physician, astronomer, and organist to Philip the Good, Duke of Burgundy. Arnaut invented a small organ with a softer sound suitable for private chambers—the antithesis of the thundering bellows of Pepin's massive, church-bound organ.[7]

One of the most important influences on music and musical instruments in Renaissance Italy was Isabella D'Este (1474–1539), a musician, musical instrument collector, and Renaissance arts patron and ruler. By the age of sixteen, when she married a prince—Francesco Gonzaga III, Duke of Mantua—Isabella was versed in Latin and Greek, and could play the lute, sing, dance, and debate with her elders. When her husband died, Isabella, a leading patron of the arts, especially music, ruled the city on her own. In 1509, she became chief of state in Mantua.

Early on, Isabella became devoted to music and to playing stringed instruments. No one knows exactly when an anonymous maker developed the viol and the "chest of viols" family of different-sized viols. But as early as 1490, D'Este, in her passion for acquiring the newest stringed instruments, developed an extensive correspondence with the master luthier Lorenzo Gusnasco, known better as Lorenzo da Pavia, whose fame had spread all over Lombardy and Venice. Gusnasco made organs, organetti, harpsichords, spinettes, clavichords, lutes, citerns, viols, and most likely, *lira da braccio*. Early letters indicate that Isabella commissioned Lorenzo to make a *lira da braccio* and a special ebony-and-ivory lute. In 1495, Isabella ordered three "viole," which referred not to a fiddle or *lira da braccio* but to a new type of viol. Later references to Isabella's request for a "viola grande" imply that by then there were at least two different sizes of viols. By 1497, the Ferrarese painter Lorenzo Costa painted an altarpiece featuring two angel musicians playing viols.

By the end of the 1490s, Isabella had become an accomplished and versatile string player able to sing and play *vihuela de mano*, *lira da braccio*, viol, and keyboard instruments, strictly adhering to the edicts of Castiglione's famous treatise on the ideal courtier. In his *Book of the Courtier* (1528, 1561), Castiglione noted that wind instruments were unsuitable for a courtier—and even more so for a lady—because classical antiquity associated them with accompanying a prince into battle and Dionysiac erotic meanings, as well as plainly phallic associations.[8]

As Plato and Aristotle considered winds to be less noble than strings, a tradition that was carried through to the Renaissance, noblewomen like Isabella valued two Greek myths that pitted wind against strings: Apollo versus Pan and Apollo versus Marsyas, stories of epic battles prized by the nobility of the Quattrocento. In both contests, Apollo's lyre is deemed victorious. In the first battle, the ears of King Midas are turned to those of an ass for having considered Pan's pipes superior to the "intellectual" stringed instrument of Apollo. In the second myth, Pallas Athena invents the pipes, then discards them because her fellow gods ridicule her for her puffed cheeks. When Marsyas, the river god, takes up the pipes, thereby challenging Apollo to a musical contest, Apollo is victorious, while Marsyas is flayed alive. Isabella not only knew these myths, she valued them and even designed her studiolo around this theme by commissioning a series of paintings depicting this musical battle. In particular, two paintings in her studiolo, the *Allegory of the Virtues* and the *Allegory of the Vices* by Correggio, show Virtue with a lyre and Vice with a pipe.[9]

Prowess in music signified power for a Renaissance noblewoman like Isabella, and so music rapidly became her idée fixe, an essential part of her self-image. In a world that severely constricted a woman's chance for achievement and fame, Isabella developed her mastery of various musical instruments as a permissible way to excel that resulted in celebrity and personal distinction.[10]

But beyond the positive associations of stringed instruments with Greek antiquity, these instruments also inspired scientific interest in acoustics, particularly among music theorists like composer Franchinus Gaffurius and close friend Leonardo da Vinci, a virtuoso on the *lira da braccio*. Improvisation on stringed instruments provided an informal laboratory in which to explore acoustics, harmony, consonance, and dissonance. The *lira da braccio*, with its elegantly curved profile and its absence of frets, is viewed as one of the three main instruments from which the modern violin derived its form.[11]

4 ∫ *Luthier*

In September 1945, Carleen had newly returned to Brearley from her exhilarating experience at P.S. 33. The day before school began, she met Helen Rice, the newly appointed head of the Music Department. It was the quiet before the storm, the day before the return of students to Brearley, the perfect time to meet new faculty.

Helen Rice and Carleen Hutchins had much in common. Both had been passionate and versatile college athletes. Both loved music—though on considerably different levels of talent—and each had a deep appreciation for science. But Helen, ten years Carleen's senior, had been born into a social aristocracy Carleen had never known. The granddaughter of a Dartmouth organist and Handel Society oratorio singer on one side and a Columbia physics professor on the other, Helen lived her entire life at 15 West 67th Street, a grand-scale Manhattan apartment purchased by her father in 1902, when Helen was just one year old. The apartment had a large, two-story-high living room, ideal for recitals and chamber music. Her father was not only a passionate amateur cellist but also a lawyer in service of the arts; his clients included the Flonzaley and Kneisel Quartets. The Rice family summered at their nineteenth-century family farm in Stockbridge, Massachusetts, which served as a second chamber music venue for family and friends.

As her father invited scores of musicians to 67th Street and to Stockbridge for informal quartet and quintet concerts in which he played cello, Helen grew up in a music-infused world and began taking violin lessons at an early age. She would later recall the angst of being invited to perform with her father's quartets when she was just fourteen—a memory that served her well in her lifetime encouragement of young players, both amateur and professional. In 1945, when she assumed leadership at Brearley, Helen felt trepidation about stepping into the shoes of her predecessor, Berta Elsmith, whose impressive talents included a penchant for putting on operas. Nevertheless, Helen accepted the position at Brearley in hopes that her passion for chamber music would help her grow into the job.

Unbeknownst to Carleen, the first step in Helen's mind for making herself at home at Brearley was to engage the interest of Carleen Hutchins —in a barter of sorts, as, at the moment, back at Helen's farm in Stockbridge, there was a very pregnant sow about to deliver. Within minutes of meeting the lower grades science teacher, Helen had hatched a plan, pitched it to Carleen, and sealed the deal before the two had even finished their first lunch together.

"I understand you teach Science to the younger children and that you keep quite a lot of animals in your science lab," Helen began.

"Yes, I do," said Carleen.

"Would you by chance be interested in a baby pig for your science classes?"

"Of course, I'd love to have a baby pig but we'd better check to see if it's all right with the powers that be," said Carleen, clearly astonished.

Helen continued: "I will give you the pig—if you promise to come play viola with my students after school."[1]

What began as a most unlikely lunchtime bargain eventually led to what Helen Rice later declared was one of her favorite stories—the story of "Susie the Pig." Carleen kept a menagerie of animals in her lab, including guinea pigs, fish, and rabbits, even a rooster. Though Rice later admitted she had not taken their pact too seriously, it became an undeniable reality when Mrs. Mac approved and the sow delivered.

The children named the pig Susie Snowwhite—because she was "immaculate and looked as if she were walking on high white heels." Susie was soon shortened to "Sus" by the Latin Department—*sus* is the Latin word for *pig*—a nickname that stuck in more than one way. The Brearley housekeepers were so used to the great messes created by the animal farm in Carleen's science room that they demanded that the pig not be allowed to stay at the school over the weekend. Carleen promptly established Susie in an old chicken cage that had housed rabbits and set up the policy that any girl who wanted to take Susie home on a weekend had to produce a written invitation from her mother. One governess actually quit one family because she wouldn't stay with a family that had a pig in the kitchen. When there was no place for Susie on the weekend, Carleen brought her home to the apartment and horrified Mort. Carleen asked: "Who's going to know whether a pig is here or not?" After figuring that the tub was the best place to keep Susie, Mort offered some old pajamas to make her more comfortable. In the middle of the night, they were both awakened by the most awful screeches of a pig stuck in a sleeve while rooting in the pajamas!

When Carleen brought Susie home to visit at 112 Essex, the piglet romped with the family's two cocker spaniels, Kimmy and Johnny. Carleen recalled: "My mother was always patient and would take in a strange arrangement of livestock I had brought in over the years, but finally looked at me and said: 'You know, we've had snakes, turtles, alligators, rats, mice, frogs, but I never expected to have a pig in my living room!'"

Susie became quite a Brearley celebrity during the six weeks she visited, tearing up and down the second floor hallway, skidding a little and pirouetting like a lamb, or making her presence known by untying shoelaces and sashes of the Grade 3 girls as they did their arithmetic. Carleen would take Susie out to the basketball court on the pier facing the East River to run with the nursery school children playing in structures they built out of boxes and boards. Susie would squeal when the cardboard mess came tumbling down, aptly disturbing the seniors taking exams. Mostly Susie lived in 2J, the Lower School Science room, with the door shut, as her voice increased enormously.

By the time Susie had to return to the farm, Carleen was more than a couple months into her second stint at Brearley—and everything was different. Whereas she had once found the authority of Mrs. Mac inspiring, and the structure at Brearley effective, Carleen was now a different person, seeking autonomy and independence, and restless to earn the same respect at Brearley that she had known at the Chelsea School. "I had been practically running a whole school because both principal and assistants at P.S. 33 had let me make all sorts of decisions. . . . Back at Brearley, it was as if I'd gone back ten years to where I didn't know what I was doing," recalled Hutchins.[2]

Carleen could not fit herself back into the Brearley puzzle once she discovered that she would have no role in policy- or decision making and was instead assigned menial tasks like managing to get the Lower School children on the right bus. "When they rehired me at Brearley, they wanted what I could give but they didn't want me as a person. They liked my teaching style as long as I kept it under the program, contained but ladylike—not pioneerish." Consequently, Carleen needed a diversion from teaching. The chance to play in Helen's after-school string ensembles was a bonus at a time when she needed it most. She recollected: "Playing quartets was a release—good to be learning the music and learning to play viola. I had to do something creative or I'd never have gotten through it." By the spring of 1946, after-school chamber music sessions had expanded to "Brandenburg evenings" at Helen's apartment on West 67th Street. Helen would invite twenty or so friends over to her ample music room to play a few compositions for small orchestra—Bach's Third Brandenburg Concerto, or his Concerto for Two Violins and Orchestra in D Minor, or perhaps Handel's Concerti Grossi.

In February 1947, Carleen was pregnant and in even greater need of something to occupy her mind and hands besides teaching. By now Carleen had naturally befriended Petie Evans, the Brearley woodworking teacher. Petie's woodshop, an expansive high-ceilinged room overlooking the East River with windows boarded up to hold corkboards of tools soon became a second home for Carleen. Whenever Petie was absent, Carleen taught her woodworking classes. One day as she was examining more closely the $75 viola she had purchased from Wurlitzer's, Carleen decided to try to make one.

When Helen heard that Carleen was thinking of making a viola, she said: "Hutchie, if you ever make a viola, I'll eat my hat!" Clearly astonished by the idea, Helen tried to convince Carleen that the task was impossible for anyone untrained in the art of violinmaking. Hutchins recalled: "I agreed with her but decided I was going to try and make one anyway." Mort did everything to encourage Carleen in this endeavor, telling her: "There is more to life than dishes, diapers and, spinach." Carleen's uncle, William Fletcher, an amateur violinmaker, also tried to dissuade Carleen—but when she persisted, he recommended that Carleen and Mort pay a visit to Meisel Violinmaking located at 4 St. Marks Place in the Bowery. As Meisel had died, Mrs. Meisel gave Carleen a blueprint for a viola and the book *Violin-Making: As It Was, and Is* by Edward Heron-Allen. She also helped Carleen select the wood she would need to make her first viola.

Carleen read Heron-Allen avidly and tried to decipher his flowery language to make sense of the task ahead. With no other mentors, she returned to Wurlitzer's in hopes of finding someone who might take pity on someone trying to make a viola. At Wurlitzer's, she met John Fairfield, a friendly salesman who took her on informally. He would take her viola pieces downstairs and ask the violinmakers at Wurlitzer's for suggestions and then bring them back upstairs and tell her what to do next.

Throughout her pregnancy, Carleen studied, carved, and measured, meticulously working on her first viola. "When I was pregnant, I started to work on the pieces and found that every now and then there would be a bump in my lap and something would get knocked off and on to the floor, as the baby inside gave me a kick or two. This was a very memorable experience and one that has always remained with me — the idea that I could try and create two things at once." Carleen did learn that she could make two things at once. While she loved one, she was clearly seduced by the other. When it came time for Carleen to deliver, Helen Rice phoned her before coming to visit her in the hospital. "Carleen, what can I bring you?" asked Helen. Carleen scanned her hospital room and then looked at the scroll in her hands. "How about some sandpaper? I brought a scroll to work on but forgot the sandpaper!"[3] William Hutchins was born October 8, 1947 —just as Carleen was beginning to make progress on her first viola. She took a leave of absence from Brearley for the rest of the semester to focus on baby and viola. Years later Carleen likened carving her first viola to carving a bow: "Carving an archer's bow from a lemon tree — more trouble than shaving a fiddle! That's where I got the nerve to try it — make a fiddle, that is. I took the rest of the year off and sat carefully working on the pieces."[4]

Within a few months, Carleen and Mort moved to an apartment on West 69th, just off Central Park, primarily to be closer to Helen's Brandenburg evenings. "I wanted to be close to that situation because that was kind of saving my life. I was still at Brearley when we moved to West 69th and I remember taking Bill over to nursery school where he had a fine time. He climbed all over Dr. Spock — before he got to be famous." Carleen found great release in these music-making ventures with Helen, particularly while she was in the midst of learning to be a mother. Mort encouraged her every step of the way in making this first instrument. He would go with Carleen to get materials. Then, gradually, as she needed various tools and pieces of equipment, Mort would find a way, coming home with a smile on his face and a little grinder to sharpen her chisels, or some clamps that he knew she needed. Very often he would offer to get a meal so Carleen could finish working on a particular part — or take Bill out for a walk or to the stores or up to Edgemont Pond where they could watch and feed the ducks.

In October 1948, just as Bill turned one year old, Carleen finished her first viola. Helen invited Carleen and a couple dozen friends, including Brearley's music staff, to an evening party as way of celebration. Louise Rood, Smith College professor and professional violist, played the guest of honor. True to her word, Helen baked and decorated a cake shaped like a straw hat. Photographs attest to the fact that Helen then donned the hat made of cake to celebrate this new viola and the wager that had inspired Carleen to make it. Carleen recalled: "When Bill was born, the viola was finished about a year afterwards and people said, 'Are you going to have another baby and make another instrument?' Well, at that time I hadn't planned to make another instrument."

Carleen paid tribute to Susie the Pig in one lasting memento. Hutchins recalled: "Since there had been a bargain of a viola for a pig, it seemed quite natural that the instrument be christened 'Sus'—'pig' in Latin—especially in the light of the pig's outstanding voice production, which, alas, was not true for that first viola!" Carleen christened her first viola SUS #1. Henceforth, inside every Hutchins instrument is the prefix SUS—from SUS #1 to at least SUS #485. Carleen had another fond memory about a weekend when she was away Christmas caroling with friends and the wires on their Christmas tree short-circuited and set the tree on fire. The first thing Mort grabbed was not the fire extinguisher but SUS #1! "I was very touched that the first thing he thought to save was my viola," she mused.

One evening, in 1949, Carleen worked up her nerve to bring her viola over to West 67th Street, where Helen was hosting a group of professional musicians playing quartets, among them, Broadus Erle, first violinist for the New Music Quartet, who later taught at Yale. Emile Brock was playing viola; Ruth McGregor, cello; and Helen, first violin. Erle was then playing a violin made by Karl Berger. Hutchins recalled: "Broadus suggested that Karl Berger might be willing to help me if I took my viola around to him and he could teach me some violinmaking." When Helen showed Carleen's viola to another violinmaker, he described it as "the work of a good carpenter." Carleen recalled: "That's about what I was—a carpenter. My early struggles in violinmaking are one of the reasons I want to help people get started on the right track. It can be an enormous waste of time and energy, which can be saved by the right kind of instruction at the beginning." Carleen eventually sought out the workshop of Karl Berger, located in the Steinway Building on 57th Street near Carnegie Hall, with its "dirty window" (good for violinmaking) and north light. Luckily for Hutchins, Berger was a Swiss master luthier with gifted hands and a wonderful disposition, genuinely interested in people, and a most patient teacher as well. Carleen recalled her naïveté when she took her first viola to Berger: "It had taken me two years to make. It had many coats of varnish on it . . . too many coats, but at the time it had a nice color . . . and it played better than the Hornsteiner viola I had originally bought. I was quite happy with it and really proud of the work." Berger looked it over, tapped on it, blew inside it, felt it, put a bow on it, and then said to Hutchins: "Young lady, if you really would like me to help you, I'll be glad to do so. I can make some suggestions about how to make this instrument sound a lot better." When Carleen gave him the nod, she watched in horror as he dismantled her viola in front of her. He took the strings off and the bridge down, and then took a knife and went all around under the edge of the top plate, removing it very skillfully, then he handed her viola back in pieces. Hutchins recalled: "I was so upset I hardly knew what to say. Here was two years work all back in little bits again!" When he handed the pieces back to Carleen, Berger showed her what to do to the plates before putting the viola together again. Hutchins: "At the time, I had no plans to make another instrument!" But eventually, Carleen's curiosity got the better of her. After the shock wore off, she began recarving the plates in her spare time for a month or so, following Berger's instructions. When she took it back to him, she was excited that the reassembled viola did sound a great deal better.

In the meantime, Carleen was learning to balance mothering and teaching. On one memorable occasion when her babysitter did not show up, Carleen made do in her inimitable fashion. By this time, Mrs. Mac had moved from Brearley to Bryn Mawr. The new headmistress, Jean Fair Mitchell, recalled giving a tour one day. Upon opening the door to the Lower School science room, Mitchell announced to visitors, "I never know what I'll find in here." To her amazement, an eighteenth-month-old boy sitting inside the rabbit hutch clutching his blanket looked up and smiled at visitors. With nothing more to say, Miss Mitchell simply closed the door and moved on.

A few months after returning to Berger, Carleen decided to try and make a second viola. She had met the violist Eunice Wheeler at Helen's and had noticed her 1560 Gasparo da Salò viola. To Carleen's great joy, Eunice allowed her to make patterns from this very special viola. "I didn't fully realize at the time how lucky I was to get a start on such an instrument as this — an extremely beautiful viola in marvelous condition that played gorgeously." Through Rice, Carleen also met J. C. Freeman, a luthier who had built up the Wurlitzer Collection of instruments and knew more about stringed instruments than almost anyone in the world. When Carleen made an appointment with Freeman and took her bag of viola parts to his door, she was met with a look of astonishment because he was embarrassed that an unaccompanied woman would call on him. Carleen sat on one side of a dining room table and he sat on the other while she spread out the parts of her Gasparo viola. Freeman was intrigued that Hutchins was working from a Gasparo da Salò, as he felt they were the best-sounding violas ever made.

By 1949, Helen Rice had become increasingly involved in the organization she founded in 1946—the Amateur Chamber Music Players (ACMP) and had decided to leave Brearley in order to devote full energy to leading this group. At the same time, Carleen began to realize that she needed to consider a major change as well. Now pregnant with her second child and increasingly overwhelmed by child-care issues as well as teaching, Carleen also gave her notice at Brearley.

In the meantime, Grace and Thomas Maley asked Carleen to move back to Montclair. At the time, Carleen's parents slept in one bedroom while Grandma Reeves still lived in the room to the right of the stairs. "My parents needed help and they couldn't keep the place and stay that way. So I decided — we decided — well, Mort decided it. He said, 'Let's move out there.' He was the one who wanted to go," recalled Hutchins. In the fall of 1949, Carleen and Mort moved back to her childhood home. They took over the little room in the back of the house, and the front room became the playroom. Carleen once again found herself in a three-generation household — just like the one she had known as a child, but this time, she was at the hub, awaiting the birth of her second child. On April 10, 1950, Caroline Hutchins was born.

From 1950 to 1952, in between chasing after two toddlers, Carleen worked on that second viola. Shortly after she completed it, Helen introduced Carleen to William Kroll, the famous violinist and leader of the Kroll Quartet. Kroll took Hutchins to the shop of the violin dealer Emil Herrmann and introduced her to Simone Sacconi, an internationally renowned expert on the techniques of Stradivari. Sacconi looked at her Gasparo viola and said, "Bravo!"

Shortly thereafter, Helen Rice made it possible for Carleen to take her second viola to Emanuel Winternitz, curator of the Musical Instruments Collection at the Metropolitan Museum of Art. Winternitz looked closely at it, and then asked Hutchins if she would like to get a Fulbright Scholarship to go to Europe to copy instruments in museums. "At the time I was trying to raise two children, run a household, and do a few minutes of work a day on my beloved instrument making. I rather sadly told Winternitz: 'I'm sorry but I have another life that I must follow right now.'"

In the February 7, 1952, *Montclair Times*, Audrey Brown likened Hutchins to a medieval craftsman using her home as her workshop. "In her kitchen [she] does much of her work on violas at the . . . breakfast table . . . [with] tools arranged upright in the grooves of the circular condenser atop her refrigerator . . . to keep tools in sight but out of reach of her children Bill, 4½, and Caroline, 1½."[5] In the November 8, 1953, *Newark Sunday News*, Frank Eakin Jr., reported about the "housewife-craftsman . . . believed to be the only non-professional, woman viola maker in this country" who had thus far made seventeen violas in her "kitchen-pantry-dining room workshop." Eakin made the synthesis of hobby and home sound seamless: "Mrs. Hutchins, the mother of two children aged 6 and 3, does not let her hobby interfere with her household duties—or vice versa. She neatly dovetails the two activities, working on the violas just as some women work on their knitting and crocheting. . . . 'I poach two eggs each morning for the children, using a three-hole egg poacher,' she explains. 'In the third hole I put my glue pot to warm.'"[6]

Between 1949 and 1954, Carleen continued to work with Berger, making approximately thirty-five instruments, mostly violas—and one cello. When Hutchins sold her first viola for $125, viola making was purely a hobby. "I had no intention of really getting into violin research even then," she said, "but it seemed to be coming at me one piece at a time."[7]

Intermezzo

Anatomy – More Than the Sum of the Parts

> Exquisite was it in design,
> Perfect in each minutest part,
> A marvel of the lutist's art;
> And in the hollow chamber, thus
> The maker from whose hands it came
> Had written his unrivalled name —
> "Antonius Stradivarius."
> — H. W. Longfellow, *Tales of a Wayside Inn*

Longfellow greets the aspiring luthier on the inside page of *Violin-Making: As It Was, and Is,* by Edward Heron-Allen, the 1864 book regarded by many as the luthier's bible. Though word has it that Heron-Allen may actually have made only one or two instruments, he meticulously documented the process, adding plenty of flowery language to baffle even the most determined luthier.

In its very anatomy, made only of wood and string, the violin is filled with mystery, paradox, and contradiction even as it is filled with air — and the essential acoustical illusion starts there. The violin is composed of more than eighty different parts, most all of which are hand-carved. Every detail matters, as every detail can change its sound. Styled with elaborate baroque arches and serpentine curves, this graceful wooden box defies logic. How does a horsehair bow crossing sheep's gut strings attached to a wooden box sing?

Most scholars agree that the violin was an end product of Renaissance science, mathematics, and craftsmanship that somehow incorporated the laws of acoustics — a field then as yet unknown — evolving from primitive medieval stringed instruments such the *lira da braccio*, the *rebec*, the *vielle*. From the *rebec*, the violin inherited strings tuned in fifths (though the rebec had three strings, one fewer than the violin's G, D, A, and E strings), a playing position at the neck, an overhand bow, and strings anchored by lateral tuning pegs. The *lira da braccio* contributed the sound post, an arched top, a shaped waist, and F- or C-shaped sound holes. The Renaissance fiddle or *vielle* bequeathed to the violin its soprano register; a top and back with connecting ribs; a separate neck, peg box, and fingerboard; and its oval shape.

The violin — along with its cousins the viola and the cello, known properly as the violoncello — is a set of strings mounted on a wooden box that forms an almost-closed air space. Some energy from the vibrations of the bow drawn across strings is communicated to the box and its enclosed air space, producing sound waves that reach the ear. The sound produced depends on this transfer of vibration from string to box to air. But that is just the beginning of an apparently simple idea that turns out to be a conundrum of unknowns. Nothing about the design of the violin seems logical. Why the elaborate swirling scroll? Why arched plates? Why S-shaped soundholes? Why overlapping edges?

The sounding box consists of an arched, bell-shaped front plate and back plate, connected by ribs, or sides — spruce for the front; curly maple seasoned at least a decade for the back. Though they may look as if they might be steam-bent, the plates are meticulously hand-carved with small handheld chisels, scrapers, and thumb-sized planes. In fact, much of the art of violinmaking depends on the nature of these arches, which when drawn with a pencil on a piece of spruce or maple resemble the elevation contours on a map. The back plate varies in thickness from 6 millimeters at the center to 2 millimeters at the outside edges (from ¼ inch to 5/64 inch). The ribs, made of matching curly maple, thinned to a millimeter all over and then bent into shape, are then glued to spruce or willow blocks set in the corners in the forward and rear ends of the plates. The top plate, made from two conjoined pieces of spruce split lengthwise from the same log, so that the grain is bilaterally symmetrical, vary in thickness from 2 to 3 millimeters. Two beautifully shaped "f-holes" are cut into the top plate, on either side of the center seam. All around the outer edge of the plate, very near the edge, a shallow groove is cut in which the luthier inserts *purfling*, a pencil-thin strip of laminate composed of two strips of black-dyed pear wood and a strip of poplar, which essentially outlines the entire top plate. Chaucer first used the word *purfling* to refer to the ornamentation on a bishop's cuff.

Traditionally, the luthier uses curly maple for the neck, ebony for the fingerboard, rosewood or ebony for the tuning pegs and tailpiece, and hard maple for the bridge. The small maple bridge, artfully carved with two tiny legs that sit on either side of the center seam of the violin, bears an incredible tension from the four strings, made heavier by the motion of the bow—the combined tension in an average four-string violin is thirty-two pounds per square inch of pressure on the bridge. With the bow, an added force of approximately twenty pounds is brought to bear straight down through the bridge, against the delicate top plate of the sound box with a thickness amounting to that of an eggshell. To spread the load and aid the top plate in withstanding the downward motion of string tension, viol makers glued a strip of wood running down the central artery of the inside of the top plate.

An early, anonymous violinmaker, whether by accident, intention, or a stroke of genius, moved this strip of wood to one side so that one foot of the bridge rested above it. This strip is now called the *bass bar* because it sits under the foot of the bridge on the side of the lowest—or bass—string. As the asymmetrical placement of the bass bar required some balancing support for the other foot of the bridge, another genius placed a small vertical post made of spruce inside the violin, sitting under the other bridge foot—the *sound post*. The sound post is not glued but fitted inside the violin, held in place by friction. This tiniest piece of wood has generated centuries of debate among violinmakers, because makers and dealers discovered that the tone of a violin could be so greatly altered by miniscule changes in its position, tightness, and wood quality such that the French named this most invisible part of the violin *l'âme*, the "soul" of the instrument. Removing the sound post from a violin makes it sound like a guitar.

All this mystery even before the bow hits the strings. Add to this the fact that as the violin is played, the bridge is actually rocking back and forth like a fulcrum. Hutchins explained it in her first *Scientific American* article: "In spite of the vigorous vibration of the moving string, the sound from the string alone would be all but inaudible. It has too little surface area to set an appreciable amount of air into motion. Trying to make music with an unamplified string would be like trying to fan oneself with a toothpick."[1] In fact, only 1 or 2 percent of the energy that a player feeds into a fiddle emerges as sound—the rest goes off as heat. To add to the paradoxes that make up the violin, although the vibrations of the wood of the sound box matter, even more critical are the multiple air currents swirling inside the box. In its vibrational essence, the violin is actually a wind instrument!

Fortuitously, the birth of the violin in Cremona coincided with the birth of a most gifted and prolific musical genius, the composer Claudio

Monteverdi (1567–1643), also a native of Cremona. By 1600, Monteverdi became known as a premiere avant-garde composer whose reputation was made with his February 24, 1607, performance of his opera *Orfeo* at the Gonzaga Palace in Mantua.[2] Monteverdi set a new standard in *Orfeo*, as the performance marked the debut of the first truly modern orchestra. Prior to this time, if a harpsichord and lute were used to accompany vocal pieces, they were considered an "outlandish" collection of instruments. In the debut of *Orfeo*, Monteverdi featured up to a dozen musical instruments, including two harpsichord-type instruments, two double basses, ten arm-viols, a double-strung harp, two small (or French) violins, three violas da gamba, two bass lutes, two wooden pipe organs, a portable organ, four trombones, two cornets, a flute, and four trumpets. This unwieldy number of musical instruments was such a hit that it became a model for all orchestras that followed.[3]

Today, violins constitute nearly one-third the instruments in a symphony orchestra, and they figure prominently in the solo and chamber music repertoire. With the possible exception of the piano, the violin is the instrument most written for in the classical tradition. Nearly every major composer, from the eighteenth century onward, has composed solo violin music, including Bach, Mozart, Beethoven, Mendelssohn, Schumann, Brahms, Grieg, Bartók, and Schoenberg.[4]

Part of the idiosyncrasies of violin design may relate to its context, built as it was in the tradition of the Italian baroque, where the "S" appears everywhere in sculpture, painting, and architecture. At virtually every juncture, the violin echoes this curving configuration — S-shaped sound holes, curved archings, fluted margins, a spiraling scroll. As such, the violin is a kind of sustained metaphor reflecting its time, a time in which luthiers in some mysterious way intuited the undulating characteristics of sound and found its parallel expression in the world of design around them, thereby allowing their perceptions to guide their hands. Somehow, they transposed some understanding of the oscillatory nature of sound into visual and tactile features of the violin that has remained unchanged for four centuries. Therein lies its genius.

Aristotle said of metaphor: "The greatest thing by far is to have a command of metaphor. This alone cannot be imparted by another. It is the mark of genius, for to make good metaphors implies an eye for resemblances."[5]

An eye for resemblances suggests the intuitive powers that enable us to see similarity in dissimilars, to make connections between seemingly opposite things — the true genius of the poet. Yet the marvel and the challenge of the luthiers' craft make it even more formidable than the composition of a sonnet. While poets must thrust their inspiration into a rigid box of fourteen lines, they can at least use their own language.

But, as Antonio Pace suggests in his essay "Violin Making as an Exercise in Creative Anachronism," luthiers must execute their craft while adhering to the southern European baroque tradition — a tradition that is far removed from anyone except the European maker. And while the baroque is the idiom, luthiers have one further challenge — to hew out their own unique mark and imbue their violins with their own identity within the time-honored baroque mold. Because the language of the baroque is foreign to so many makers — American and Chinese, for instance — they risk either lifeless imitation or exaggeration that comes from only partial understanding. Metaphor comes to life only to the degree to which the maker breathes his or her own essence into the creation. It is the true luthier's lonely internal struggle — not a technique or path that can be easily explained in a manual.

Under such conditions, it is easy to understand how violinmaking might be regarded as a combination of cabinetmaking and acoustical engineering, approached first with a methodical, step-by-step, highly detailed recipe book. No wonder this puzzle has been canonized for those who would follow it, imitate or exaggerate it, and declare war on those who would change it. Antonio Pace eloquently describes the violin and violinmaking as "creative anachronism": "The violin, however, continues to flourish, very much a graceful and lively little dinosaur in an alien environment, in a form given to it by the 17th and 18th century makers; and any attempt to modify that form draws only indifference, scorn or wrath from the musical establishment."[6]

Stretto

Entry of a motive
in a second voice
before the first voice
has finished

Timothy A. Smith, "Anatomy of a Fugue"

5 ∫ *Scientist*

In mid-May 1949, Carleen sat under an old apple tree on the edge of Helen's garden at her Stockbridge farm, skimming the papers in her hands, reprints of articles given to her by the retired Harvard physicist Frederick A. Saunders, whom she had met just moments before. It had been roughly six months since Carleen had taken her first viola to Karl Berger. Each spring Carleen came out to Stockbridge to help Helen plow her garden. It was the perfect time to venture to South Hadley for an afternoon, as Helen Rice and Louise Rood had proposed that Carleen accompany them to meet Saunders, a physicist and string player—with orders to bring her precious viola along.

Saunders had retired from Harvard in 1941 and was teaching part-time at Smith and Mount Holyoke while continuing his violin research in a small lab at Mount Holyoke. The Smith College professor and violist Louise Rood had played chamber music with Helen in New York and in Stockbridge and had also worked extensively with Saunders over the years, testing instruments and playing them for him as he took measurements. As of the spring of 1949, Hutchins and Saunders had only heard of each other through Rood. Though Rice and Saunders had many common friends in chamber music circles, they had not met as yet either. On May 12, Saunders wrote to "Mrs. Hutchins" that he would be honored to meet her, observing that he had not yet made a better fiddle and that, to the best of his knowledge, his experiments had not proved to be of any tangible use. He also mentioned the great variability between one violin and another, given the instrument's hybrid nature.[1]

Sometime after mid-May 1949, Rice and Hutchins took a break from plowing to visit Saunders and his wife at their home. Hutchins recalled: "Saunders tapped around on my instrument, blew in the f-holes and listened to it. Then he said: 'Young lady, I shall be interested to see your next one.' At the time, I had no plans to make another one! I was only interested in making one for myself to play."[2] Saunders told Hutchins a great deal about his work testing instruments and gave her some reprints of articles he had written. Though she did not understand much of the physics terminology, one thing spoke to her. "I realized Saunders had never been able to test anything but fancy, finished instruments. He had never been able to change the wood of the box. I thought then that maybe he could use instruments he could cut into." Within a day or so of their meeting, Hutchins offered to make some expendable instruments for Saunders that could be cut up. But Saunders didn't think much of the idea, saying that it looked like a great deal of work for not much in return. Then he asked what violinmaker would be crazy enough to put so much time and energy into making instruments that would then be demolished in experiments? Hutchins recalled: "I volunteered to do just that!"[3]

By June, when Carleen returned from meeting Saunders, Berger's advice had grabbed her attention, and she had begun to make her second viola. After collecting her thoughts about meeting Saunders, Carleen wrote her first letter to him to ask for advice. In a letter dated July 20, Saunders not only replied to Carleen; he set up her first experiment, recommending that she make a thicker viola. He noted that, historically, the viola had been made by cutting down the viol and that while it was obvious that viola tone could not be improved on by making the viola smaller, it made sense to try making one with deeper ribs to see what would happen acoustically.

By October, as her son turned two years old, Carleen, pregnant once again, was hard at work getting the "right" resonances for her next viola, heeding the advice of Saunders as she worked on her Gasparo viola. Each letter from Saunders proved denser than the last. When he was not talking technical points about resonances and body lengths, he was sharing his research and his observations in less formal ways.

In a letter dated November 17, 1949, just five months after their first meeting, Saunders wondered whether the air resonance of a set of viols made by Thomas Smith of Cleveland might give some clue as to the correct air resonances in violas. Saunders was excited by the prospect that Carleen might soon be able to determine if it would work to locate the air and body resonances for the viola in the same places where they occur in the violin. Saunders wrote to Hutchins that it was most fortuitous timing that they had met at this moment — at the very time that he had begun to ponder questions that he could not explore further without destroying instruments, something he was very reluctant to do. Yet here was a violinmaker willing to make experimental instruments!

Despite the wide gap in their professional and academic training, on an instinctive, emotional, gut-level plane, the violinmaker Carleen Hutchins and the physicist Frederick Saunders had much common ground. They both loved music and science. Each had developed a lifelong passion for ornithology. They were both drawn to experiment. They both played viola, and they both loved to play chamber music. In one short paragraph, in a letter dated December 10, 1949, Saunders applauded the resonances on the Gasparo; commented on the role of f-holes; suggested a new experiment; implied his anticipation of Opus III (the next experimental viola) and congratulated Carleen on the upcoming birth of her second child! Such would be their whirlwind correspondence in letters that covered much ground and never seem to lose momentum.

By February 1950, with Carleen less than six weeks away from delivering her second child, Saunders was writing lengthy letters on violin tone to "Mrs. Hutchins," even suggesting that their work would be worth publishing. Suddenly, association with Saunders not only satisfied Carleen's scientific curiosity, it legitimized her fledgling hobby and made it more significant at a time when Hutchins was mourning the loss of her professional life rather than becoming enamored of motherhood — a tension that characterized her entire life.

In April 1950, Carleen delivered her second child — daughter Caroline, who would later be known as Cassie. Cassie's health problems as an infant necessitated that Carleen spend hours at a time by her bedside. To fill the hours, Carleen worked on violas. With a two-year-old to care for, she was grateful for the help afforded her by her parents, who still lived on the third floor at 112 Essex. They could watch Bill while she took jaunts into the city to show her work to Berger. She could also escape for an evening of chamber music at Helen's.

On November 14, 1950 — more than a year after they had met, and after fifteen letters addressed to "Mrs. Hutchins," Saunders wrote to Hutchins that Helen Rice had suggested he call her "Hutchie" — the nickname Rice herself had coined — and what did Carleen think of the idea? Thereafter, a bond formed: Saunders called Carleen "Hutchie," and the two became a team. In Hutchins, Saunders suddenly had found a very skillful and practical ally who willingly volunteered to carve instruments for experimentation. For Hutchins, violinmaking was her oasis, her escape and comfort when domestic demands of a husband, a three-generation household, and two children seemed to surround her. She relished the questions and every word of encouragement that her prestigious mentor offered in his frequent letters.

In the meantime, the new focus for Saunders and Hutchins was for Hutchins to make a flat-top viola as a way to experiment with certain elements—bass bar placement; f-hole size, shape and, location; different bridges; different kinds of wood; the placement and depth of the purfling—without having to take the instrument apart each time. Hutchins made bridges from thirty-five different woods. Their goal was to begin to define what a player means by "violin tone," which actually includes the whole impression he or she gets from an instrument—loudness, ease of playing, tone-color or timbre, even the way a tone starts. Carleen recalled: "We did more than a hundred experiments on this box itself—that's what got me excited and got me into acoustics. It represented the elements that are necessary for good sound, with none of the fancy stuff that everybody thinks is so important."[4]

Beginning in 1953, in addition to the flat-top viola, Hutchins and Saunders completed a long series of experiments with violas of different sizes, from seventeen inches to just under thirteen inches, whereby each viola was adjusted to have a good loudness curve. They devised a "sound meter" composed of a little box containing a microphone for picking up sound and an electrical circuit to amplify it and cause the motion of a pointer over a loudness scale. The loudest tones appear as peaks in the curve, with valleys ascribed to the weakest tones. Through thousands of tone-color analyses, Saunders and Hutchins found that the tones at the peaks are rich in the fundamental tone or the lower overtones, and that these peaks, to which listeners respond positively, had a great deal to do with the overall tone impression characteristic of a violin.[5]

Any free violin plate gives several musical tones when held at different points and tapped at other points. But, after the plate is glued to the ribs and back to form the sound box, the violin plate displays somewhat different natural tones because it is part of a larger structure and is no longer free to vibrate as a simple plate. These loudness curves are caused by the natural vibrations of the top plate of the instrument combined with the air inside the box.[6]

In the process of these investigations, Saunders and Hutchins elucidated the cause and nature of the air tone of the violin. They found that the air tone forms at the peak of lowest pitch, caused by the vibration of the air inside the box as it rushes in and out of the two sound holes at a rate of about 280 vibrations per second in violins. They determined that the naturally occurring air tone of a violin generally occurs near the low C-sharp and that it possesses a tone color or timbre that is unique.[7] The air tone is one *simple pattern* that occurs when the air inside the chamber of the violin vibrates in its natural way. As the air moves in and out of the f-holes simultaneously, the body of the violin expands and contracts with changes in air pressure inside so that the tone produced is "very nearly pure," without overtones. They found that even when they poured heavy carbon dioxide gas into the f-holes of a horizontal violin, this did not affect the positions of the body peaks.[8]

Saunders and Hutchins found that players — even expert professional violinists — did not always appreciate their findings, as they were convinced of the tonal uniformity of their excellent instruments up and down the scale. One amusing instance involved a group of professional players listening to a colleague play a slow scale of semitones up the lowest octave as it passed through the air tone peak. Saunders reported that despite the fact that the sound meter showed a noticeable increase of 10 decibels as the player reached the air tone, then fell, both players and listeners insisted that the scale was uniformly loud, declaring that the General Radio meter must be at fault. They were "suspicious" of anyone suggesting that their firm, yet supremely subjective, perceptions might be flawed.[9]

Saunders and Hutchins concluded that there is "a good physical reason" that, for more than three centuries, the air tone has consistently been located at the same part of the scale; it is badly needed to strengthen the fundamental of the low tones. In addition, they found that because the air tone is unimpeded, carried to the ears by air both inside and outside the box, they could raise or lower the pitch of the air tone by either narrowing the depth of the ribs to lessen the volume of the box or by increasing the total area of the f-holes. Consequently, they found they could lower the pitch of the body vibrations by thinning the top of the violin or (temporarily) adding a mute to the bridge.[10]

Drawn in by the questions Saunders asked, Carleen began to teach herself acoustics by carving violins, perhaps reinforcing an observation made by one of her friends that had so impressed Carleen, she had recorded the comment in the family log. The friend had said that Carleen had "an incredibly arrogant mind."[11] Is it hubris, curiosity, naïveté, or ignorance that blinds one to doubt or propels one past it? The luck and lore of the outsider in any field is that he or she does not know the jargon of the canon, so is less likely to fall prey to false assumptions. To the newcomer, there are no silly questions, no preconceived notions. One has left behind the inner editor and the restrictions of the mind that thinks it knows. Another aspect of an arrogant mind is the total lack of need for approval from others. This kind of single-mindedness provides its own momentum, regardless of territory, credentials, authority, or approval.

In seeking to uncover the viola tone, Saunders and Hutchins began by testing the theories of Félix Savart, a French physicist, who wrote in 1837 that the viola air peak ought to occupy a place similar to the one it inhabits in the violin—at F-sharp on the C string. They eventually got a viola into this condition but were disappointed with their results. To follow Savart's ideas, the sound holes had to be so small or the depth of the ribs so great the viola would not fit under the chin. They finally abandoned Savart's idea. Next, in searching for the ideal "viola tone," Carleen made an especially small viola—14⅞ inches long, with ribs 1⅛ inches high, such that its internal volume (the air peak) came up to D, as in the Heifetz violin. This viola proved "unbelievably powerful," resulting from a very successful combination of air and body tones.[12]

When Carleen made a very large viola that produced a striking "wolf" tone, the research team began to study these troublesome sounds. A wolf tone occurs at a particular note when the vibration of the wood and the vibration of the string get out of sync and cancel each other out. The result is that the note that has barely begun to sound suddenly disappears, resulting in a stuttering sound caused by a beating action when energy is shuttled back and forth between them.[13] First, they tried replacing the arched top plate with a flat top made from less expensive wood, but the wolf tones remained. Next they sprinkled sand on the top and found a strong visual pattern of the viola's natural vibration. After about fifty experiments with loudness curves, Hutchins and Saunders managed to prove that the bass bar was stiff enough, that the long sound holes (as long as four inches) were better than short ones and that they "could kill the wolf tones only by suppressing them altogether" but found that doing so weakened the overall tone of the viola.[14]

Surmising that the unstable nature of the wolf tone occurred because the top plate was not free to vibrate, they developed a process to allow the top to vibrate more freely—a process they called "ditching." Hutchins cut a millimeter-wide and millimeter-deep ditch along the thin edge of the plate inside where the plate is glued to the body. Their ditching process freed up the plate. As a result, the wolf tones almost disappeared, and the tone increased in volume. All at once they found that ditching even their flat-top, experimental viola suddenly and dramatically improved its tone to such an extent that they could call it a "good" viola.[15]

Hutchins treated several violas, violins, and cellos in this way, and each time "ditching" produced a marked improvement in tone, much improved in most cases. One outstanding case occurred with the "$5-fiddle" that Saunders had named "Pygmalion" and was using as his "standard of badness" in violin tone. Ditching so improved this violin that a musical group preferred it to an old Italian violin when each was played behind a screen.[16] It was not a great leap for Saunders and Hutchins to consider the link between thin edges, flexibility, and old Italian violins. Saunders reasoned that the infamous "secret" of old Cremonese and Italian instruments must involve small refinements and that one such refinement could simply be the thickness and flexibility of the top plate. Thinning the top plate would allow it to vibrate more vigorously, which might possibly result in producing a better distribution of loudness over the violin's entire tonal range. Whether or not Hutchins and Saunders had found the "secret," they had, at the very least, discovered a technique that could greatly improve the tone of a violin.[17]

Hutchins soon realized that the ripple effect of her work to "improve" fiddles might mean stepping on toes. Saunders soon wrote to her about how quickly such a technique could upset the violin market. What's more, Saunders argued, even if he and Hutchins managed to convince Wurlitzer, the most celebrated American violin dealer, about the effectiveness of ditching, making new, improved violins and violas by this method would soon make people less inclined to buy a venerable, old instrument. This would inevitably displease the dealers bent on preserving high prices on old violins.[18]

Meanwhile, despite—or perhaps because of—her family challenges, Carleen found her own release by making fiddles. In fact, she worked so fast carving plates that Saunders had trouble keeping up with her. By this time Carleen had built her fourth viola — a medium-size instrument — and was making SUS #5 on the pattern of #2, while she had #7, #8, and #9 in the works. In fact, she was working so fast that Saunders told her he had begun to catalogue her instruments. He also asked Hutchins to bring her detached flat-top, experimental viola plate to him, as he wanted to use it in a lecture-demonstration.[19] In fact, early on, in order to accommodate the constant interruptions in a household, Carleen decided it was much easier and she could be more consistent if she carved multiple plates, performing the same step on a number of plates before going on to the next step. She could easily return to where she was because she was using the same tools involved in the same process whether on plate 1 or 6. The added benefit was that she found that multiple plates allowed for more accurate tests.

As Saunders's letters flew at least weekly, and sometimes every other day, to 112 Essex, Carleen replied on hastily written postcards composed on the fly. Meanwhile, Saunders continued to explore and test out their "ditching" technique with professors, players, and dealers. In July 1952, he visited the Philadelphia Orchestra violinist Schima Kaufman and the violin dealer William Moennig, also of Philadelphia, bringing along with him Pygmalion and a few Hutchins violas in order to showcase the benefits of "ditching." Saunders wrote to Hutchie that even if they could convince other luthiers to thin the edges of their inexpensive fiddles so they could get more money for them, these same makers would soon realize that transforming poor violins into good ones endangered their livelihood, which depended on preserving the status quo that placed the highest value on old violins.[20] By August 19, Saunders and Hutchins seemed to have hit upon a mutually acceptable version of their first joint article about improving violins, which they had decided to pitch to *Violins and Violinists*. A month later, on September 11, the editor wrote to Saunders saying that he wanted to hold the article for further consultation in light of its conceivably provocative implications.[21]

About this time, Robert Fryxell entered the Rice-Saunders-Hutchins triumvirate. Fryxell, a young chemist and avid amateur cellist, had driven east from Chicago to the Berkshires to take his first job. When his car was burglarized, the thieves stole everything except his cello. When Fryxell went to a haberdashery in Pittsfield to buy clothes, he met the owner, Jay Rosenthal, who happened to be a string player. He invited Fryxell to play quartets at Helen Rice's farm. In the spring of 1951, Fryxell began to play quartets with Helen Rice and became a regular for the next two decades. In the fall of 1952, Helen invited Fryxell to meet two of her friends—a retired physicist and a New York City science teacher who had begun to make fiddles.

On November 2, 1952, the New Music Quartet came to perform at Smith College, and Saunders took advantage of the opportunity, engaging the renowned viola soloist and teacher Walter Trampler and the violinist Broadus Erle to see some of Hutchins's violas.[22] As a physicist, Saunders was fearless in his conviction that Hutchins was "improving" the acoustics of the fiddle—the viola in particular—and showed no hesitation about trying to persuade other makers of the validity of her techniques.

Saunders considered himself a cantankerous muckraker unafraid to rock the boat of the violin world. At the same time, as a player and as a physicist, he also knew how important accolades from established players could prove for a luthier learning the craft. Saunders was delighted to report what Gil Ross—a University of Michigan professor of violin, formerly at Smith—had said to him: that Ross and his quartet colleagues remained profoundly interested in Saunders and Hutchins's violin and viola experiments, were open to the discoveries they had been making, and sent congratulations for work well done. Such a letter highlighting the interest of professional players of the caliber of the Stanley Quartet was special indeed.[23]

Still, in a letter of January 1953, Saunders foresaw challenges that Carleen might encounter because of her collaboration with him. As he had watched the Stanley Quartet perform in one of Helen Rice's Brandenburg sessions, Saunders sensed that these players could not help but consider him—and his scientific study of the violin—a curiosity, to say the least. Saunders wrote to Hutchins that he had overheard the second violist suggest that perhaps Saunders might be a bit of a "crackpot." Saunders then joked that Carleen's reputation might be tainted by her association with him. But since neither he nor Hutchins had any inclination to stop their research out of concern for criticism from other luthiers, players, or dealers, Saunders suggested that Carleen could view such guilt by association as "fashionable."[24]

Intermezzo

Science – the Organ, Polyphony, and the Science of Sound

If musicians and scientists were more conscious
of each other's approaches and needs, there would be
more rewarding collaborations.
— Mary Harbold, physicist,
"Summary of Current Developments in Musical Acoustics,"
March 15, 1964

Music has always been a science. In fact, early pioneers in sound and acoustics were nearly all musically minded scientists, many of whom made musical instruments in the process of their study.

In Alexandria around 270 BC, a curious engineer by the name of Ktesibios began experimenting with an intermittent birdsong whistle device that worked by regulating the flow of water into a cistern. Problems with the faintness of the birdsong and lack of a continuous source of pressurized air led Ktesibios to experiment further, resulting in his invention of a novel musical instrument — the organ, called a *hydraulis* because of the crucial role water played in producing its sound. Ktesibios developed a pump to supply air, a wind chest to distribute it, and a manual keyboard to allow the player to control it — innovations that have remained unchanged for two millennia.[1]

This first organ served as a kind of technological marvel, a carnival instrument that sounded forth flutes and trumpets amid the background of gurgling water and provided its own kind of musical theater for banquets, gladiatorial contests, and other entertainment. The first reference to it actually being played involved a performance at the Delphic games in 90 BC. Evidently, Nero was an organist. The oldest archaeological fragments of an organ — dedicated in AD 228 to the college of weavers at the Roman Acquincum near Budapest — attest to the popularity of this odd musical contraption.[2]

But Ktesibios's organ was much more than entertainment. It provided living proof of the link between abstract numbers, the proportionate length of the pipes, and musical consonance — the absolute relationship between number and harmony. This knowledge of the Greeks, though it would all but disappear within a few centuries during the Dark Ages, eventually became the foundation for Western science.[3] But it took some time for the organ to emerge into the harmonious instrument it would become. Initially, the organ was massive and loud, more a feat of technology and engineering than an instrument of harmony. Its initial job was to awe and to overwhelm, which the early organs easily did.[4]

One such organ was the one in Winchester Cathedral, south of London, built in the 990s and described by a monk named Wulstan as "a spectacular machine." It possessed twenty-six bellows, operated by seventy men who pumped air into the massive wind-chest supporting four hundred pipes, controlled by forty sliding rods played by two men, each at his own manual. Each sound was produced by ten pipes blowing simultaneously. Nevertheless, the tenth-century Winchester organ was difficult to play because it did not possess a keyboard like its ancient predecessor. Levenson explains: "To play a note the organist would have to pull on a long rod and then push it back into place to cut off the flow of air to the pipes—a one-hand-one-sound motion, compared with the one-finger-one-sound action of a modern keyboard." This setup necessitated a team approach so that two brothers were needed to play an instrument that possessed just forty notes. Even so, there would have been wild fluctuations in pitch. The result would have been more monstrous than musical.[5]

By 1050, the Church had embraced the organ as a substantial new musical instrument that could be of liturgical use. Renewed interest in the organ by the Church spurred craftsmen and instrument builders to improve upon it. Medieval organ builders enhanced the action of the bellows by devising animal hide bellows laid on the floor. By placing their entire weight on each downstroke, the organist's assistants produced the necessary air by performing a kind of rhythmic dance on the bellows. Drawings show one such marvelous pump room for the organ in the Halberstadt Cathedral in Germany, installed in 1361.[6] Still the medieval organ was difficult to play. Around the eleventh century an anonymous innovator proposed a slider mechanism connecting to a key, essentially rediscovering a solution the Greeks had already devised centuries earlier.[7]

The organ itself demonstrated the mathematics and science of music simultaneously. In addition, the perception of the sounds emanating from these early organs provided the foundation for polyphony. The practice of sounding more than one organ pipe with a single slider key provided built-in polyphony. In fact, early uses of the church organ involved doubling the vocal line of the chant. Perhaps of greater importance, a keyboard allowed a player to play two separate lines of music.[8]

Early polyphony led medieval society to new challenges and a new contemplation of the mathematics of acoustics. Though the construction of an organ's pipes was simple enough, following the principles of Pythagoras, the practical sound that resulted was not so simple. When an organist tried to play two or more notes in the polyphonic style, some notes would clash viciously. The flaw lay not in the organ but in the arithmetic of sound itself. In his book *Measure for Measure*, Thomas Levenson elegantly describes the imbedded imperfection of the Western octave scale:

> The twelve notes of the Western octave can be derived by leaping up through the cycle of fifths, as Leonard Bernstein demonstrated on the keyboard of a grand piano to his Harvard audience. Begin with a C, go up a fifth to G, then up another fifth to D, D to A, and so on. As the series continues, it picks out all twelve notes of the scale before returning to the original note, seven octaves up from the starting tone. But the two sums —twelve fifths and seven octaves—don't line up perfectly. The cycle of fifths lands slightly higher than the octave, creating a scale with an error of about 2 percent off the perfect ratio of 2:1, a gap named the Pythagorean comma. The essential scaffolding of the twelve-note scale, that is, does not fit the abstract idea of arithmetical perfection.[9]

Levenson explains the significance of such a small gap when it occurs amidst predictable musical intervals:

> In practice such gaps don't always matter. As long as music is purely melody, in fact, the goal of a kind of perfection remains attainable. A choir singing a Gregorian chant can keep each succeeding note in a perfect numerical relationship to the preceding one. Even the simplest kinds of polyphony could survive; purely parallel harmony, with two voices singing the same melody separated by a fifth, or an octave, for example, could march through the tune in lockstep, adjusting each note on the fly to preserve Pythagoras's perfect consonances. But as soon as a composer constructs two lines of music that differ from each other, the incompati-

bility of the different intervals comes into play. If all the octaves were kept pure and perfect then other intervals must fall out of tune by greater or lesser amounts. To this day every scale we use is 'out of tune' in this sense. From the moment that harmony seemed a good idea, the only issue was where to put the dissonances, the imperfections, imposed by the arithmetic of sound.[10]

The invention of multipart music forced instrument builders and medieval musicians to face a basic flaw in the concept of number that is central to all of Western music. Although two notes sounded together at intervals of fifths, fourths, thirds, and so on create vertical harmony as long as one note follows another, when a composer devises two differing lines of music, the incompatibility of different intervals occurs. Pure and perfect octaves naturally reveal innate discrepancies of greater or lesser amounts in the intervals.

Meanwhile, the expansion of the Church's political power indirectly supported scientific inquiry. As the organ became important to the monastery and Church, it was studied more carefully. Music became the new laboratory for examining not only the laws of sound but the laws of nature. Through the manipulation of number, music led directly back to scientific inquiry. Humanity looked to music not only for the sound itself but beyond music, to unlock the secrets it might expose about creation.[11]

By viewing music in scientific terms and treating a musical challenge as a scientific experiment, Henri Arnaut invented the portable organ. In the process he unraveled a solution to the riddle of the Pythagorean comma and the innate numerical dissonance of pure intervals. In addition, the wolf tone spurred musical and scientific experimentation. Pursuing the goal of harmonic freedom, other musicians continued to experiment and developed "mean-tone" tuning by spreading dissonance over a large number of intervals in order to maximize the number of playable keys.[12]

Around 1590, the music theorist, lutenist, and composer Vincenzo Galilei (1520–91) studied pitch and string tension and performed what may have been the first experiments in acoustics.[13] In the seventeenth century, it was his son, Galileo, who would prove that the ratio of musical intervals was the result of sound waves hitting the ear rather than the tension or thickness of the string. The French priest-scientist Marin Mersenne (1588–1648) investigated the relationship between pitch and frequency.

At about this time, experimentation went hand in hand with collecting all sorts of things. Scientists ranging from the curious inventor to Oxford-educated cleric-scientists might each have a "cabinet of curiosities." Collections encouraged comparisons, reasons for experimentation, and further discussion. In this atmosphere, Oxford was ripe for developing a more formal forum. In 1648, John Wilkins, the English clergyman appointed warden of Wadham College, first encouraged a collegiate group of like-minded gentlemen (no ladies allowed) to meet for the common purpose of interrogating nature through experiment and formed the Royal Society, the bedrock of modern Western science. Initially, the Royal Academy welcomed all "natural philosophers" — the term used to describe anyone studying nature — including the self-taught inventors and craftsmen who had no formal schooling. Wilkins himself set the threshold for just how wild the musings could be for this "invisible college" when he wrote a paper titled "How One Might Fly to the Moon."

But the institution's egalitarian roots did not go very deep. A century later, the Royal Society changed dramatically under the leadership of Joseph Banks, president from 1778 to 1820, when it slipped and "slumped into the leather armchairs of unearned privilege of an ossified princeling court."[14] In doing so, the Royal Society turned its back on its roots and left behind the craftsmen — the self-taught inventors and artisans who intuited investigation through hands-on work and experimentation.[15]

Hanging in the central staircase of the Old Ashmolean Museum, now the History of Science Museum, is a painting by an anonymous sixteenth-century artist titled *The Measurers* that illustrates the words of the Roman poet Horace: "Est modus in rebus" (There is measure in all things). The painting is rare in that it places the instrument maker — a common craftsman — at center stage, surrounded by the tools of his trade — compasses, a geometric square, a pair of surveying dividers, a polyhedral sundial. By not including the "fancy" instruments of astronomy or navigation, the painter depicts the yeoman's ordinary world of measuring. Indeed, though academe eventually constructed walls to separate art and science, craft remains a synthesis of both.

Luthiers use both art and science in their craft. Early makers perfecting the violin intuited acoustics through trial and error. One source surmises that one reason their knowledge of how to create such beautifully toned stringed instruments was lost may be that, in order to avoid taxes in the early eighteenth century, many craft guilds went underground and stored their knowledge as "trade secrets."[16]

6 ∫ *Apprentice*

"What is the feminine of Stradivari?" When Saunders actually asked Hutchins this question in a letter dated March 9, 1953, he added a postscript saying that just as Stradivari had attracted students and found "great fame," Hutchie would surely to do the same![1] Such praise from Saunders was both exciting and unsettling for Carleen. There were so many different directions to go.

How do you apprentice to two trades? Within one year of making her first viola, Carleen had begun her informal apprenticeship with Berger—she would make thirty-five instruments under his guidance. But just a few months later, on nearly the same day that she met Saunders—almost overnight—she had decided to make experimental fiddles, too. She had taken on two apprenticeships simultaneously. Carleen now had two mentors, and suddenly everything multiplied—including the fiddle plates she was carving—conventional violas, her first cello with Berger, and experimental fiddles for Saunders.

Then there was the mothering apprenticeship that happened in and around these two endeavors. Mort picked up the slack in virtually every corner of the household from cooking, cleaning, and household repairs to overseeing Bill and Cassie. Carleen would later recall this time in her life in rather simple terms: "I was raising two kids and taking care of two elderly parents and my husband and keeping a household going and doing this at that same time. But it saved my life because I just didn't want to settle down. As my husband said, you don't need to just settle down to dishes, diapers and spinach."[2]

In reality, Carleen found herself immersed in another informal apprenticeship to the violin world itself, a world that included all kinds of unexpected direct and indirect encounters with professional musicians, music professors, dealers, quartets, and patent lawyers, as well as other luthiers—spawned primarily by the network Saunders had built during twenty years of research.

An apprentice is a person who learns a job or skill by working a fixed period of time for someone who is very good at that job or skill. But unlike a conventional apprenticeship, Hutchins's double apprenticeship had no structure, and it certainly offered no pay. In addition, Carleen had no boundaries to bump up against except the constraints of time, energy, and focus, given the other distractions surrounding a mother. In addition, there seemed to be no limits to the unbounded enthusiasm of Saunders, who had increasing confidence in Carleen's intuitive violinmaking abilities. Though honored to have the confidence of so prestigious a mentor as Saunders, Carleen found it at times increasingly difficult to keep pace. And as usual, Mort remained supremely tolerant, patient, and totally supportive of any direction Carleen chose.

On February 13, 1953, Saunders wrote to Hutchins that their "ditching" idea was catching on. Saunders sent a copy of a letter he had received from the renowned cellist Oliver Edel, a revered professor at the University of Michigan School of Music, who wrote that "ditching" had been tried successfully by two other luthiers — Halvarson and Meyers, of Nashville, Michigan. Saunders thus considered these two to be the first expert violin producers to be persuaded of the value of his and Carleen's new technique.

In May, the "scientific" version of their joint article, "On Improving Violins," published by the *Acoustical Society Journal*, caught some attention even as hopes for a patent diminished when Verne S. Swan, presumably a patent lawyer, located an 1858 patent granted to John Robertson of Edinburgh for improving the volume and quality of violin tone by "grooving the back and breast."[3]

On a return trip from Halifax in October 1953, Saunders went by Cambridge and stayed overnight with his friend Wolfensohn and wrote to Hutchins about even greater prospects for spreading the news of the success of her work thus far.[4] Saunders said that in "Wolfy's" quartet, both the Boston Symphony Orchestra violist Eugene Lehner and Wolfensohn himself wanted to purchase Hutchins violas. Also during this visit, Saunders had met a Harvard Observatory physicist who was taking a violin lesson and told Saunders he would like to buy a Hutchins violin. Consequently, Saunders reported that all three musicians were planning to drive to Montclair in a few weeks in order to visit Hutchins, view the laboratory at 112 Essex, and try out her instruments.

By the fall of 1953, Carleen, age forty-two, had a two-year-old daughter and a five-year-old son. By then, she had made seventeen violas in all —

seven built to sell, and ten other "very weird looking" instruments. One reporter described the curiosities resulting from the Hutchins-Saunders experiments: "One looks like a child's violin that has been sat on and another has a deep sound box that makes it look almost like a guitar, and still another looks like a stringed cigar box. Yet all sound like violas."[5]

At about this time, at the invitation of the violinist and Juilliard teacher William "Fritz" Kroll, whom Carleen had met through chamber music with Helen Rice, Mort and Carleen took twelve of her violas and a few violins to the Krolls' apartment. By this time, Carleen had a fair amount of information from her experiments with free plates. Carleen and Mort conversed with Mrs. Kroll, while Fritz tried out the different violas and violins. Afterward, Kroll held up one viola and said, "This has it — the feel we look for in a fine instrument. When I play it, I can feel the whole instrument vibrate. The back vibrates; the top vibrates. I can feel it all through my shoulder and my arm and there's a response that comes quickly. It's not the case in any of the other instruments you've brought here."[6]

So Carleen packed up her fiddles and pondered Kroll's comments for a long time. She finally decided the only way to find out what was going on in the one best-sounding viola was to take it apart and test the two plates. This was the beginning of Carleen's interest in studying tap tones.[7] The tap tone is the sound produced by a detached violin plate when it is held at a specific point and tapped lightly at another point obtained by generating a magnetic driving pulse observed in a photo strip. Saunders and Hutchins used various methods in their magnetic driving experiments, testing as many as forty violins, including two Stradivarius. In one method, they installed a wire in lieu of the G string and sent current at a specific frequency through it, recording sound levels over the whole range of the frequency in a series of peaks and valleys.[8]

A second method, developed by A. S. Hopping, a former Westinghouse electronics expert who joined research efforts at 112 Essex for a time, consisted of fastening a piece of thin iron to the violin bridge. Modified by current from an audio generator, the magnetic driver was attracted to this piece of iron, causing the violin to sing with a nearly pure tone that was then picked up to drive an oscilloscope spot vertically, recording the amplitude of motion on a moving strip of photographic film. These "photostrips" produced visual images chronicling the condition of a violin plate at various stages of development—for example, demonstrating how it changed tonally in the process of thinning it.

Hutchins found that tap tones are often multiple and that there were two optimal arrangements—to have the highest tap tone of the top plate differ (a little higher or a little lower) from the highest tone of the back plate and that the difference should be about a semitone. The tap tones of front and back plates should never coincide.

Saunders and Hutchins came to some conclusions about carrying power, ease of playing, quickness of response, and the effect of varnish and age. "Carrying power" is defined as the sound emitted by the violin in unit time. Acoustically, the violin is extremely inefficient in producing sound in comparison with the power spent to play it. That is to say, only 2 percent of the energy that a player feeds into a violin actually emerges as sound. To add to the complexity, there is no easy way to replicate a "pure" measurement of musical sound, because there is no way to direct the sound waves, as a player might throw a ball to a target. In accordance with the physical nature of wave motion, when one hears a musical instrument in a concert hall, one hears both the direct sound from the violin in combination with other sounds reflected from interior surfaces. Saunders and Hutchins found that the loss of sound attributable to reflection usually varies with frequency—a fact that can work with or against the instrument, depending on its own qualities. "Carrying power" depends on the power of the instrument, the nature of the hall, and especially the size of the audience, which tends to absorb sound greatly.[9]

A physicist would define "ease of playing" as the amount of mechanical power necessary to cause a violin to "speak properly." To test for this concept, Saunders and Hutchins used the automatic bow to obtain data. They measured the minimum power necessary to produce a proper tone and were pleased to discover that this proved to be a repeatable amount. They then plotted the power against the frequency. Their results showed that the weight of the string was the most important factor, with the weight of the whole violin as the second-most important influence, concluding that in order to make the violin "speak," the player creates the loudest tone by using a short bow distance combined with high speed.[10]

In considering "quickness of response," Saunders and Hutchins used a high-speed camera (more than ten feet per second) with a high-speed amplifier and managed to obtain good pictures of the vertical motion of the oscilloscope activated by the listening microphone. They concluded that the inexpensive violin reached its maximum tone more quickly than the Guarnerius but that the maximum tone reached by the Guarnerius was greater, indicating that the quickness of response was not an indicator of excellence.[11]

With respect to the variable of varnish, Saunders and Hutchins tackled the conclusion of H. Meinel in Germany, who observed that varnish produced such a small change in the response curve that it was not ordinarily detected by the ear. After testing the tap tones of two similar strips of wood, then varnishing them, Hutchins and Saunders found that their tests agreed with those of Meinel.[12]

The effect of age on violin tone is a complex issue, because different age variables cannot be separated out — there is the length of time between the cutting of the tree and the making of the violin; the age of the completed instrument; and the number of years it has been played. In addition, there is only one violin — the "Messiah," which sits in its display case in the Ashmolean Museum in Oxford in a beautiful state of preservation — that might reveal something about the effect of age alone.[13]

In the spring of 1954, Saunders received news that he had been selected to receive the Honorary Fellowship, the highest award given by the Acoustical Society of America. Suddenly he was reluctant to include Hutchins, saying to her, as Hutchins recalled later: "You don't need to come to the meeting — you probably wouldn't understand most of it."[14] Having grown up in a home dominated by the accomplishments of his father and four brothers — all of them professional scientists and musicians — Saunders might view Hutchins in a different light as a woman teaching herself physics. Even though he welcomed experimenting on her instruments and genuinely enjoyed the camaraderie, it was another matter to include his self-taught female apprentice in the academic arena of the Acoustical Society of America. Regardless, their correspondence expanded as Hutchins became more and more a colleague of Saunders and her understanding of violin acoustics grew. Saunders continued writing long letters as Carleen penned postcards.

Another labor-intensive set of experiments involved thirty-five instruments that Hutchins had in the making. With each one, the top and back were intentionally left too thick. Saunders would test the plates, and then

Hutchins would assemble the plates into instruments and get feedback from players, particularly Louise Rood and John Di Janni, the first violist of the Metropolitan Opera Orchestra. Both Rood and Di Janni were known for their extremely consistent auditory memory. Then Hutchins would take the instrument apart, carve more off the plate, and retest.[15]

In June 1954, Carleen could celebrate selling SUS #15 — to Robert Courte of the Stanley Quartet.[16] Reading between the lines of the family log and observing comments from Saunders, one can surmise that the Hutchins household had gone through a tough time. Even so, fiddlemaking continued, no matter what. On May 10, 1955, Saunders wrote Hutchins a letter commiserating about the family's bout with illness but applauding the fact that she had nevertheless continued to produce instruments.[17]

On August 1, Saunders wrote to Hutchins about another session of trying her instruments at the home of Gertrude Smith, the pianist at Smith College, where Saunders had joined Smith and Louise Rood and played music for two violas and piano. According to Saunders's account, both Smith and Rood startled at the sound emanating from SUS #26 when Rood first played it, and Rood later pronounced it "perfect!" Saunders not only sent his congratulations to Hutchins on obtaining such a response, he even suggested that this viola might be the one that would finally garner the interest of the Boston Symphony violist Eugene Lehner, who had been showing interest in Hutchins's instruments but had not yet purchased one.[18]

Sometime during the summer of 1955, Carleen began another experiment that involved making a shallow cello — the "pancake cello." On September 23, Saunders wrote that he had great faith in the potential acoustical properties of "pancake" stringed instruments. One week later, he wrote that SUS #11 — a flat cello — had surpassed his expectations.[19] On November 9, a letter arrived from Saunders describing in great detail his music session at Smith with the Stanley Quartet, where the musicians tried out violin SUS #29; violas 11, 27, 22, and 30; and the X-1 flat "pancake" cello. Saunders wrote that everyone got excited about the experimental cello because no one could fathom that a flat cello could produce such a monstrous tone, and that Oliver Edel, the Stanley Quartet cellist, gave the cello a workout, describing its C string as stupendous.[20]

The same day, Carleen's father went into the hospital. Less than a month later, on December 1, 1955, Thomas Maley was admitted yet again. For various reasons, the Saunders-Hutchins correspondence went dormant for six months. The Saunderses were relocating to a new home, while Carleen was coping with the illness of her father. But on April 13, 1956, Saunders picked up where he had left off, writing that he had been going over loudness curves for SUS #26 and 28 and that Louise Rood was also working with Carleen's violas. Saunders wrote that Rood not only approved of all of Carleen's work but continued to find new things to praise about her latest crop of violas. Priding herself on giving Hutchins specific feedback about each viola she tried, Rood declared that while SUS #27 had a big, rich viola tone, it was too big to play; SUS #26 was good but had a bad C string; and SUS #28 was so perfect in evenness and power despite its small size that she wanted to keep it!

From January 3, 1956, through late February, Carleen's father was transported in and out of the hospital several times via ambulance. Then on February 24, Thomas William Maley died at 3:20 a.m. He was buried three days later. The family log mentions nothing else. On March 6, Bill joined the Cub Scouts, and on April 17, Carleen and Mort hosted Bill's first Cub Scout meeting at their house. A week later, Saunders was abuzz about the growing interest of William Lincer, the principal violist for the New York Philharmonic. Saunders often played quartets with his colleagues at Smith and Mount Holyoke—and brought along Hutchins's instruments to test in chamber music sessions. In one letter, Saunders lamented the negativity of Mount Holyoke professor and violinist Milton Aronson, who had complained about the unevenness of the G string.[21] But then, just ten days later, when Saunders took SUS #22 to another chamber music session, Aronson had nothing but praise for it, both when he played it and when he heard Saunders play it. Saunders loved reporting such progress in changing people's perceptions, applauding the fact that Hutchins was getting better and better at her craft. In fact, Saunders wrote that he considered SUS #22 to be Hutchins' best viola yet—much superior to the one he currently played.[22]

Even as he peppered his letters with compliments for Hutchins's success thus far, Saunders always found a way to push for the next experiment. On May 15, 1956, he managed to fit a whirlwind list of compliments on one small postcard, ending this litany with a suggestion about the next experiment. Would she consider altering her Gasparo model viola to make it less difficult for a player to reach the high positions?[23] Even a sale! On August 14, Saunders congratulated Hutchins on selling SUS #22. Throughout thirty years of entries in the family logs, Hutchins very seldom recorded the prices of the instruments she sold. Early efforts most likely went for under $300 to $1,000. But as she expanded her output, prices rose to as much as $5,000 or more.

Saunders and Hutchins were constantly aware that many luthiers, dealers, and players looked askance at their experiments. In one instance, E. W. Lavender, the editor of *Strad* magazine, asked Saunders to write an article about his 1930s testing of old violins, including Heifetz's Guarneri and Stradivari instruments. Saunders agreed but warned Lavender that he hoped he would not mind Saunders's candid remarks about some flaws in the Stradivari instruments.[24] In a letter to Hutchins dated October 15, 1956, Saunders observed that Lavender had agreed, saying he could not object to printing technical data regarding Heifetz's violins because he was certain that any scientific evaluation of their tonal qualities would have absolutely no influence on the opinion of any artist.[25] In other words, as Saunders had observed for more than a decade, not only were players subjective about their views of certain instruments, but they often showed nothing but disdain for scientific analysis.

Now that Saunders and Hutchins were keenly aware that they were shaking up preconceived notions about old versus new violins, no territory was sacred, especially the work of contemporary viola makers like Englishman Lionel Tertis, one of the first violists to promote the viola as a solo instrument and the latest luthier claiming to have solved the viola puzzle with his own model. While large violas measuring 17⅛ inches often have great power and deep tone, they are difficult to play. To address this problem, Tertis claimed to have developed a way to make a slightly smaller viola measuring 16¾ inches that still retained the tone of a larger instrument.

On October 19, 1956, Hutchins wrote of meeting Tertis in the family log: "He has the courage of conviction and has tried everything he can think of to make the form of a viola easier to play and with more tone — especially on the C string. . . . [I]nterested in a lopsided model." In late October, Saunders wrote to Hutchins about meeting with Tertis and suggested that perhaps the only way to discover what was wrong with a Tertis-model viola was for Hutchins to make one according to the Tertis specifications.[26] By then Tertis had given Hutchins a blueprint and a set of instructions, and

Hutchins accepted the challenge, reserving rights to run her own experiment with varying plate thicknesses.[27]

Years later, Hutchins reflected on comments from luthiers about how science was "demystifying" their art. "I tell them I am helping the art . . . taking the mystique out of it, but giving them solid facts to explain why when you change a fingerboard you can either help, or destroy the sound of the instrument. . . . [T]here are tests to show exactly what happens when you change the mass and stiffness of the fingerboard."[28]

Hutchins remained forever fascinated by one of the great puzzles that has challenged luthiers since Amati first designed the violin: the mystery of wood itself. Because wood is not a uniform substance, acoustical measurements of two pieces cut from the same section of the same tree can differ drastically, leading luthiers to wonder if the Old Masters were somehow able to take these variations into account when they selected violin wood — another unsolved conundrum at the center of the luthier's world.

On Friday, March 13, 1959, Carleen wrote: "Eugene Lehner swapped his Tertis-Richardson viola for my #31. Will play in Boston Symphony. Yippee!!!!"[29]

Intermezzo

Acoustics – Sound Waves and Sand Patterns

The essential problem of research in musical acoustics
in recent years has been to find ways to prevent the
divorce of music as an art from music as a science.
— Acoustical Society of America Citation, 1981

A century before Frederick Saunders began bowing violins in a sound booth, in Paris at the turn of the nineteenth century, the birth of violin acoustics began in the sand, glass, wood, and string acoustical experiments performed by two musically minded scientists and two scientifically minded luthiers bent on exploring sound and making music in the process. The result was a *euphon* and *clavicylinder* made by Ernst Chladni; a *guitar-violin* by François Chanot; a *trapezoid violin* made by Félix Savart; and a *de Jullien* (small violin), *contralto viola*, and *octobasse* made by Jean-Baptiste Vuillaume.

Though Leonardo da Vinci, Robert Hooke, and Georg Christoph Lichtenberg had each observed how grains of sand vibrated in varied geometric patterns, it was the German physicist and amateur musician Ernst F. F. Chladni who made these "sound figures" famous. Chladni toured Europe giving lectures and demonstrating these sound patterns to live audiences so extensively that they became known as "Chladni figures," consequently earning him the title of "the father of acoustics."[1] As Chladni drew a violin bow perpendicularly across the edge of a piece of metal covered lightly with a coating of sand, he observed that at certain resonances, the sand formed into geometric patterns as it settled into the nodal regions of the metal plate. Furthermore, he observed that the plates vibrated at pure audible pitches, each pitch producing a unique nodal pattern. The patterns formed were symmetrical and often intricate and spectacular — lines of sand forming circles, stars, waves and other complex geometric shapes. Chladni painstakingly diagrammed the patterns that occurred at different frequencies and classified them according to geometric shape and corresponding pitch.

In this way, Chladni devised a repeatable, practical, and visual way of demonstrating how sound affects physical matter. In 1787, Chladni published this technique of generating sound figures in his book *Entdeckungen über die Theorie des Klanges* (Discoveries in the theory of sound). In the process, Chladni invented two musical instruments — the *euphon*, a modified version of Benjamin Franklin's *armonica*, and the *clavicylinder*, a keyboard instrument with keys connected to glass cylinders, turned by a pedal and loaded wheel, an improvement of Hooke's "musical cylinder."[2] In 1808, Chladni visited the Paris Academy and demonstrated his sound patterns to an audience that included not only leading French scientists but Napoleon as well. Still, the full explanation for the occurrence of "Chladni figures" remains elusive — part of the mystery of modern waves research that remains unsolved today.

At about the same time that Chladni was demonstrating sound figures in Paris, François Chanot, who had grown up in a Mirecourt violinmaking family, left Mirecourt for Paris to study mathematics and graduated from the École Polytechnique. In 1812, Chanot, a naval engineer, began studying stringed instrument acoustics. Theorizing that sound production involved the wood fibers of the violin, Chanot changed the shape and position of the f-holes; centered the bass and the sound post; transformed the tailpiece to a guitar bridge pattern; and reversed the curve of the scroll. All in all, the instrument he created looked much like a guitar, hence its name — "guitar-violin."

Chanot summed up his research in a thesis, "Mémoire d'un essay tendant à perfectionner les violins, altos, basses, et contrebasses," a thesis about "a trial to improve the violin, viola, cello, and double bass." In 1817, when he sent it to the Beaux-Arts Academy with a violin made according to his principles, Chanot was granted a patent free of charge. But shortly thereafter, upon deciding instead to rejoin the navy, Chanot sought out a serious violinmaker to manufacture his guitar-violins. Chanot chose J. B. Vuillaume, who had also been born into a Mirecourt violinmaking family and had most likely begun his training, by tradition, at age thirteen. By 1818, Vuillaume had spent four years as a journeyman, and set to work for Chanot.[3] The guitar-violins were initially successful, but they proved fragile at a time when musicians required increased tension on the strings to project sound in larger concert halls. Construction of these guitar-violins halted in 1823.

Meanwhile, at about the same time Vuillaume was working on Chanot violins, the physician Felix Savart became fascinated by the acoustics of stringed instruments and began to build violins based on the mathematical principles he wrote about in his thesis on stringed and bowed instruments. In 1819, Savart went to Paris to meet the French physicist and astronomer Jean-Baptiste Biot. Biot was so impressed with Savart's memoir that he presented Savart's paper to the Academy of Sciences, where it was published in that same year—a seminal work titled *Mémoire des instruments à cordes et à archet*. Savart was the first physicist to devote study to violin acoustics and the first to give an explanation about the function of certain parts of the violin.

By 1823, Vuillaume had begun to come into his own as a violinmaker. At the 1827 Fair of Industrial Products in Paris, Vuillaume for the first time presented instruments under his own name. He exhibited copies he had made of violins by Stradivari, the Amati, and the Guarneri. As a result of his acoustical experiments, Vuillaume also made several experimental instruments. The *de Jullien* was a small violin tuned an octave above the viola, named for the dance master who commissioned it. He also made a great pattern, deep-ribbed *contralto* viola, and the *octobasse*—a twelve-foot-tall contrabass that required two people to play it—one to bow while the other controlled the strings via pedals.

In 1830, Savart invented a toothed frequency wheel for determining the number of variations in a given musical tone—a device that aided all those who would come after him in violin acoustics, as it provided a simplified method for generating tones at controllable frequencies.[4] At the beginning of his career, Savart had held out great hopes that the mystery of the violin would be solved. In fact, so confident was he at this time about the merits of violin acoustics research, Savart ended his memoir with this conclusion: "We have arrived at a time when the efforts of scientists and artists will be united to bring to perfection an art which, till now, was limited to a blind routine."[5] But more than a decade later Savart had given up his experiments with the trapezoidal violin. In 1831, he wrote of his chagrin about the riddle of violin acoustics to his brother Nicolas: "The business of violins . . . is getting so complicated that I think I will never understand anything. Air plays the devil's part, which I can more or less understand. But I cannot make out the laws. The nature of the wood also has an influence . . . which complicates the manufacturing process. . . . You will see that this is the devil and the conditions that have to be met to succeed are so complicated that it seems inconceivable that good violins can ever have been made other than through sheer luck."[6]

Meanwhile, in the nineteenth century, luthiers made a few substantial changes in the modern violin in order to address the rise in frequency of the pitch reference for musical note A from approximately 370 Hz to 440–450 Hz and to create instruments that would project better in larger concert halls.[7] In response to these new requirements, luthiers intuited a way to get greater sound from the violin. They lengthened the neck and strings; adjusted the angle of the neck to allow for tighter string tension; built a higher bridge to allow for maneuvering of the bow; and installed a heavier bass bar to strengthen the top plate. The collaboration between Savart and Vuillaume most likely developed because Vuillaume was taking apart old violins in order to make these changes.

At the 1839 Fair of Industrial Products, Vuillaume got the highest award — a gold medal — for two violins, two violas, and a cello. He was now on par with the best piano builders — Erard and Pape. Sylvette Milliot, Vuillaume's biographer, wrote of Savart's influence on Vuillaume: "Apparently, the collaboration with Savart had given him the necessary scientific groundings to reach his goal: the rediscovery of the famous Italian tone. In so doing, he passed from the imitation of his models to their true replica."[8]

After Savart and Vuillaume, little research into violin acoustics was done for nearly a century. Then twentieth-century electronic devices facilitated further study of violin acoustics. In his monumental work *Sensations of Tone*, the German physicist Herman von Helmholtz (1821–94) focused on the physiological sensation of sound and psychological investigation of perception, using a set of sphere resonators of graduated sizes that he developed. Lord Rayleigh (John William Strutt, 1842–1919) made significant contributions to the practical understanding of musical acoustics in his *Theory of Sound* (1877) by using electrical circuit theory analogies to understand vibrations of acoustical resonators. In the 1890s, the Russian luthier Anatoly Ivanovich Leman applied scientific training to lutherie and made instruments considered comparable in design, beauty, and workmanship to those of Stradivari. Leman wrote *Acoustics of the Violin* in 1903.

In the early part of his career, the Indian physicist C. V. Raman (1888–1970) studied the bowed string. In the 1930s, Hermann Backhaus (1885–1958) studied acoustical properties of the violin and was the first to map vibrational modes of the arched top and back plates of a violin, vibrated by an automatic bowing device. Hermann Meinel (1904–77), a student of

Backhaus, was also a master violinmaker from a lineage of makers. Meinel made and tested his own instruments under a range of conditions, varying wood thickness, arching, and varnish. He also studied the properties of outstanding instruments and published his findings in articles in 1937, 1957, and 1975.

In 1930, when Frederick Saunders became curious about exploring violin acoustics, he was the virtually the only American physicist in the field. Following in the footsteps of European scientist-luthiers Chanot and Savart and the master luthier J.-B. Vuillaume, Carleen Hutchins was the first twentieth-century American luthier to merge acoustical physics with violinmaking. For this reason, she remains controversial among luthiers, many of whom have shown distrust of the application of science to lutherie.

On the Violinist.com blog, on March 3, 2012, an entry titled "The 'Secret' of the Strad: It's in Scientific American 1981" was posted by the violinist Anna Heifetz to begin a discussion about Hutchins's 1981 *Scientific American* cover article, "Acoustics of Violin Plates." Heifetz quotes Hutchins: "Modern tests of the vibrational properties of the unassembled top and back plates of a violin reveal something of what violinmakers do by 'feel' and lead to the making of consistently good violins."

David Burgess posted his reaction to Hutchins's work on the vibration of violin plates. "Carleen was quite convinced and passionate about her methods. Unfortunately, others were much less impressed by the goodness of her violins than she was. However, she helped stimulate interest in scientific investigation of violin sound, which continues today, but with more sophisticated methods, better engineers, and better data acquired from the old instruments.[9] Minutes later, Marc Cicchetto posted the following: "It has been my experience that Ernst Chladni's use of vibrating particles on a plate, violin or other, will indeed show you a pattern of active and dead zones for a given frequency. However this is of little use in tuning plates while they are being made. . . . [Nevertheless] I have great respect for the findings of Carleen. . . ."[10] A few hours later, John Soloninka said of Hutchins: "Carleen Hutchins needs to be acknowledged for the contributions she made to the 'science' of understanding violins. However, later research on 'tap tones' revealed them to be less prescriptive of violin quality than that article suggested."[11]

The next day, Bob Spear, a well-known American luthier who originally studied violin acoustics with Carleen and later made an entire violin octet, posted:

> My God! Where do I start? . . . But David, Carleen only "stimulated" interest in violin research? Man, she drove it from the start. That woman was like 100 tons of locomotive on rails — a force to be reckoned with! No Carleen, no Catgut Acoustical Society, no Oberlin Acoustics Workshops, no nuthin'!
>
> Marc, Chladni patterns of little use in tuning a violin plate? . . . The violin world is awash in schemes that seek to tune the parts of the instrument to specific tones or even chords. It seems as though something intuitively correct, but if plate tuning as Carleen taught it fails because of what happens when the parts are assembled then pretty much all the other approaches fail as well.
>
> John — matching the modes of free plates is indeed not prescriptive, but it is indicative. Perhaps a little elbow in the ribs to makers who graduate plates because it's really all they can do and it makes them feel good is tolerable, but just consider what happens to a violin when the plates are not tuned! Reminds me of the little joke about the airplane passenger who hopes that the engines don't fail or he'll be up in the sky all day![12]

Pedal Point

Suspension of one pitch
in such a manner that it
is alternately consonant
then dissonant with the
chord progression

Timothy A. Smith, "Anatomy of a Fugue"

7 ∫ *Musicmonger*

Hundreds of conflicting air currents swirl inside the violin. The rush of air exiting through the f-holes amounts to a ten mile per hour wind, most of which escapes as heat rather than sound. But there would be no sound without the escape hatch of the sound-holes. By 1956, Carleen Hutchins had so much going on in her life as she tried to balance work and family that she felt overwhelmed. She had no escape hatch — so something had to give.

On December 2, 1956, Carleen sat in hospital room 756 at Columbia Presbyterian, the day before surgery, having stowed away viola SUS #23 in her closet.[1] Just five days before, on Wednesday, November 28, Mort had recorded rather inconspicuously in the family log: "Carleen phoned office of Dr. Haagenson, who has advised her to have operation on Monday. Got family together to tell them of plans at suppertime tonight. Arrangements have been made for Lulu Harrison [housekeeper and babysitter] to stay here through Thursday of next week to help with household."[2]

The diagnosis was breast cancer, though it was never named. And the doctor's recommendation had been immediate surgery. Carleen had reason for concern: "This really shook the family up because my mother had a sister who had died of breast cancer and they were sure that that was the end of me."[3] Saunders tried to sound reassuring, writing to Carleen that he had had many friends and relatives who had fared the operation just fine and so, he assured her, there was nothing to be afraid of.[4] Though she had had a little less than a week to comprehend the diagnosis, in one sense, Carleen was the least surprised of all. There had been nothing out of the ordinary about life at 112 Essex, yet that was part of the problem — something had to give. Chasing down tools at bargain hardware stores; treating deerskins with lime; canning applesauce; tending to the turtle pen and the menagerie of animals; tending to two children, ages six and nine, who were frequently home sick with allergies; traveling into New York City to work as science consultant for Coward-McCann Publishing and the Girl Scouts; rebuilding a stone fireplace and chimney; carving a cello top; graduating violas with differing thicknesses; playing quartets at a neighbor's house — these were the activities that constituted a normal day for Carleen Hutchins.

Carleen had her own ideas about why her body was speaking to her. She had long ago concluded that her breast cancer was evidence of the stress she felt in balancing a three-generation household while mourning the professional paths she might have taken. Hutchins recalled the career options she had been required to turn down: "These were big jobs, not peanuts but this was 1945–46, before we had Bill. I made a list of what would happen if I took each job—any one of those jobs—or called it quits, and I figured I couldn't stay married. I just decided: forget it. I went back to Brearley and was miserable there because I knew what I could have done. I had a radical mastectomy. It took that long for the stress to really take me to pieces."[5]

Whereas the norm for many housewives in the 1950s was defined by traditional roles, ever since Cornell, Carleen had surrounded herself with women pursuing nontraditional paths—professional, educated women with careers. This circle of professional female friends included lawyer Margaret Sachter, Girl Scout Director Edith Conant, publisher Alice Torrey, social worker Harriet Bartlett, musician and ACMP founder Helen Rice, Smith music professor and violist Louise Rood, and woodworking teacher Petie Evans—all of whom provided strong alternative female role models. If anything, Carleen's peers pressured her to continue her work, outside the domestic realm. In addition, most of these women were single and so became extended family at 112 Essex.

Given her sense of loss about what careers she might have pursued, Carleen clung even more to her work with Saunders. Her collaboration with him had suddenly added prestige and importance to an obsession that had begun as a pipe dream hobby. And Saunders was clearly as interested in their work as Carleen was—an unexpected bonus. In the same letter in which Saunders voiced his reassurances about the upcoming operation, he soon veered off to the topic at hand—the latest findings on the fiddles. Saunders assured Carleen that he had not shared her latest research on tap tones. For now, he urged her to keep her results private, lest her untested theory be released too soon. Then Saunders took on the issue of volume and tone by comparing his overtone measurements of an accordion with that of a Guarneri violin. Even though the accordion had, at minimum, ten more measurable overtones, its tone was not better, so Saunders concluded that some criterion other than the overtones and volume must be important to optimal violin tone.[6]

These were ideas Carleen was mulling over as she contemplated her operation. Just a few weeks before, on November 5, Carleen wrote in the family log: "Letter from Saunders on his plans for more experiments on fiddles. Most exciting ideas in many moons. Much to digest and think about."[7] So, no matter what the circumstances, no matter what Carleen was thinking or doing, fiddles were never far away. Drawn toward the magnet of her violin research with Saunders, Carleen already faced the daily temptation to get lost in violinmaking and research in order to escape the much less exciting realms of a household and raising children. The latest opportunity for distraction and escape came in the form of a chance meeting under most dire circumstances between a doctor and patient, spawning a friendship that began in a hospital room with viola SUS #23 and a piece of curly maple that culminated in the creation of an entire string quartet.

Virginia Apgar and Carleen Hutchins had much in common. Apgar had wanted to be a doctor since high school, inspired by the illness of a brother and the early death of another brother to tuberculosis. A zoology major, violinist, and cellist at Mount Holyoke, Apgar enrolled in the College of Physicians and Surgeons at Columbia University and finished fourth in her class in 1933. Though Apgar won a surgical internship at Columbia and excelled, her mentor discouraged her from surgery because women had failed to establish careers in the field. Instead, he urged Apgar to pursue the fledgling field of surgical anesthesiology, a responsibility that until then had been delegated to nurses.

But in 1938, when Apgar became director of the division of anesthesia at the Columbia-Presbyterian Medical Center, surgeons did not accept or pay anesthesiologists as equals, so Apgar struggled to recruit doctors, and she remained virtually the only staff member in the field until the mid-1940s. In 1946, when anesthesiology became an acknowledged medical specialty, Apgar became the first woman appointed to full professor at Columbia University College of Physicians and Surgeons. Apgar took obstetrical anesthesiology to a new level of expertise by devising the first standardized method for evaluating the health of a newborn. The APGAR Score evaluates five indicators of newborn health one minute after delivery — Appearance, Pulse, Grimace, Activity, and Respiration. Formally presented in 1952, the APGAR score has since been accepted as an international standard throughout the world to measure newborn health at birth.

Both Hutchins and Apgar, biologist and zoologist, had needed to carve their way through unknown territory. Both had wanted to be doctors, but only one would succeed. Each was a lone female in a branch of science in its infancy—musical acoustics and anesthesiology. Both loved string music. Both played viola—and one made violas. On the day before surgery, Carleen sat in her hospital room, staring at the closet, awaiting a visit from her anesthesiologist. Through her surgeon, Dr. Cushman Haagenson, who was also a friend, Hutchins had learned that Apgar played viola!

As a result, Carleen had stowed her SUS #23 viola out of sight in her closet. On the night before the operation, Apgar poked her head around the corner to ask if Carleen was the patient of Dr. Haagenson. Before they even discussed the upcoming operation, Carleen went for the jugular: "You know, Dr. Haagenson suggested you might be interested in one of my violas, and I brought it; it's in the closet. Would you like to see it?" Where upon Apgar took up the viola and spent the rest of the time playing it right in the middle of Clarkman Pavilion, much to the enjoyment of nurses on the floor.[8] Later Apgar admitted that she had been so distracted with playing the viola that she had to return to room 756 to finish gathering her patient's medical history.

The next morning, on Monday, December 3, 1956, upon seeing the results of the biopsy during the operation, Haagenson performed an immediate mastectomy. Hutchins recalled: "It was a rugged time, but Dr. Apgar was very helpful and pleasant after the operation and kept coming in to see me. We talked, and occasionally my special nurse, Mrs. Kirk, would serve tea to both of us in the afternoon."[9]

Meanwhile, Mort was dealing with chaos at 112 Essex. He returned home to discover that both the dishwasher and refrigerator had broken down. He was terribly relieved that Lulu was coming in to help, as both Bill and Cassie were home sick with colds. Two days later when Carleen phoned the family, she suggested they not visit her the next day. Meanwhile, Apgar kept dropping by to see Carleen. And they must have been discussing violas because on Sunday, December 9, just eight days into her hospital stay, when Carleen phoned to talk to Mort, Bill, and Cassie, she asked them to bring viola SUS #28 to the hospital the following day.[10] On the 10th, when Mort went to have dinner with Carleen in the hospital, he received a "to do" list, mostly related to fiddle work and Carleen's efforts at pulling away from commitments in viola testing and Cub Scouts.[11]

The idea of escaping the commotion, the broken-down appliances, and the tasks awaiting her at home spurred Carleen to readily accept the offer for her to spend a week recuperating at Helen's 67th Street apartment. Without consulting Mort or the family, Carleen just made the plan, and Mort accepted whatever she chose to do.[12] On Saturday, December 15, 1956, Carleen went directly from the hospital to stay with Helen and her mother. Staying with Helen proved to be a double blessing because they played music together—doctor's orders: "I practiced the viola a bit each day and managed to play the Corelli *Christmas Concerto* last night. Haagenson says to exercise the arm—flap like a bird, but boy, it pulls all the muscles!"[13]

On Saturday, December 20, Mort, along with Bill and Cassie, drove over to bring Carleen home from New York. Carleen wrote in the family log: "Home! And am I ever glad to be back. Everyone has been wonderful to me—good care at the hospital—lots of interesting conversations about violas with the Doctors. . . . [T]his past week so good at Rice's with Helen and her mother doing everything they could for me—what friends!"[14] Even Carleen was aware of changes in both Bill and Cassie. "Mostly I just want to hug Bill and Cassie and Mort and Nanny and look at them. A short conversation with Bill about television shows me how much he has grown up since I left. Miss Gamble, his teacher, has done a wonderful job. Cassie, very self-contained, showing me lots of things she has done, loving and a bit wistful."[15]

Meanwhile, violas had evidently sparked a fast friendship between Hutchins and Apgar. One week later, on December 28, Apgar asked Carleen to come with Mort and Bill to lunch at the Medical Center. A week later, Apgar stopped by 112 Essex for the first time—"to see Carleen, fiddles and have drinks."[16] A few days later, on January 8, 1957, Mort returned to work; Bill and Cassie were home with colds. Nevertheless, that afternoon Carleen made her first "public" appearance since her operation by hosting a quartet at 112 Essex.[17] Playing viola—flapping her wings—was not only following doctor's orders, it proved to be an outlet that became increasingly difficult to resist. Playing quartets soon became both therapy and escape. A few days later, Apgar phoned Carleen with the good news that the pathology report showed no sign of cancer, so Dr. Haagenson had decided that there was no need for radiation therapy.[18]

Within three months of Carleen's operation, Apgar seemed to have become part of the Hutchins family. On Saturday, March 2, at Apgar's invitation, Carleen and Mort went to her home for supper, followed by a New York performance of *My Fair Lady*.[19] That next Friday, Carleen left for New York on the morning bus to have lunch with Edith Conant, but not before she had worked out household logistics, with her mother (Nanny) watching the children so she could go to Virginia's to play quartets that evening. A few days later, Carleen hosted quartets and reported on assembling SUS #36.[20] The next day, Virginia joined the family for dinner.

The following day, after visiting Helen and her mother in New York, Carleen stopped by the Medical Center. Virginia surprised Carleen with the question: "Do you want to see a baby born?" Carleen jumped at the chance, donned a hospital gown and skated around after Apgar in and out of operating rooms, up and down stairs. She reported in the family log: "Finally the baby made it, but very limp, needed resuscitation. Amazing teamwork by everyone in the room but me."[21] The next day, Carleen told Cassie she should try and stay quiet so as to get rid of her cold. Cassie, nearing her seventh birthday, told her mother: "How could I help bouncing around? Virginia was here. She's bouncy and she makes people bouncy — she makes everyone bounce around!"[22]

In the spring of 1957, during one of her post-op check-ups, Carleen got up the nerve to ask Virginia about a piece of wood she had seen in the hospital — the curly maple shelf in the Harkness Pavilion first-floor telephone booth. Carleen thought it would make great wood for a viola and asked Apgar about whether she could have it. Hutchins recalled that after Apgar talked about options among a few of her associates, "finally the consensus was that the only way to really get it was to help ourselves to it."[23] So Hutchins and Apgar hatched a plan to steal the phone booth shelf! First, Carleen had to make a replacement shelf. To her surprise, on the mission to the hardware store to replicate the stain, a man sorting paint at the back of the store overheard the conversation about Harkness Pavilion and rushed to the front counter, saying: "If you will use this number of our stain and this number in these proportions, you will get that color — I mixed the stain for that job 27 years ago!"[24] On March 20, Carleen went off to play quartets at Virginia's around three o'clock. That evening, Apgar, Hutchins, and Petie Evans took advantage of a dark night and rode to the hospital in Apgar's blue roadster—with Hutchins toting her son's briefcase filled with carpenter's tools, jimmy tools, pry bars, and the stained piece of maple. Apgar left the getaway car at the ambulance entrance and donned her white doctor's coat.

It was quite a job for Evans and Hutchins to pry the old shelf loose without ruining the whole plaster wall while Apgar stood in the main corridor between the elevators and the doctors' lunch room, distracting curious onlookers. Carleen remembered: "Every time someone came by, Virginia knocked on the glass door of the phone booth, and I would be busy putting dimes in the telephone. When the night watchman came by asking what all the racket was about, Dr. Apgar convinced him everything was fine."

When Carleen tried to replace the shelf, she realized she had not noticed a hidden dovetail joint that made her shelf too long. To remedy the situation, Carleen had to saw the end off an eight-inch long, one-inch thick piece of maple with a dovetail saw, the only one she had with her. The only possible place to do this, to get any leverage at all was to put the board across the top of a toilet seat in the ladies room. While Carleen was sawing on the toilet, Dr. Apgar appeased the curious nurses who kept coming by the ladies room, saying that this was the only time workmen could access the ladies room without embarrassing anyone. Meanwhile, Hutchins installed the new shelf, and Apgar took the old shelf with all the nails sticking out of it under her coat and out the ambulance entrance to her car. Hutchins concluded: "Presbyterian Hospital now had a brand new telephone shelf without cigarette burns or chewing gum, no dimes behind the shelf, and no scratches or fingernail marks of worried fathers reporting about their babies being born."

By ten o'clock that evening, the mission had been accomplished. Carleen, exhausted from having spent so much energy such a short time after her operation, returned home, surprised to see the horror on nine-year-old Bill's face when he learned his briefcase had been used in the sting. Hutchins recalled: "He felt his mother was going to end up in a New York jail . . . swiping things from the hospital using *his* briefcase full of jimmy tools! Mother saved the day, and said: 'A little nonsense now and then is relished by the best of men.' Nanny convinced Bill his mother wasn't quite so bad after all."[25]

The shelf-stealing escapade proved the beginning of a close friendship between Hutchins and Apgar. In fact, stealing the maple shelf inspired Apgar to ask Hutchins to teach her how to make a viola. What better piece of wood to use than the coveted piece of curly maple that she had just helped to steal? Shortly thereafter, the Hutchins-Apgar violamaking lessons began. It was the first time that Hutchins had a pupil in violinmaking. Hutchins said that Apgar was an apt pupil who learned quickly. The only problem was that Virginia loved to take pictures every step of the way, and sometimes, in the course of trying to photograph her viola, it would get dropped — requiring several weeks' worth of repairs.

On Sunday, March 31, 1957, Carleen was excited to report that a Mr. Grossman, who played second viola at the Metropolitan Opera, visited 112 Essex to try violas and "took one to try." That same afternoon, Saunders invited Hutchins and A. S. Hopping to join him for dinner at the Marlboro Inn, just down the street from 112 Essex. On this crystal clear night, while Carleen was out discussing fiddles, Mort wrote in the family log that he got out the telescope, and he, Cassie, and Bill spied the nebula in Orion and Jupiter and four moons.[26]

When she wasn't playing quartets with Carleen or stopping by 112 Essex to work on her viola, Apgar found other ways to fit into life with Carleen and Mort — weeding the gardens, pouring a concrete floor for the turtle pen, doing errands for the family, taking Mort to the airport. Pardoxically, while Apgar, a single doctor without family, latched on to the Hutchins family, Carleen took her family largely for granted. The fiddle became the thing that allowed Carleen permission to flap her wing and escape everything, freed by the good will of Mort, Nanny, and Lulu, who would keep things going at home. For instance, on April 11, even though Bill was sick and away from school for most of the week, Carleen and Virginia took a weeklong trip north to the cabin in New Hampshire by way of South Hadley, staying over with the Saunders to talk fiddles. On Saturday, May 4, 1957, the family celebrated Mort's birthday with a party that included Virginia, Petie Evans, Alice Culver, Mary Steward — and a new turtle pen for Mort that was christened by breaking a bottle of root beer. On Mother's Day, May 12, Mort helped Carleen set up a workbench in the cellar. But that evening, Carleen went out to play quartets with Mr. and Mrs. Piggins and Apgar.

The family log also recorded an insightful comment by Cassie. When

Nanny asked Cassie where her mother was, she said: "She's out getting something she can't find." From out of the mouths of babes — for Carleen was usually elsewhere, even when she was right at home carving or measuring or talking fiddles. Except for the occasional Cub Scout meeting at 112 Essex and rare moments like the one when Carleen might blow taps to close a meeting, Mort was the one attending Brookside School Field Day and watching Cassie finish fifth in the first-grade fifty-yard dash or fourth in the potato race.

In the meantime, on Monday, September 16, 1957, when Carleen went to play quartets, Virginia invited her to join her in a rehearsal with the Teaneck Symphony. Carleen loved it so much, that when she returned home, she called Isabel Richter to arrange weekly viola lessons — a routine that often included playing quartets in the afternoon at 112 Essex or at Virginia's in the evening, when she was not rehearsing with the Teaneck Symphony. (Hutchins later described herself as a mediocre violist.) Even the children's birthdays seldom seemed free of fiddle business. On Thursday, April 10, 1958, Cassie's eighth birthday, Virginia joined the family for the celebration — yet the log recorded: "Cassie very much excited. CMH: took the back off #30 viola this morning. Will test it to determine sound peaks after 3 years of aging of the varnish."[27] It seemed as if Carleen was always taking her leave, chasing intertwining trails that incorporated fiddle tests or carving plates or playing quartets or writing fiddle articles.

Over the years, Apgar remained an adopted member of the Hutchins family. Hutchins helped Apgar make three other instruments — a violin, a mezzo, and a cello, but Apgar never completed the cello; Hutchins finished it when Apgar died in 1974. These four instruments became known as the Apgar String Quartet, now housed at Columbia-Presbyterian Medical Center. The back plate of the Apgar viola made from the maple phone booth shelf turned out to have a nice sound, but not as good as it might have had, because the wood had been kiln-dried.

Carleen could be kiln-dried in showing emotion, a stoic who at this point in her life seldom really saw all that she was ignoring on the home front in favor of following her fiddles. She kept turning her back on everything else happening at home. On Saturday, May 17, 1958, Cassie went with the Moore family to the Brookside School Field Day. She took first prize in the relay race and finished third in the fifty-yard dash for girls in grades 1–3 — all dutifully recorded by Mort in the family log. Carleen returned home late that evening after an overnight music outing at a Bach Festival in Pennsylvania. In recording the day, Carleen is all sunshine about her stay in an immaculate Pennsylvania Dutch house with Apgar, Stan James, and Connie Berren; she wrote in the family log on the very same page: "Soaked up music and sun and wind. Music out of this world lovely — Passion, Harpsichord, Brass Choir in steeple, the whole B minor Mass — several thousand happy people . . . picnicked . . . cooked breakfast by a trout stream in a park full of girl scouts and bird watchers."[28]

Even in her happiest moments, Carleen never seemed to separate her fiddle work from her personal life — they were one and the same. On her birthday in 1958, Carleen spent the day outside putting finishing touches on her cello as she watched Bill and Cassie in the yard. She wrote in the family log: "A wonderful day in all ways. Family busy and happy. Sky blue and gold day. Dougie here to play with Bill and Cassie. I sat out in yard and watched activities . . . finished adjusting cello. Galley proof from *STRAD* . . . *VA* came and worked in garden . . . I'm grateful for so much!"[29]

Despite a home environment that seldom if ever offered a day free of "fiddle business," Bill and Cassie nevertheless excelled. In moments of personal success, both showed humility and sensitivity to others — qualities they certainly saw modeled every day in their father, who witnessed nearly everything and recorded it faithfully in the family log. On June 4, 1958, Mort wrote that Bill had been elected "best citizen" of his fifth-grade class by a vote of 16 to 1, the only dissenting ballot being his own. Cassie tied with Rickie Ripley for first honors of second grade but awarded it to Ricky, as he was younger and not absent as much as Cassie had been.[30]

How do we mark — or do we always see — the milestones of our children? Often they are not momentous at first glance, with progress measured in baby steps sometimes barely visible to a busy parent. On Monday, March 10, 1958, Mort recorded Carleen's activities, and then two small milestones for Bill, age eleven, and Cassie, a month away from her eighth birthday: "Music lesson this morning — Mrs. Richter's. Bill to Red Cross meeting — got out earlier than usual, started to walk home by himself. Is now on his own around town. Cassie built herself another campfire in side yard this afternoon."[31] Somehow, children grow up despite what parents do or do not notice. Suffice it to say, Mort was more likely to see these changes in Bill and Cassie than Carleen was. Even benign neglect is still neglect.

Intermezzo

Lutherie – a Spanish Lute Maker Settles in Cremona

The luthier who knows nothing about acoustics
of stringed instruments is nothing more than a carpenter.
—Antoine Marius Richelme, *Renaissance du violon*
et de ses analogues, 1883

One of the most precious artifacts located in the center of the Metropolitan Museum of Art is neither an object nor an exhibit but a room—the Gubbio Studiolo. The finest Italian Renaissance room in North America, built in 1496 in Florence, the Gubbio Studiolo served as the study for Duke Federico da Montefeltro, Renaissance statesman, warrior, scholar, and connoisseur of the arts, one the fifteenth century's most cultured and educated military leaders. A hidden treasure in plain sight, the Gubbio plays with vision through the magical mathematics of linear perspective, a brand new device in the fifteenth-century artisan's toolbox. Through the style of trompe l'oeil, we stand in an empty room and see things that are not there: benches, bookshelves, and closets holding the duke's treasures—books, armor and library tools, and scientific and musical instruments. The room itself is the illusion, as two-dimensional walls depict three-dimensional artifacts. A visitor to the Gubbio sees everything differently; it embodies the common ground where artist, scientist, and musician met with mutual interest and equal status, and music was the metaphor that combined all three. Stepping inside the Gubbio is like stepping into the time and mindset that birthed the violin.

The tallest bell tower in Italy stands at the iconic center of Cremona. The Gothic Torrazzo, built in 1309—the oldest brick tower over one hundred meters still standing, the second-oldest brick tower in all of Europe—houses the world's largest astronomical clock. But in the famed "City of Violins," in one respect, time stopped in Cremona at the time of death of its most famous native son—Antonio Stradivari.

Cremona comes by its romance honestly. If, in one small section of this provincial town perched on the bank of the Po River, time were to be compressed across two centuries, the very air would be dense with violinmaking genius. A couple of hundred yards away from Piazza San Domenico, Stradivari lived in Number 5 (the old house is gone) in an area now renamed Piazza Roma. One side street over one would find the parish of San Faustino, the patrician house of the Amatis. Even closer to Stradivari's house, in San Matteo parish, was the home and workshop of Andrea Guarneri. Giuseppe del Gesù lived not five minutes from Stradivari. Carlo Bergonzi and Francesco Ruggieri also lived nearby. That is to say, most of the world's great violins were made in this small section of Cremona over a span of less than two hundred years—perhaps one the greatest mysteries of the violin world.[1]

The tree of life for the violin has many branches—the ninth-century Arabian *rabab*, a two-string, fretless, pear-shaped gourd held in the lap and played with a bow, and the eleventh-century wooden, three-string Spanish *rebec*, played at the shoulder. The oval-shaped thirteenth-century French *vielle* had five strings, a front and back with ribs, a soprano register, and a separate neck, pegbox, and fingerboard. The many-stringed fifteenth-century Italian *lira da braccio* or "arm-lyre" contributed an arched top, a shaped waist for easier playing and f- or C-shaped sound holes.

But why was the violin born in Cremona? One factor may have been topography. Late-fifteenth- and early-sixteenth-century Cremona, owing to its location on the Po River, had close ties to Venice and became a major center of cultural activity during the Renaissance, enhanced by the fact that it possessed an advanced river system to facilitate the transport of wood from the mountains to other regions, a circumstance that might have helped local luthiers.[2]

But another answer, if legend has a corner on truth, is far more personal and engaging, though it came out of the suffering of exiled refugees. During the Spanish Inquisition, on July 30, 1492, the entire Jewish community—two hundred thousand people—were expelled from Spain. The sudden mass expulsion of Sephardic Jews (referred to as *Sephardim*, derived from the Hebrew word for Spain, *Sepharad*), orchestrated by Father Tomas de Torquemada, was so cataclysmic that ever since, the year 1492 has been an important date in Jewish history. Tens of thousands of refugees died while trying to escape. Spanish ship captains charged Jewish passengers exorbitant sums, then dumped them overboard in the middle of the ocean. When rumors spread throughout Spain that the fleeing refugees had swallowed gold and diamonds, many Jews were "knifed to death by brigands hoping to find treasures in their stomachs."[3] Among the survivors was a lutemaker named Giovanni Leonardo da Martinengo, who according to census records, arrived in Cremona in 1499.

In her book *Color: A Natural History of the Palette*, Victoria Finlay imagines his entrance into the town, based on the few facts that are known about this luthier:

> We know almost nothing about this lute-maker except the year he arrived, the fact that he must have been one of the thousands of Jews expelled from Spain in 1492, and that by the time of a census in 1526 he had the two Amatis (Andrea would have been twenty-one then) working in his shop. We don't even know his real name: Martinengo is a town in Austrian Italy where he may have lived for a while, Leonardo could have been his baptismal name—if he had been one of the thousands of Spanish Jews who turned Christian—and Giovanni is an Italian version of Juan. So our luthier's name was itself a collection of stories. He was a composite man—made up of many different parts, rather like one of his lutes.
>
> I think of him that first day in Cremona not as a man exhausted after a long journey, but as a storyteller walking proudly along the Via Brescia toward the center of town, surely attracting the attention of local urchins, who would be fascinated by the strange deep-bellied beast that he carried and which they would have pestered him to play. And perhaps he would have sat down and strummed them a ballad. Not for too long: like many instrument-makers he would probably never have thought of himself as a musician; but also he may not have wanted to think too much about the home he had lost. It would hurt too much.
>
> What could this man have seen in those seven years? Had the terrible times won out, or had the experience of journeying through Europe just as the Renaissance was starting brought him and his art alive? Either way, something happened, because the skills taught by this refugee to those Italian boys had not been taught before.[4]

The time was ripe for Andrea Amati—born in Cremona, and a product of Renaissance science, mathematics, and craftsmanship—to intuitively employ the laws of acoustics and create the unique features of the violin that attest to his innovative genius: the curvature of arched top and back, sound holes, sound post, and the asymmetrically placed bass bar. It is no small truth that none of these elements can be changed without enhancing or disturbing the delicate equilibrium between air and wood. Indeed, violin virtuoso Yehudi Menuhin wrote: "The violin maker is perhaps one of the supreme magicians of the void, shaping the enclosed space of the violin . . . with the finest sounds of honey and gold that the human ear can ever imagine."[5]

Amati's design was so glorious that it survives to this day, a design that neither his sons Antonio and Girolamo, his grandson Niccolò, nor Niccolò's famous pupils Andrea Guarneri and Antonio Stradivari could improve upon — surely a sign of genius.[6] While Amati is commonly referred to as the father of the violin, Gasparo da Salò of Brescia was swimming in the same current. If it is the job of the poet to give form to ideas that already exist but are yet to be expressed, then certainly, Andrea Amati and Gasparo da Salò were "early poets of the violin."[7]

By about 1550, violinmaking schools had been established in Cremona, Brescia, and Venice, and four strings had become standard. In 1555, the Marshal de Brissac brought several violinists to the French royal court. Their leader was Balthazar de Beaujoyeux, referred to at the time as "the best violinist in Christendom." The work of Andrea Amati soon became famous all over Europe. In fact, documents exist that show a sale of twenty-four violins by Andrea Amati to King Charles IX of France in 1560.

When Niccolò Amati, grandson of Andrea, lost most of his family to the plague, he took on two apprentices — Bartolomeo Giuseppe Guarneri (del Gesù) and Antonio Stradivari. At age twenty-two, Stradivari began putting his own labels inside his violins. Like his contemporary del Gesù, Stradivari experimented by making larger violins and using different varnishes; he also designed and redesigned pegs, fingerboards, and tailpieces. With the death of his mentor in 1684, Stradivari's fame grew. Around 1690, Stradivari made his first so-called long violin. By 1700, he had settled on pleasing proportions for his violins and thus began what was later called his golden period of violinmaking, during which time he perfected his orange-brown colored varnish, the recipe for which has never been found. While a varnish cannot improve a violin's tone, it can adversely affect it. Stradivari soon became known as the finest luthier of his day.

Ironically, by 1737, ten years after the death of Stradivari and just as the reputation of the violin was blossoming, the tradition of Italian violinmaking entered its greatest decline. For a century after the death of Stradivari, the violinmaker's legacy went dormant, and the traditional knowledge was almost completely lost. Then in 1937, fascist dictator Benito Mussolini, to stimulate his version of nationalism to coincide with the two hundredth anniversary of the death of Cremona's famous native son, started a school for violinmaking. At the same time he opened a museum to celebrate the legacy of Stradivari. In 1997, as part of the city's efforts to reclaim its celebrated history, Cremona renamed a piazza after its master luthier.

Between 1550, when Andrea Amati was in his prime, and 1883, when Enrico Ceruit died, there were easily perhaps ten thousand stringed instruments produced in Cremona—given the fact that Stradivari made more than 1,100 instruments on his own and he was a fourth-generation Cremonese luthier. The testament to their resilience is that half of them still exist—and many are being treasured as artifacts or played by lucky virtuosos. So the common ground of violinmaking soon became sacred ground for the violin world, as it revered the lore surrounding the Old Cremonese Masters.

In fact, part of the aura of performances by several contemporary violinists involves the fact that they perform and record with Stradivari instruments. Joshua Bell plays the 1732 Tom Taylor; Gil Shaham, his 1699 Countess Polignac; Itzhak Perlman, the 1714 Soil and the 1721 Sinsheimer; and Yo-Yo Ma, the Davidoff Stradivari.

Mecca is alive and well in the violinmaking world. Today, there are approximately 125 professional luthiers working in Cremona, plus another 100 non-tax-paying makers who are paid under the table. Do the luthiers in Cremona get along, communicate, or socialize with each other? According to one of them, Lorenzo Cassi, all the luthiers in Cremona fall into two philosophical camps—the handful of violinmakers who studied under Bissolotti—a meticulous craftsman who practices and teaches the slower, "Old World" methods most like those of Stradivari—and everyone else—those who are less interested in that tradition. "Many who studied Bisso's way of making have since changed to the other way because Bisso's way takes much longer, is much slower, so we are among a handful of violinmakers who still use methods taught by Bissolotti. So there is this tension between philosophies of violinmaking," Lorenzo explained in an interview in 2004. His wife, Kathryn, also makes violins.

When asked about the local organization of Cremonese makers, Lorenzo became pensive. "I would think that it would be good for violinmakers in Cremona to work together, to buy bridges, for instance, so the price would be better. But instead they fight among themselves. What is the purpose of an organization if it is to fight with each other rather than to help each other? So after two years of belonging, we decided not to join, but to be on our own."[8]

The Stradivari museum is informative for unexpected reasons — not because of any valuable Stradivari violins housed there, but because it offers plenty of documentation that shows that Stradivari was consistently experimenting with different-sized violins. On display in glass cases are diverse drawings: a paper dye (a cutout drawing) for a *piccoloe viole, soprano da braccio* and another paper dye model for a *viola d'amore* and a *viola da gamba*. There also numerous wood forms — one for a *viola tenor* and a *viola contralto*, both dated October 4, 1690. There is another wood form for a tiny, five-inch-long *piccolo violino* and one more for a *violino un quarto*.

Stradivari was always experimenting. By challenging 350 years of history and tradition, Hutchins was actually following in the footsteps of the master.

Carleen Maley Hutchins, circa 1990. Courtesy of Hutchins estate.

Carleen Maley, age nine, standing in front of 112 Essex Avenue, Montclair, New Jersey, 1921. Courtesy of Hutchins estate.

Carleen Maley, age fourteen, bugler at Girl Scout Camp Watchung, 1925. Courtesy of Hutchins estate.

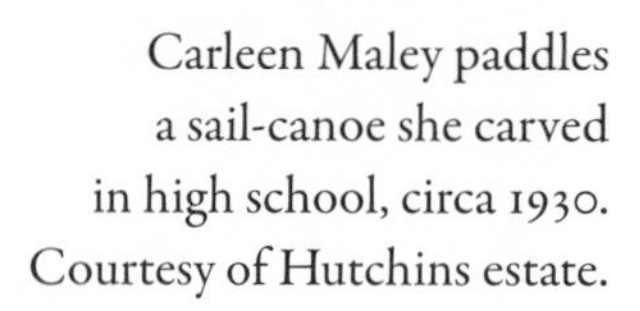

Carleen Maley paddles a sail-canoe she carved in high school, circa 1930. Courtesy of Hutchins estate.

Carleen Maley Hutchins with Susie the pig, Brearley School,
New York City, fall 1945. Courtesy of Hutchins estate.

Carleen Hutchins carving fiddles in her kitchen, circa 1955.
Photographer, Russell Kingman. Courtesy of Hutchins estate.

Hutchins measuring the thickness of a violin plate, circa 1960. Courtesy of Hutchins estate.

"The Physics of Violins," *Scientific American* cover, November 1962. Artist: Walter Tandy Murch. Reproduced with permission. Copyright © 1962 Scientific American, Inc. All rights reserved.

Carleen testing a plate in her basement lab, described by one neighbor as her "anechoic root cellar." Photographer: H. Grossman, October 25, 1963.

The first trial of the entire new violin family at the studio apartment of Kellum Smith, New York City, on Carleen's birthday, May 24, 1964. *Left to right*: Sonya Monosoft, treble; William Kroll, soprano; Louis Zerbe, mezzo; India Zerbe, alto; Sterling Hunkins, tenor; Peter Rosenfeld, baritone; Julius Levine, small bass; Ronald Naspo, contrabass; Henry Brant in the right corner. The photo was taken from the balcony. Courtesy of Hutchins estate.

The Hutchins violin octet in the living room at 112 Essex Avenue, 1965.
This photo graces the cover of *Research Papers in Violin Acoustics 1975–1993*.
Courtesy of Hutchins estate.

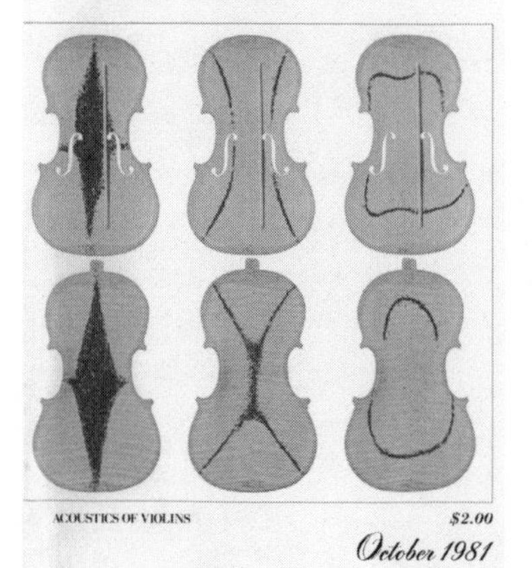

"Acoustics of Violins," *Scientific American* cover, October 1981. Artist: Marvin Mattelson. Reproduced with permission. Copyright © 1981 Scientific American, Inc. All rights reserved.

"Symphony of Strings: Rich in Fundamental," *New Yorker* cover, March 6, 1989. Artist: John O'Brien, the *New Yorker*, courtesy of Condé Nast Collection.

Mort and Carleen Hutchins in the garage workshop at 112 Essex Avenue, 1995. Courtesy of Hutchins estate.

The Hutchins Consort, founded in 2000 by bassist Joe McNalley.
Opening season concert, October 5, 2014, Newport Beach, California.
Courtesy of Hutchins Consort, 2014.

Fergus O'Flaherty plays the banjo with the Hutchins Consort at
O'Flaherty's Pub, Dingle Town, County Kerry, Ireland, March 15, 2014.
Courtesy of Hutchins Consort.

Augmentation

Statement of a motive
in rhythmic durations
that are doubled

Timothy A. Smith, "Anatomy of a Fugue"

8 ∫ *Inventor*

Sometimes the only thing that aligns opportunity with achievement is the missing question that arrives at just the right time.

"Can you create a family of violins across the tonal range of the piano?" That was the question that greeted Carleen Hutchins on August 21, 1958, when Mr. and Mrs. Henry Brant and Sterling Hunkins called at 112 Essex. Brant was a composer from Bennington, Vermont. Hunkins, a friend of Brant's and an accomplished cellist in his own right, was the one responsible for bringing Brant to Montclair. Many years hence, Carleen recalled the moment of Brant's challenge with her wry sense of humor. Brant "wanted to have the sound of the violin, the clarity and the full rich tones of the violin projected into seven other tone ranges starting with the double bass at the bottom and going up to an instrument an octave above the violin. . . . I realized what would probably be needed was to work out various sized instruments in order to put resonances in certain places. . . . Within half an hour, I agreed. . . . Little did I realize how much of a project I was getting into, and how it would become practically a life work."[1]

By this time, Carleen had made nearly fifty instruments, mostly violas, plus ten violins and one cello. In October 1958, at the same time that Carleen accepted Brant's challenge, she decided to apply for a Guggenheim Fellowship, as the Brant project certainly added new focus and depth to her proposal. In early 1959, Carleen made the first "new" violin—the Alto—by cutting down an enlarged viola that itself had been a cut-down sixteenth-sized child's cello sold to Hutchins by cellist Carl Aue. When Hutchins and Saunders found that the air resonance was too low, Hutchins cut the ribs down two inches at a time—until the Helmholtz air mode occurred on the open D, or third string. Hutchins and Saunders found that when the main wood resonance and the main air resonance occurred on the two open middle strings, they were pleased with its sound.[2] Then, on April 11, 1959, Carleen received a special delivery letter from the Guggenheim Foundation granting her $1,500 a year for three years to carry out her work on testing musical instruments.

Synchronicity was at work, because at just this moment Louise Rood had sent Carleen a copy of a brochure titled *Bridging the Gaps in the Violin Family*, produced by Connecticut luthier Fred Dautrich, who, unbeknownst to Carleen, had already taken on the challenge in the 1930s and come up with his own solution. Immediately, Carleen began trying to find Dautrich. Eventually she located Fred's son Jean Dautrich, who still had his father's instruments. On May 16, Hutchins drove with Apgar to a lecture in Hartford, after which they ventured to Torrington to meet Dautrich.[3]

When they arrived, Hutchins and Apgar were amazed to see the Dautrich instruments spread across the living room—violin, *Vilonia*, *Vilon*, cello, *Vilono*. Pleased with the sudden interest from Hutchins, Jean Dautrich agreed to lend her a *Vilonia*, *Vilon*, and *Vilono*. The same day, Hutchins officially acknowledged receipt of three Dautrich instruments and one bass bow on loan, listing the insurance values of each: *Vilonia*, $200; *Vilon*, $200; *Vilono*, $350; and the bass bow, $30—for a total cost of $780. She right then offered to purchase them.

On February 20, 1960, Dautrich wrote to Hutchins saying that though he felt the insured values fell far short of the true value of the violins, considering the work and skill involved, he accepted the offer in order to promote rather than discourage interest in his father's work.[4] On March 18, Carleen responded with a check for $780 and great enthusiasm: "I am glad you have decided to sell your instruments at the insured values because our group . . . could not go higher. . . . This will give us a chance to develop and publicize the work you and your father did so that it can achieve its rightful place in music of today."[5]

In late 1960, as Hutchins contemplated the next violin—the Tenor—she reasoned that the tenor should ostensibly be twice the size of the standard violin. But when she and Saunders worked it out, they discovered they did not have to make the body twice as long as the violin to get the desired pitch. Size in relation to the tuning was what mattered. To her delight, she discovered that the Dautrich *Vilon* was close to the desired tenor size, but the ribs were too deep. So she cut down the ribs, working by trial and error to get the right air mode. Eventually, Hutchins and Saunders found that the first tenor she made from the Dautrich *Vilon* was still a bit too short to get the optimal air mode, so Hutchins designed and built a slightly larger tenor from scratch.

In the meantime, through Saunders and Helen Rice, Hutchins was introduced to John Schelleng, a recently retired sound engineer and director of radio research at Bell Telephone, who also happened to be a cellist. Schelleng had read Saunders's articles over the years and had begun corresponding with him but had never met him. On January 12, 1961, Schelleng met Hutchins and Saunders for the first time while playing quartets at Helen Rice's house in Stockbridge. Schelleng and Hutchins clicked because that spring Schelleng began sending Hutchins drafts of his article about the violin as a circuit. Schelleng was applying elementary circuit ideas to explain the acoustics of bowed stringed instruments, that is, the movement of energy inside the violin.

Not everyone in Carleen's circle liked Brant's idea. Both Saunders and Schelleng doubted Hutchins could make stringed instruments with good tone and playing qualities. Hutchins recalled in many interviews that at first, the challenge from Brant had looked insurmountable to her colleagues. Carleen vividly recalled the consternation on Schelleng's face when he looked at the new alto violin: "Schelleng was willing to try it with some misgivings. When he put a bow on it, he was amazed and excited because it had wonderfully expressive sounds especially in its lower range that we had never heard from a viola before. Saunders and Schelleng became convinced I had something valid to work with, so we set to work to try and develop the other instruments."

On May 2, 1961, when Schelleng came to 112 Essex for the first time, he left a revised version of his "The Violin as a Circuit" article. By July, Hutchins had become an avid correspondent with him. The magic of the Hutchins-Schelleng teamwork lay in the fact that they were both pragmatists, not academics. As a biologist teaching herself acoustical physics by the trial and error of making violins, Carleen Hutchins was, above all, a pragmatist. While Schelleng, an engineer and mathematician, worked out the scaling theoretically to help Carleen figure out the dimensions of each of the next six octet instruments, he never wanted it published because the actual measurements and the theoretical ones did not always agree. For while the Helmholtz mode can be calculated from the value of the violin box, measurements of the area of the f-holes and the flexibility and arching of the walls in a violin are extremely variable and hard to calculate. Hutchins explained: "So we were working primarily with empirical findings starting with existing instruments of various sizes."

The next violin was the Soprano. Hutchins made the Soprano from a three-quarter violin that Henry Brant had tried unsuccessfully to tune in that range. She recalled: "The first soprano worked out pretty well. It looked funny and didn't have the full sound it ought to have had. I don't think we got the plates tuned right at that range at the time. The others were lots better than that one." Next came the Baritone. Hutchins discovered Dautrich had tuned his *Vilonio* to the right wood resonance for the baritone. "So we simply moved his *Violonio* up to this frequency," she recalled. "That's how we got our first baritone, and got the length of it right — it had a very good sound in that range." In a letter dated April 1, 1965, to Bob Fryxell, Hutchins credited Dautrich: "I certainly feel we should stress the importance of the Dautrich instruments, especially the job he did in designing them on his theory of 'Bridging the Gaps in the Violin Family.' His work has literally saved us years of cut and try."[6]

The Small Bass was developed next. When aspiring luthier Gordon McDonald of Erie, Pennsylvania, visited Montclair, he told Carleen about Donald Blatter, a retired engineer and bass maker. When Blatter learned about the new violin project, he offered to let Hutchins use bass parts he already had under construction. Hutchins said: "Without the help of Donald Blatter, we would have been many more years working out the new violin family."[7]

In 1961, Helen Rice hosted two early concerts featuring the first five octet violins — soprano, alto, tenor, baritone, and small bass — one at her farm in Stockbridge. At the other concert at her studio on 67th Street, William Kroll played his Stradivarius violin, with cellists George Finckel, Sterling Hunkins, Bob Fryxell, and violist Louise Rood. Hutchins would never forget the reaction of George Finckel: "He had tears running down his face. He said: 'This is the first time I have ever been able to talk back to the piano in a Brahms sonata.'" In other words, stringed instruments have traditionally not had the power and volume to compete with the sonorities of wind or percussion instruments like the piano. This is the reason that there are so many more string instruments in an orchestra. The improved resonance and sonority of Hutchins's instruments signified a striking change in that dynamic. For the first time, the Hutchins baritone or tenor violin could "speak back" to a piano. In this way, the Hutchins violin octet signified a whole new paradigm shift in the power of string instruments.

In fact, it was during one of these early concerts, when violinist William Kroll was playing his Stradivarius alongside the alto, tenor, and baritone, that pianist Rosita Levine, while sitting in the audience, said to Kroll: "Fritz, I can't hear that Stradivarius of yours. What's the matter?" Levine was questioning why she could not hear the Strad next to the Hutchins octet violins. The incident got Carleen thinking that perhaps the traditional violin was no longer compatible with the new violins—it was not loud enough, for one thing. As a result, Hutchins and Schelleng began designing a "new" slightly larger violin that would become the Mezzo, the violin closest in dimension to the traditional violin. The mezzo—later nicknamed the "He-Man" violin—came into being when Hutchins added violin strings to a sixteen-inch viola-patterned instrument that she had already made with violin resonances. To make it more playable, Hutchins later designed a fifteen-inch mezzo. She recounted: "By measurement, this instrument has twice the power output of a normal violin. I sold it to a concertmaster some years back when we first developed it. He said he has to play every note correctly because everyone can hear him!"

The next challenge was the big Contrabass. To make the biggest fiddle, Hutchins first turned back to Savart but found Savart's frequency wheel was only partly effective for testing violin resonances. She explained: "Instead of making the dimensions proportional, we have made the resonant frequencies proportional to its tuning. If it were dimensional only, the large bass would have had to be 6 times the length of the 14-inch violin or seven feet tall, and the body length of the treble only 7 inches."[8] The big contrabass violin began with a Prescott bass with a body length of forty-eight inches that Henry Brant had loaned to Carleen, but it was so full of cracks that it was impossible for her to identify the pitch of the enclosed air inside the box. When she discovered that electronic driving equipment was not powerful enough to activate the air inside to obtain the cavity resonance, Hutchins resorted to a makeshift solution, using a vacuum cleaner hose to blow across the sound-holes. In this way, she learned that in order to obtain the right air resonances, the ideal contrabass violin would need to be even bigger than the huge Prescott.

With this and other scaling factors in mind, Hutchins and Schelleng projected a theoretical body length of fifty-one inches for the contrabass violin. With the help of bassists Julius Levine, Charles Traeger, and Ronald

Naspo, Hutchins figured out how to arrange the mensur—the gauging of the length of the neck and strings so the instrument is playable—so it would be adequate for a single musician to manage. Creating the big contrabass was truly a team effort. Schelleng figured the scaling; architect Maxwell Kimball helped develop a design based on the violin shape rather than the conventional bass; Carleen, aided by Donald Blatter, provided the craftsmanship; Stuart Hegeman produced the huge electronic testing equipment powerful enough to shake the huge fifty-one-inch plates of spruce and maple.[9] When the new contrabass possessed about 80 percent of the tone quality hoped for, the only constructional feature left to consider was rib thickness. Hutchins then took the big fiddle apart, removed the linings and hand-planned the ribs, thinning them from three millimeters down to two millimeters throughout, a meticulous carving job that took her ten days. Bassist Julius Levine was delighted by the tone and responsiveness of the new contrabass. This was the first time a string bass had been developed using tuned plates related to tonal range.[10]

The Treble violin—nicknamed "Treble Trouble"—was the last and most difficult to make because there was no prototype for it. Using the design of a quarter-size child's violin, Hutchins and Schelleng figured a method to make deep ribs and then put holes in the ribs to raise the frequency of the enclosed air.[11] Schelleng eventually hit upon using aluminum ribs. Carleen made the ribs out of the soft aluminum edging she had used to finish her curved kitchen countertop. When Carleen found that epoxy resins would not hold the ribs under vibration, she put rivets in the corners to hold them together.[12]

Further problems involved finding the right material for the highest E string. Upon reading a *Scientific American* article, Carleen even paid a visit to a researcher experimenting with the tensile strength of spider webs—though it turned out to be a dead-end in terms of fiddle strings. Schelleng and Hutchins eventually tried National String Company carbon rocket wire, which had the right tensile strength but rusted almost immediately from the perspiration of the player's fingers. They eventually used brass-coated rocket wire and shortened the string length by lengthening the nut to tune it one octave above the violin.[13] When it sounded "tinny," Hutchins figured it had to do with the inflexibility of the ribs, so she filed them down from the outside. Then, after experimenting with enlarging the f-holes and raising the chin rest, Carleen still had to fiddle with the bridge. "Sometime I got the bridges so thin they just cracked across and I had to start over again — and the treble was the hardest one to do on that basis, too."[14]

With the creation of the first successful violin octet, a discussion naturally arose about patents and the idea of producing other octet violins. Dautrich had already lost a fortune trying to obtain a patent, and history is littered with other instrument makers who had just as much trauma related to patents. Hutchins eventually asked the advice of Earl Kent, director of the C. G. Conn Instrument Company, the primary band and orchestra instrument maker in the country at the time. Kent told her: "There isn't any sense in trying to patent these things because a patent in this game is nothing but a ticket to court — there's no way to prove anything."[15]

According to Carleen, four areas of research had made the new violin family possible — the placement of the main wood and air resonances, taptone relationships, methods of putting resonances at desired frequencies, and dimensional scaling.[16] In retrospect, Carleen remained mildly amused at the circuitous path of research, such that one is often looking for one thing and finds another. "We did the right things for the wrong reasons, which was luck. We thought we were scaling to the length of the wood of the box, and actually we were scaling to the length of the box on which these frequencies depended. We were able to get a successful result because we were doing it empirically. We were getting instruments that had the sounds and frequencies we wanted and then went to work."[17]

Meanwhile, in early 1961, Carleen recorded another thrill — her Carnegie Hall debut. "Lehman played #41—re-varnished a dark red by some Boston violin maker — very excited by seeing him play it at Carnegie Hall stage — almost feel as if it were my Carnegie Debut!"[18]

Intermezzo

Consorts – da Vinci's Dream

La figurazione delle cose invisibili.
(The figuration of things unseen.)
— Leonardo da Vinci

Leonardo da Vinci wrote these words next to a musical staff on which he had notated a musical phrase — a rare instance for a virtuoso on the *lira da braccio* used to improvising his melodies rather than recalling them and writing them down. Even as he was performing, Leonardo continued to explore the unique sound emanating from his *lira*. As one of the earliest stringed instruments played with a bow, the *lira da braccio* represented the ideal string sound because it most closely mimicked the human voice. Bowed stringed instruments constituted a major musical milestone in the history of Western European music because the effect of the bow surpassed that of fingers on a plucked instrument. The bow allowed the musician to elongate the tone, to play it out, control it, manipulate between soft and loud — all the nuances for which the violin would be heralded a century later.

Da Vinci was so taken with this tone — and the idea of replicating the sound of a group of bowed stringed instruments — that he invented two musical instruments to further explore it. The first was a silver lyre in the shape of a horse's skull.[1] The second instrument resulted from Leonardo's musings that the ideal musical instrument would combine bowed stringed instrument harmony with the ease of a keyboard — his *viola organista*. Sketches of this instrument appear on ten pages of da Vinci's notebooks, accompanied by elaborate, detailed illustrations of a stringed instrument with a keyboard that set the strings into motion via a mechanical device, either a wheel or endless bow. Such an instrument would ostensibly combine the polyphonic possibilities of the keyboard with the tone color of strings, "something like an organ with string timbre instead of wind timbre . . . which amounted to nothing less than a one-man orchestra."[2] Such a comprehensive design must have been a dream of instrument builders for centuries, because it surpassed the organ in that it offered flexible dynamics — gradations of volume — as is possible today on a pianoforte. But the *viola organista* would have been superior to the pianoforte in one regard. "The striking of the hammers produces a tone that immediately begins to fade away . . . whereas the bowed strings of the *viola organista* would produce tones that crescendo and decrescendo but do not die away."[3]

In November 2013, a YouTube presentation featured a version of da Vinci's *viola organista*, the first of its kind, constructed by Sławomir Zubrzycki, a young Polish luthier who built the instrument according to da Vinci's notes and drawings. The live performance revealed truly amazing sounds. The *viola organista* was a hybrid between an organ, a set of viols, and a clavichord — truly a mini-orchestra with just one keyboard. The sounds emanating from that instrument changed in nuance with each piece. One moment, it sounded like an organ, the next, a string ensemble; then another piece made it sound like a plucked keyboard instrument. The truly amazing moments occurred when the instrument plunged into another realm in between these sounds, creating a new palette of sound like nothing else.[4]

Emanuel Winternitz, musicologist and former curator at the Metropolitan Museum of Art, surmised that this musical instrument in Leonardo's mind and notebooks also represented a kind of collective idea that inspired many other instrument builders — the idea of a multitude of bowed strings playing in harmony — like a family of viols but with more sonority than viols provided. In 1581, Vincenzo Galilei, himself a virtuoso lutenist, wrote of a most remarkable keyboard stringed instrument that Elector Augustus, Duke of Saxony presented to Albert of Bavaria. "This instrument has strings similar to those of the lute . . . bowed like those of a viola by a strand made ingeniously of the same hairs of which are made the hair of viola bows . . . made to revolve by the foot of a player . . . by means of a wheel over which it passes, the number of strings wanted [controlled] by the fingers of the player." Galilei further explained: "I tuned this instrument in lute-like fashion and when well played it produced the sweetest sound, not different from an ensemble of Viols."[5]

Surely long before the birth of the violin — or coincidental with it — in the workshop of Amati, luthiers were experimenting. The four instruments that compose the Amati Quartet in the National Music Museum demonstrate that Amati was experimenting with different-sized violin-type instruments — no doubt seeking this idea of a multitudinous string sound. In fact, by 1619, German musicologist Michael Praetorius (1571–1621) wrote of the same idea, in his *Syntagma Musicum*. In its second volume, *De Organographia*, Praetorius described two stringed instrument families, including woodcut illustrations of each. Plate 20 presents an illustration of "Viols and Violins." About it, Praetorius wrote:

> There are two kinds of viols and violins, the viols da gamba and the viols da braccio. The viola da gamba is so called because it is held between the legs, gamba being the Italian term for leg. . . . Because the viols da gamba are much the larger and have longer necks and strings, they produce the far lovelier sound than the viols da braccio, held on the arm. Musicians differentiate between these two types of instruments by calling the viols da gamba simply viols and the viols da braccio, violins—or Polish fiddles, perhaps because they are supposed to have originated in Poland, or else while the best players of these instruments are found here.[6]

It is clear that Praetorius thought of the viols as the older, more formal family of strings with the sweeter sound. Ironically, the violin, used in less formal settings by the dance master, was so common at this time that Praetorius almost took it for granted. Indeed, it is interesting to note that though Praetorius, in his description of plate 21, devotes only a few words to this group of Geigen, he mentions several sizes of Geige. This second group of instruments—the viols da braccio—remains the clear historical precedent of the Hutchins violin octet. Alongside this plate, Praetorius wrote:

> The Viol da Braccio, or Violino da Brazzo, is also called Violin and is named Fiddle by the common folk. It is named da braccio because it is held on the arm.
>
> The bass, tenor, and descant of this instrument (the last of which is called violino, violetta piccola and rebecchino) all have four strings, and the very small violin (called pochette in French—see Plate 16) has three. All these strings are tuned in fifths. Since everyone is familiar with these instruments it is unnecessary to deal further with them here.[7]

As the duke's kapellmeister—a word that implies a leader of stringed instruments—Praetorius may even have been leading some sort of "violin band," a precursor to the idea of a family of violins. According to musicologist Peter Holman, Praetorius's *Terpsichore*, composed in 1612, was a collection of French courtly dance music reflective of the French court violin band, the group known as the Vingt-Quatre Violons du Roy. "According to [French musicologist] Mersenne, groups of this sort could consist of '500 different violins, though twenty-four suffice, consisting of six trebles, six bass, four *hautecontres*, four *tailles*, and four *quintes*.' Thus the group played in five parts, with six violins on the top part, four violas on each of the three inner parts, using instruments 'of different sizes, even though they were in unison.'"[8]

What happened to all those different-sized violins? Who invented the string quartet? More than a century later, in 1755 in Vienna, Joseph Haydn, just twenty-three years old, debuted his first string quartet composition, thereby conjuring up a new form that would forever change chamber music. Haydn wrote eighty-three string quartets in all, earning him the title of "father of the string quartet."

Two centuries later, the idea of a true family of violins resurfaced again in the work of three visionary luthiers who kept thinking about that violin band—the French father-and-son team (both named Leo Sir), and American luthier Frederick Dautrich. Sometime around the turn of the twentieth century, the Sirs invented a series of stringed instruments they called the *dixtour* to create a comprehensive string tone across the musical scale of a piano. The Sirs created six stringed instruments: *Sursoprano*, *mezzo-soprano*, *contralto*, *tenor*, *baryton*, and *sans-basse*. When added to the string quartet, the ten instruments formed the Sirs' *double quintette*—a group of ten violins across the range of written music—*sursoprano*, *soprano*, *mezzo-soprano*, *alto*, *haute-contre*, *tenor*, *baryton*, *basse*, *sousbasse*, *contrebasse*—a palette of sound reflecting all the timbres of the human voice.

In 1905, the Dixtour Leo Sir won a silver medal at Liège and in 1907, the Grand Prize at Bordeaux. Sir argued that the conventional quartet was, by its very nature, incomplete because it had no tenor voice. Despite the fact that Italian composers understood the role of this essential timbre and persisted in composing for the tenor voice in opera, luthiers answered the need by delegating the tenor voice to the alto. To support this idea, Sir cited a letter of Marquis Ariberti of Cremona, dated September 19, 1690, ordering from Stradivari "two altos to complete his quintet. One played the part of the contralto and the other part of the tenor!" According to Sir, luthiers "did absolutely nothing to overcome that gap which obliges composers to borrow more or less successfully, from the other groups of instruments, or to overburden the four instruments which compose the quartet."[9]

In 1935, in his pamphlet titled *Bridging the Gaps in the Violin Family*, Dautrich argued that the gaps in the string family related to the inherent troubles of the viola, the missing tenor voice, and an essential problem with the quartet in that the second violin is a soprano instrument yet used to produce a "true" alto quality: "No matter what part the viola is given to play, it can never be more than an under-sized *alto* instrument, tuned an octave above the cello. *Where then is the tenor instrument?*"[10] Dautrich's solution was to create three intermediary violin-shaped instruments — the *Vilonia*, or new "alto" violin; the *Vilon*, his answer for the tenor range; and the *Vilono*, or small bass. Evidently, beginning in 1933, the "Fred L. Dautrich Quintet" had a short time in the limelight with at least a dozen performances in distinguished venues, including Juilliard and Carnegie Hall, to mostly favorable reviews.

The Hutchins violin octet addresses these same concerns about gaps in the string quartet. Tonally speaking, the violin octet — composed of treble, soprano, mezzo, alto, tenor, baritone, small bass, and contrabass violins — is a homogeneous "true" family of eight violins spanning the entire range of a piano. By way of comparison, the traditional violin, viola, cello, and bass differ substantially from each other because their resonances fall in different places on each instrument. In terms of timbre or sound color, the string quartet instruments differ in shade and value, and might be described in visual terms as combining the colors lavender and red, whereas the violin octet offers eight "true" violin tones, creating a rainbow palette of sound never before heard from a family of stringed instruments.

The most unusual and enigmatic violin at the center of this rainbow of fiddles is the alto violin — slightly larger than and tonally comparable to a viola but too large for most players to play *da braccio*, so most often played vertically like a cello — hence, a "vertical viola." Despite the fact that the viola is often made fun of for its difficult ergonomics and unstandardized size and tone, it remains a tonal mentor, balance wheel, and backbone to the string quartet.[11] No one understood the role of the viola better than Haydn. In the City Museum of Vienna, a painting, *Joseph Haydn Playing with a Quartet*, depicts the composer conducting while he is playing viola. The composer, dwelling in the heart of the quartet, hears the voices of the first and second violins while simultaneously attuning to the cello's grounded harmonic.

Biographer and avid amateur chamber music player Catherine Drinker Bowen, in her book *Friends and Fiddlers* — a personal tribute to amateur chamber music — describes the unique role of the viola as the enigmatic but essential part of the string quartet:

> Approach a professional string quartet after a concert; congratulate first the violist, and watch the others grin. "Anybody," a violist admitted to me on such an occasion, "knows the viola is the backbone of the quartet"—and his three colleagues nodded rapid assent. It was not for himself the violist spoke, but for his instrument. Your violist has, as a rule, neither melody nor base; he is . . . in the middle of the music; he can hear everything that goes on. When he has the melody, it is heavenly. . . . When the viola plays bass, the ensemble, lacking the cello's deep finality, has another quality, a strange, tremulous something that projects us at once into an unknown place, into a fourth auditory dimension, fascinating Erewhon full of half lights, half sounds; of breaths, as it were, half drawn.[12]

Carleen began her fascination with chamber music by playing viola. While only an average amateur violist, she nevertheless found herself at the center of the sound and was irresistibly drawn to chamber music. In fact, without the passion for playing amateur chamber music, Saunders, Schelleng, and Fryxell would never have connected with Rice or Hutchins, and the violin octet would not exist. Bowen spent many joyful hours performing at Helen Rice's Brandenburg evenings, where she met and played quartets with Carleen Hutchins. Bowen described the irresistible, intangible thrill of playing chamber music in a group, a kind of universal draw that beguiles professional and amateur alike:

> Only the true musician knows how to take music seriously enough to be able to take it lightly. If prayer is an art, so is flirtation: only your true artist, to whom music is a thing serious as his own life—only he knows how to flirt with music, to follow up a Bach fugue with a café waltz and derive, as it were, equal pleasure from both. The giant can afford to laugh at Lilliput; perversely enough, it is more often the pygmy who is heard cracking jokes at the giant. . . . As for me, I am neither strong nor wise, and my performance on the violin is so unequal to my passion for that instrument as to make the gods themselves laugh.[13]

9 ∫ Author

Writing about the unseen is no easy task, and so much of studying nature involves deciphering the invisible in order to understand it — whether it is describing how a Luna moth feels its way in the dark, visualizing the structure of DNA, or describing the air currents swirling inside the fiddle. Carleen wrote about all these things. As a science consultant for the Girl Scouts, she wrote *Luna Moth* (1957) and *Life's Key — DNA: A Biological Adventure into the Unknown* (1959), both published by Coward-McCann.

On January 7, 1959, Carleen had another chance to follow the moth to the flame. "Mr. Rembert Wurlitzer to see my work. Had lunch and asked if I would like to work with Sacconi — Whee!!!!"[1] So few words to signify that on one January morning, Carleen Hutchins had finally become visible to Rembert Wurlitzer. On this wintry Wednesday, Hutchins was most amazed to see the celebrated, internationally known instrument dealer standing on her doorstep — quite unannounced. Hutchins recalled: "It was a fascinating day. He found my instruments hanging all over the place, from the curtain rods, in the breakfront and down in the cellar. He just went through them one after another looking each one over as fast as he could. At the time, I couldn't quite figure what he was up to." Then, after discussing instrument construction over lunch in the kitchen, Wurlitzer suddenly asked Hutchins: "How would you like to work with Sacconi?" She remembers: "I was floored! This was more than I had ever expected — I was overjoyed at the possibility. By this time, I had started to work on some of the new instruments of the violin family."[2]

In the violin world, Stradivari was the flame, and Simone Fernando Sacconi was the torchbearer for Stradivari. A renowned expert on violin restoration and the author of *The Secrets of Stradivari*, Sacconi was the master luthier of Wurlitzer's workshop on 42nd Street, where he trained many of the day's leading makers, restorers, and experts, including René Morel, Hans Nebel, Luiz Bellini, Bill Salchow, and Charles Beare.[3] Consequently, like moths to a flame, all the greatest string players of the day were drawn to Wurlitzer's — Heifetz, Piatigorsky, Kreisler, Menuhin, Rostropovich —

clients of the greatest team of stringed instrument experts, restorers, and connoisseurs in America.

According to Charles Beare, the renowned British violin expert, Wurlitzer believed there should be no secrets, that knowledge should be shared. Given Wurlitzer's philosophy, he must have been more than curious about the Hutchins-Saunders experiments. Why else would he have dropped by unannounced at 112 Essex? The opportunity for Carleen Hutchins to work with Sacconi was rare indeed. On Thursday, March 12, Carleen received word that she would be able to meet Sacconi for the first time on Saturday. She began going to Wurlitzer's shop — on 42nd Street between 7th and 8th Avenues on the south side of the street — where the workshop was on the lower level, below the street. Carleen followed explicit instructions from Wurlitzer to bypass the lower floor and to come to the third floor *only*, so as not to upset the other violinmakers if they saw a *woman* working with Sacconi![4]

Hutchins worked with Sacconi intermittently every few weeks from 1959 to 1963 — always taking the "back stairs" to remain invisible, staying away from the scrutiny of the other luthiers. In her contribution to Sacconi's book *The Secrets of Stradivari*, Hutchins recalled:

> Sacconi wanted me to follow as closely as possible the methods he had evolved from the work of Stradivari — the molds, the designs, the tools and the ways of using them. I worked from the MacDonald viola and Sacconi's drawings of it using willow for the blocks and liners. Much to Sacconi's amusement, my willow blocks came from two polo balls I purchased since willow is not commercially available in the USA. When it came time for me to make the purfling, Sacconi got a twinkle in his eye and said he hoped I liked Chianti wine — for I should go to the liquor store and get a crate in which Chianti came. The crates were then made of Italian Lombardy poplar that I should cut to make 0.6 mm thick white strips of the purfling.
>
> Sacconi had a wonderful sense of humor, but mostly he radiated complete dedication to every aspect of his work. . . . I am one of the lucky ones to have known him. The violin makers of the world owe a deep debt of gratitude to Fernando Sacconi for all he did to understand, interpret and perpetuate the finest traditions of Italian violin making."[5]

For years, other luthiers — some of whom had worked at Wurlitzer's — accused Hutchins of fabricating stories about working with Sacconi. In fact, in 1988, Morton Hutchins recorded in the family log the fact that Thomas Weinberg, editor of *The Dictionary of American Violin Makers*, had taken out any reference to both Karl Berger and Simone Sacconi in the Carleen Hutchins biographical sketch published in the current volume. When Carleen spoke to Weinberg about the omission at the 1988 Cello Congress, Weinberg asked Hutchins for written evidence of her work with Sacconi. The logbook shows that on June 30, 1989, Carleen had a phone conversation with Mrs. Wurlitzer about obtaining information from logbook records and copies of drawings to show that Hutchins had worked with Sacconi over a period of years. Later, a letter from Lee Wurlitzer corroborated the fact that Carleen Hutchins had studied violinmaking with Sacconi on the premises of her father's workshop. Drawn to Sacconi's light, Hutchins settled for working in the shadows of Wurlitzer's shop. The fact that she had to be secretive about it spurred her interest even more.

In spring 1959, as Carleen came around the corner of Columbus Avenue and 67th Street, her arms full of lilac and dogwood branches to bring to Helen Rice and her mother, she nearly fell over a woman walking a little black cocker spaniel, and recognized Mrs. Kroll. After an exchange of pleasantries, Mrs. Kroll mentioned that Fritz had a student looking for a viola and asked if Carleen could bring one over for inspection. The next week Carleen brought over SUS #34—a 16¾-inch viola based on a Gasparo pattern — the "best viola I could lay my hands on with a lovely sound that seemed very responsive and easy to play." It just so happened that on this particular day, the Kroll Quartet was rehearsing in the Krolls' apartment. When Carleen came by, they stopped playing for a few minutes as she opened the case. First Kroll tried the viola, followed by violist David Mankovitz. "He played it for a little while, and played his own instrument and the quartet exchanged some knowing glances. Within ten minutes, David Mankovitz asked me what I wanted for the viola and wrote a check for it!" Mankovitz played SUS #34 with the Kroll Quartet for more than ten years, all over the world alongside Kroll's Stradivarius and two other early Italian instruments.[6]

In the meantime, while the photographic method of visualizing tap-tone frequency developed by A. S. Hopping made it possible to determine tap-tone frequencies in free violin plates with considerable accuracy, it was difficult and cumbersome to tune a hanging violin plate. Hutchins began to investigate using Chladni patterns on horizontal free violin plates by placing the violin plate over a microphone inserted into a hole in a table. At the suggestion of Arthur Methot, who came to 112 Essex to learn violinmaking, Hutchins began using Christmas glitter to visualize Chladni patterns on free violin plates. The geometric patterns that appear at different frequencies indicated to Hutchins where she needed to carve off more wood in order to improve the arching of the plate, which thereby helps the luthier gauge the balance between flexibility and stiffness in the violin plate.

As was the habit of both Mort and Carleen, comments on major health events were barely mentioned in the family logbook. But on July 24, 1960, Mort took Carleen to the Harkness Pavilion of Columbia-Presbyterian Hospital.[7] The next morning, Carleen had a hysterectomy. She remained in the hospital for eleven days, from July 26 to August 5. When Carleen left the hospital, she went directly to Helen Rice's home, where she stayed for more than two weeks recuperating, returning home on August 21.

On May 14, 1961, Nanny, Carleen's mother, was in a state of collapse. The next evening Grace Fletcher Maley died of a stroke. No other mention is made in the family log. But just two days after her mother's funeral, Carleen went off to New Hampshire with Virginia Apgar (and the cat!) — recorded faithfully in the family log by Mort.[8] Many years later, Carleen credited Grace with giving her the gift of freedom. Carleen often remarked about how much she owed her mother, who was always making things possible for her only child, supporting and encouraging Carleen in whatever task she undertook. Indeed, the same role that Carleen credited to her mother in her young life, she credited to Mort much later in life — when she began to realize, in bits and pieces, the personal price of her passion.

Family life at 112 Essex was not unlike Carleen's science classroom in its array of household pets and animals. On September 30, 1961, the family log first mentions Satan, the injured crow that came to live there, thanks to Mary Arne, a childhood playmate of Carleen's who taught biology at Montclair State and was always rescuing animals. One day Mary came to the Hutchinses' house with an emaciated, featherless crow on a hawk strap, a crow she had already named Satan. Carleen recalled this story many times, saying that when Mary tried to leave with Satan, the bald crow jumped off the hawk's strap and came running back up the step to the front door, whereupon Mary smiled and said to Carleen: "She's yours!" Satan took immediately to Cassie, who took the crow out in the yard for exercise then a bath in a pool of water inside an inverted garbage can cover. That night, perhaps as if it might be a sign that Satan had come to stay, Mort recorded a spectacular aurora that spanned across the entire sky.[9] By October 22, Hutchins had devised a cage for Satan. The following winter Mary Arne included an update on Cassie and Satan in her wildlife column in the *Montclair Times*: "We have good news of the bedraggled crow which we told you about last spring. Cassie Hutchins is the one who has worked the miracle and produced the magnificence!"[10] Satan became a part of the Hutchins family and lived with them for twenty-six years. Two years before Satan died, another crow named Elijah came to live at 112 Essex.

Meanwhile, on April 18, 1962, Carleen received a special delivery letter —her second grant from the Guggenheim Foundation—awarding her $4,500 a year for three years. Carleen became ever more intrigued by the idea of studying old instruments as a reference point for her research.[11] In May, after months of correspondence with the Musical Instruments Department at the Library of Congress, she finally hit gold. Harold Svevack agreed to allow Carleen to visit the library's Whitall Musical Instruments Collection of Stradivari instruments to make patterns and drawings from the Cassaviti viola.

At the time, the Budapest Quartet was the quartet-in-residence at the Library of Congress. Three years before, Hutchins had attended a Budapest Quartet concert in Montclair. A few days later, violist Boris Kroyt had come to 112 Essex, and then Carleen had met Kroyt at LaGuardia Airport to loan him three violas. Boris now agreed to accompany her to visit the Cassaviti, largely to assuage the fears of museum personnel about her even touching the viola. One morning Carleen went to listen to the Budapest Quartet rehearsing in the Library of Congress auditorium. She had been listening closely to the Strad cello being played by Mischa Schneider—the one with the knotted poplar back. Afterward, out in the hall as they were carrying the instruments to their storage place, they stopped to talk to Hutchins. When Hutchins said she had a cello in her car that sounded "as good if not better" than his Strad, Schneider suggested she bring it by his home so he could try it. "Much to my delight, he found that it was very similar to his own cello and that he liked it very much," Carleen later recalled.

As it happened, the Budapest Quartet was presenting a concert at Montclair High School the following week. Schneider, delighted to avoid traveling with his cello case, told Carleen he would be happy to bring with him only his bow and asked her to meet him at the auditorium door with her cello prior to performance. On May 25, 1962, Carleen took cellos, a viola, and a violin to the high school auditorium, where she and Mort met the Budapest Quartet and gave a cello to Schneider to use in performance that afternoon.[12] Carleen recalled the excitement: "You can imagine how thrilled I was to sit in the audience and listen to that cello sing. Several times the quartet compared notes silently and I thought they were fussing about the cello." Afterward, when Carleen went to retrieve her cello, she asked Schneider, with fear and trembling, "'How did it go?' He said one word—'Magnifico!' This was indeed the thrill of a lifetime!"[13]

On June 15, 1962, a *Time* Magazine article titled "The Strads of Montclair" summarized Carleen's path thus far—from housewife violinmaker to successful inventor of the violin octet. A few weeks later, in the July–August 1962 issue of *Sound* magazine, Saunders covered the horizons of the field in his article "Violins Old and New: An Experimental Study." Saunders discussed the history of violin acoustics—air tones and subharmonics—and then his work with Hutchins: the magnetic driving of fiddle plates, violin qualities, tap tones, effects of age and varnish, and mathematical scaling for the violin octet.[14]

This was the last article that Saunders would write, capping a career that had spanned four decades. Still, Saunders, the uncontested American "grandfather" of violin acoustics, must have been a bit shocked by the ripple effect of an article published just three months later. In November 1962, *Scientific American* published "The Physics of Violins" by Carleen Hutchins as its cover article. Given the circumstances that led up to this event, Hutchins was the most surprised of all. The timing was auspicious because Hutchins had submitted her article at just the moment when the lead article for the November issue had not held up under scrutiny, so editors were clamoring to fill the gap. She modestly remembered: "I blundered into the right spot. . . . [T]hey were looking for something else, and the physics of the violin struck their fancy."[15]

While the editors went to work dissecting the manuscript, photographer-artist Irving Gist arrived at 112 Essex to make drawings. Gist spent six weeks commuting from New York City to Montclair, so excited about the illustrations that he lost track of time. Hutchins recalled that Gist worked all day, "keeping us jumping up and down, moving everything under the sun, taking photographs of parts of instruments, whole instruments, making sketches, designing things as he went along. At 11:00 at night we'd say, 'Look, Irving, you've got to go home—you can come back tomorrow.'" These expansive illustrations by Gist, along with the Praetorius 1619 woodcut illustration, transformed Carleen's article. The image from Praetorius's *Syntagma Musicum* aptly demonstrated that the violin family was an old idea. Stradivari's 1690 pattern drawing for the sound holes of a tenor violin proved that the tenor violin was an old idea as well. The double-page spread of Gist's "Anatomy of a Violin" illustration brought the reader—any reader—inside the violin itself. The image of eight octet fiddles in cascading sizes set against a piano keyboard summarized the tonal range of each octet violin. Another image of the violin octet juxtaposed against the string quartet instruments showed the octet violin sizes.

To top it off, the cover featured a stunningly beautiful painting by the *Scientific American* illustrator Walter Tandy Murch. Throughout his career, Murch focused his attention on objects, devoted to capturing the "spirit" of things. At some point during the time that Gist was visiting Montclair, Murch visited 112 Essex as well. For his still life painting of a violin, Murch composed a montage of images, combining a violin experiment that he had seen in one of Carleen's basement vibration test chambers with a scroll sitting in the background. The synergy between the two—the scientific experiment poised with the hand-carved scroll—set in a mysterious, almost ethereal atmosphere, perfectly summarized the science and art of the violin, capturing the passion that had led Carleen for more than a decade. Carleen could not have orchestrated a better image to adorn the cover of *Scientific American*. This article put Carleen Maley Hutchins on the map in the violin world. As of 1979, *Scientific American* had distributed nearly thirty thousand reprints, and the Catgut Acoustical Society had supplied several thousand more.

If ever there was a manifesto for the work of Carleen Maley Hutchins, this was it—and the fact that it became the cover story was both surprising and serendipitous. Along with illustrations that encapsulated the entire story of the violin octet in a few images, the wording of the article revealed the forthright, no-nonsense character of a most determined housewife–violinmaker–science teacher who had made it into the *Scientific American* limelight—for the first time by herself, with no coauthor. Carleen clearly stated her position: "To sum up, I believe that, without ignoring the precious heritage of centuries, the violinmaker should become more conscious of the science of his instrument. We really ought to learn how to make consistently better instruments than the old masters did. If that challenge cannot be fulfilled, we should find out the reasons for our limitations." In the concluding paragraph of her article, Hutchins laid down the gauntlet. It was no wonder that in this article, Hutchins managed to inadvertently alienate, and in some cases anger, some traditional violinmakers who wanted nothing to do with science and held fast to the "mystique" of their craft.

Not only had Carleen Hutchins sparked the conversation about violin acoustics, she had done so with a bang.

Sequence

Repetition of a motive at another pitch level, usually up or down a step

Timothy A. Smith, "Anatomy of a Fugue"

10 ∫ Catalyst

Catalyst, orchestrator, yeoman — Carleen Hutchins resonated with anyone who would talk fiddles. When she wasn't carving, she was thinking fiddles, dreaming of the next experiment or playing chamber music. Through the front door, down the back steps, into the garage, or down to the catacombs of the basement, not to mention the kitchen, the dining room table, and especially the concert hall, she followed any connection to a player, a composer — even a conductor.

Sometime prior to the summer of 1962, word of Carleen's new violin family reached conductor Leopold Stokowski, celebrated for his innovative repertoire and pioneering broadcast techniques. From 1917 to 1977, Stokowski's orchestral recording career spanned the acoustic to the quadraphonic eras and then included high fidelity and stereophonic recording.[1] On June 19, 1962, Stokowski wrote to Hutchins to inquire about the vertical viola. Hutchins answered promptly two days later, sending him size charts comparing the vertical viola to conventional stringed instruments. By December 28, Hutchins had redesigned and made a second viola with a revised mensur suitable for viola fingering and easier performance. She proposed several dates to arrange for musicians to play this instrument for Stokowski.

Meanwhile, Hutchins had been sowing other seeds as well. Several years before, after playing hundreds of quartets for more than a decade with Helen Rice, Robert Fryxell relocated back to Ohio. And he might have stopped coming east, except for two things — his friendship with Helen and the fact that Carleen had loaned him her first cello indefinitely, thereby establishing a bond between Fryxell and Hutchins and all the violin acoustics activities occurring at 112 Essex. By 1961, Schelleng had finally met Saunders. In early 1962, Fryxell met Schelleng. The circle was complete: Saunders — a violinist and violist; Schelleng and Fryxell — both cellists — and Carleen Hutchins made an intense foursome — a foursome that John Schelleng once jokingly called the "catgut acoustical society."[2]

Meanwhile, Carleen's November 1962 *Scientific American* cover article was a breakthrough in the whole process of violin acoustics research because it offered to a wide audience a vivid illustration of the practical application of science to violinmaking and introduced a new family of violins, thereby fulfilling the dreams of luthiers and players dating back to the Renaissance. In addition, the article was publicized around the world beyond anyone's wildest possible hopes — the kind of overnight publicity of which any pioneer could only dream.

First, Hutchins had been caught off-guard by the luck and serendipity of making the *Scientific American* cover. Not only had she not expected it, she certainly had no inkling there would be such a noticeable response. Instead, Hutchins received more than two hundred letters expressing interest in all facets of the experimental work, letters that Saunders and primarily Schelleng helped her to answer. In fact, as a result of the article, just two weeks later, the Acoustical Society of America asked Hutchins to give a paper at the next ASA meeting in New York City the following spring. Given the proximity of Montclair to New York City and the recent flurry of interest caused by her *Scientific American* article, it occurred to Carleen that the timing was right to orchestrate a new organization. Why not coordinate its first meeting with the upcoming Acoustical Society of America (ASA) meeting, in order to lure people already coming to New York City?

Carleen Hutchins had a gift for perceiving other people's gifts, igniting their passions, finding common ground, and then providing the energy of enthusiasm that she powered like the wind. On Friday, May 15, 1963 (the night before the first "catgut" group would gather at Carleen's home), Bob Fryxell, who had just arrived in New York from Ohio, was barely out of his car when he was immediately caught up in one of Carleen's crosswinds. Carleen had brought some of her instruments — new and conventional — to this Friday night meeting on the last day of a weeklong conference sponsored by the Acoustical Society of America. Though the commute to the Hotel New Yorker from Montclair was easy enough for Carleen, it was slightly complicated by the fact that she was bringing along a collection of fiddles.

For cellist Bob Fryxell, it was a night to remember, but at the time he had no reason to think so. About one hundred people were crammed into a hot, sweaty, smoky room — one of the side dining rooms in the Hotel New Yorker. Carleen pulled Fryxell aside, put one of her tenor violins in his face, and asked: "Have you ever seen one of these?" Fryxell, who had arrived just a half hour before the meeting was to start, recalled his reaction to Carleen on that night.

> Carleen said: "We're going to have some demonstrations tonight. William Kroll has promised to demonstrate the mezzo. You know who he is, right?" One of the big names! And she mentioned the Zerbes whom I had met only once. He played viola and she played cello. They were competent professional musicians. And William Kroll—one of the superb artists of New York. And Carleen said: "Here's a tenor—you're going to play it, aren't you?' I had never seen one before. So I had to hole up in the next room and practice like a dog—and try to at least not play out of tune. And sure enough, later in the evening, I was on stage center with William Kroll trying to fake duets."[3]

The next morning, on Saturday, May 16, 1963, the Catgut Acoustical Society was born, as twelve members of the original technical group gathered around a Ping-Pong table in the side yard at 112 Essex, talking violin acoustics all day around a jug of wine and lunch provided by "four cooperative wives" (as the *CAS Newsletter* would later report)—Virginia Benade, Connie Hegeman, Elinor Schelleng, and Sally Smith. The original group consisted of Robert Fryxell, president; Carleen Hutchins, secretary; Virginia Apgar, treasurer; and Arthur Benade, William Carboni, Louis Condax, Donald Fletcher, Stuart Hegeman, Maxwell Kimball, J. C. Schelleng, Eugene J. Skudrzyk, and J. Kellum Smith. Four additional members were unable to attend the original meeting: Frederick A. Saunders (elected president in absentia), Jean Dautrich, Louise Rood, and Rembert Wurlitzer. Though Saunders was unwell and unable to attend this debut CAS meeting, CAS membership certificates had been prepared for each new member, signed by Saunders.

On June 9, 1963, less than a month after the founding of CAS, Frederick Saunders died. With the sudden death of Saunders, Fryxell, who had had extensive discussions with Saunders about the importance of keeping a violin acoustics archive, took on the task of CAS organization with new urgency, a responsibility that he took personally and conscientiously. The true value of CAS membership, as Fryxell saw it, lay in gathering and keeping track of information and presenting it in a consolidated, digested, evaluated form that would make it more accessible so that it might "trigger the next guy."[4]

The *Scientific American* article sparked other interest: in the fall of 1963, a *Life* magazine reporter visited Montclair, as the magazine was planning a significant feature on Hutchins and her fiddles. But the Kennedy assassination seized the spotlight, and the New Jersey housewife-violinmaker was pushed inside, her abridged story told with a few engaging photographs. Whether it was the *Life* article, the *Scientific American* splash, or perhaps the founding of CAS, activities at 112 Essex suddenly drew the interest of the California Academy of Sciences, in San Francisco.

On April 14, 1964, a film crew of five, headed by Dr. Earl S. Herald of the California Academy of Sciences and Dr. David Park of Stanford University, spent a few days filming Carleen at home for an educational program titled *Science in Action*. In the film, Herald introduced Hutchins: "For the past thirty years, a group of physicists, chemists, and musicians have been exploring this aspect of the Science of Music. . . . [T]hey are organized informally as the Catgut Acoustical Society. Our guest is currently the catalyst of this society."[5] The next day, the crew filmed a concert-demonstration at Montclair State featuring three professors performing on the octet violins —violinist Louis Zerbe, cellist India Zerbe, and bassist Ronald Naspo. The California Academy of Sciences documentary—the first film on the violin octet—aired June 4, 1964, in California and later that year in the east; it became a valuable marketing tool for Hutchins and the CAS.

By May 1, with the printing of the first Catgut Acoustical Society newsletter, Carleen had all eight violins in playable condition with the exception of the small bass, for which a regular bass was being substituted until the small bass was complete.[6] This publication acknowledged the passing of four very significant members—Saunders (June 1963); Jean Dautrich (September 1963); Rembert Wurlitzer (October 1963); and Louise Rood (February 1964). Consequently, the current CAS officers were John Schelleng, president; Robert Fryxell, vice president; Carleen Hutchins, secretary; and Virginia Apgar, treasurer. By the time the *CAS Newsletter*'s second issue was published on November 1, 1964, it had doubled in size from six to twelve pages.

The premiere concert featuring the new violin family took place on May 20, 1965, at the 92nd Street YMHA, as part of the "Music in Our Time" series developed and conducted by violinist Max Polikoff. Henry Brant composed a piece for the violin octet titled *Consort for True Violins*. The program was taped for broadcast later over station WRVR-FM. Leopold Stokowski was in the audience. The next morning Carleen got a phone call from Stokowski, saying, "I want one of those things!" Hutchins recounted the conversation: "Stokowski said this was the sound he had always wanted from violas in his orchestra—at which I got pretty excited. And then he wanted to know how soon he could have one to try—and I had an extra one at that point." About a week later, Carleen took it over to him at his apartment on Fifth Avenue. "He looked it over and tried it and thanked me very much and I went off," she recalled.

On October 6, 1965, the maestro wrote to Hutchins that he had finally located a violist willing to try the "vertical viola"—the alto violin. He asked if he could borrow an alto, saying that he thought this was an important advance for the orchestra and chamber music.[7] Two days later, Hutchins sent viola SUS #60, valued at $2,000 and a note: "If you wish to keep this for an extended period I would appreciate your having it insured for the above amount."[8] In late 1965, Stokowski gave an extensive interview to Jay Nelson Tuck for his article "New Designs for Old Instruments" published in *BRAVO*, in which he talked extensively about the need for improvements in classical Western instruments, highlighting the work of Hutchins: "Carleen Maley Hutchins is doing research on the physical and acoustical properties of violins, violas, cellos and double basses. . . . Research is of great importance to analyze the loss of quality of tone of great instruments."[9]

The May 1966 *CAS Newsletter* announced two significant upcoming events. The first concert on May 8, at Riverdale, would feature Yale graduate students performing new music written especially for the new violins by composing departments at Riverdale and Yale. The following month on June 3, in the Paine Auditorium at Harvard, there would be a memorial concert to honor Frederick Saunders, featuring new music composed and arranged by Quincy Porter, Mel Powell, and students. On October 21, 1966, CAS celebrated another milestone, when the certificate of Incorporation for the Catgut Acoustical Society was accepted by the State of New Jersey. The November 1966 newsletter established the first CAS membership dues at $3 per year and a newsletter subscription price of $2 per year.[10]

In January 1967, Samuel L. Singer, in a *Philadelphia Inquirer* article, "New Family of Fiddles," chronicling family life at 112 Essex, wrote that though Hutchins had the approval of her husband, her children were another story.

"Not so enthusiastic are the Hutchins offspring. Son William, 19, a freshman at Haverford College majoring in history, [is] 'so tired of science I can't stand it any more.' Daughter Caroline, 16, a junior at Montclair High School, has no aspirations in science or music. She wants to raise horses some day."[11]

In the meantime, word of Hutchins's work continued to spread. Her article "Founding a Family of Fiddles" made a splash in *Physics Today* in February 1967 and caused Walter Sullivan, science editor for the *New York Times*, to phone Hutchins for an interview. Fortuitously, Sullivan was both a science writer and a cellist. After talking with Hutchins for several hours, Sullivan toured the basement lab, and then "tried one after another of the vertical instruments, and further words were not needed."[12] Two days later, on February 20, Hutchins departed on a weeklong lecture tour to Cleveland and Cincinnati. While Carleen was in Ohio, Sullivan's enthusiasm about his visit spurred him to write two articles in the span of a week. The first, "Stradivariuses by the Dozen—Maybe: Researcher Would Broaden Range of String Family," published on February 21, was particularly memorable for the photograph of Hutchins testing a violin in her acoustical test chamber. With her wild hair and furrowed brow, she looked the part of the mad scientist. Just five days later, Sullivan wrote his second piece, "Some Secrets of Stradivari," published in the *Sunday New York Times*, February 26, 1967.

When Carleen returned home after being gone just one week, she was hardly prepared for the buzz created by two back-to-back *New York Times* stories. The May 1967 *CAS Newsletter* reported:

> The ripples set up by his [Sullivan's] articles in the *New York Times* of February 21 and 26, 1967, are coming in from many parts of the country. Otto Reder [CAS colleague in Germany] sent a clipping of another article by Walter Sullivan which appeared in a Zurich, Switzerland, paper.
>
> "Radio Free Europe" and "Voice of America" are doing broadcasts using an interview along with excerpts from the WGBH "Touchstone" program taped . . . [of] the Saunders Memorial Concert of June 1966. The United States Information Agency is working on plans for a television taping and are at present reviewing the TV film made in 1964 by the California Academy of Sciences. Even the third and fourth grade news sheet *My Weekly*

Reader, that goes to millions of school children, carried Sullivan's story of the new violin family.

It begins to look as though the new instruments are coming around the corner from obscurity into the world of contemporary musicians.[13]

On March 9, 1967, Hutchins wrote to Fryxell: "So much has resulted from the recent publicity that I am gaga. Radio Free Europe—piles of mail, two radio shows—and my inclination is to duck them all and make fiddles. . . . Right now I have a bug and am lying low."[14]

In the meantime, Stokowski was still exploring whether there was a place for the vertical viola in his orchestra. Hutchins recalled: "I think he did play viola to a certain extent, but he wanted viola players in his orchestra to learn to play it vertically. He felt that vertical playing was much more efficient and effective than playing it under the chin—which, of course, being twenty-one inches, it certainly is. He felt that the thumb position gave players a great deal more leeway, too."[15] But eventually, resistance from viola players won out. On October 20, 1967, evidently in response to a phone conversation with Stokowski highlighting the unwillingness of violists to retool to play vertically, Hutchins proposed that she make a modified viola that could be played *da braccio*. Hutchins even sent the maestro a drawing and wrote: "I have pondered at some length your idea of giving it violin string length, thicker strings, sloping upper shoulders, and slightly broader bouts that will maintain tone quality and yet make it possible to play under the chin with some degree of ease as high as eighth and ninth positions."[16] A week later, Stokowski agreed.

The November 1, 1967, *CAS Newsletter* began with the unfortunate news of the passing of Sterling Hunkins, the cellist whose solo performance on the vertical viola had so impressed Stokowski two years earlier.

His wide reputation as a professional cellist was matched by his great generosity and understanding as a person. As reported many times, it was he who came with Henry Brant asking for the new instruments of the violin family. And it was he who conveyed the essential meaning of this request through long hours of discussion, playing and testing of instruments. Their musical success can be in great part attributed to Sterling Hunkins. When Leopold Stokowski commented: "No viola ever sounded like that

> before. It fills the whole hall," it was Sterling Hunkins playing the vertical viola in Brant's piece "Consort for True Violins." We have all lost a real friend.[17]

In the meantime, on April 9, 1968, Stokowski wrote to Hutchins to inquire about the tenor. Hutchins wrote back two days later: "Cellists find it very easy to play and many times have indicated it holds real potential as a solo instrument in a tone range that has long been missing in the violin family."[18] On April 15, Stokowski replied that whenever Carleen had the "monster" viola—as they had both come to refer to it—ready, he could meet with her at Carnegie Hall to try it out onstage, following a rehearsal.[19] Sometime prior to January 1969, Carleen met up with Stokowski and unveiled the "monster"—a cornerless vertical viola in which Hutchins turned the strings and the playing arrangement sideways so the left hand could move easily up to the bridge. The result was an unbalanced instrument that tended to flop around rather than stay steady in the player's hands. Hutchins said to Stokowski: "Maestro, when you see this, you are going to have bad dreams." He said: "No, no bad dreams!" But when she opened the case, he said, "Well, maybe!"[20]

On January 24, 1969, Hutchins wrote Stokowski: "It was indeed interesting to watch your reactions to the 'monster.' . . . As you said, musicians are extremely conventional, but the hope is that you just may be able to find one who is willing to explore its potential and provide some really constructive criticism." Three days later, on January 27, Stokowski wrote to Hutchins, saying that the "monster" viola had great tonal depth and also a kind of brilliance above this deep tone that made it very special, indeed.[21] Nevertheless, its size made it difficult for small hands to play, and the large, heavy side to the left pulled downward, making it difficult to hold. Could Hutchins think of any way to improve these two conditions? Though that was the last letter Hutchins received from "Stokey," Carleen wrote this entry in the family log on March 8, 1969: "3 Violas to Carnegie Hall for test with Stokowski: #42 'dark' and #51 'open.'" Carleen later recalled: "Stokowski had a good sense of humor. I probably went over to talk to him three or four times. He had the 'Monster' for maybe a couple of years. He said that the sound of it was very great, but that it was hard to handle, that the players didn't like it—and if you can't suit the players, you are out of luck."[22]

Stokowski, as he tried to urge his violists to rethink things, was not unlike Hutchins diligently working to orchestrate interest in her violin octet and in the work of the Catgut Acoustical Society. In discussing his philosophy for training conductors, Larry Livingston, professor of conducting and music director of Thornton Orchestras, says that the conductor is the "congealer of all of the separate threads that make this special fabric what it is. . . . In the end, all rivers flow together, so conducting an orchestra is as much about your ability to induce those people to want to go over the cliff with you as it is technique—and to do that, you need conviction, knowledge of the tune, and then you need to *be* the music!"[23] Both Stokowski and Hutchins were forever working toward "being the music" in that they were both always engaged in trying to convince others to jump off the cliff with them. Stokey's "Monster" ended up being cornerless and off-balance, but at least it was the result of both his and Hutchins's pushing the boundaries of convention, asking the next question because it needed to be asked. Asking the next question was the nature of innovation, the natural inclination of a pioneer.

Intermezzo

Collections – the Cabinet of Curiosities

The world in a glass cabinet:
how history was collected and put on display.
— Arthur MacGregor, *Curiosity and Enlightenment*, 1985

The Golden Harpsichord made by Michele Todini that sits in the musical instrument galleries of the Metropolitan Museum of Art is one extravagant example of the gilded age of baroque decorative arts, a reminder of the seventeenth-century "cabinet of curiosities" rolled into one musical instrument. In its original state, the harpsichord (only one part of which has survived) was part instrument, part sculpture, part installation, and part machine. Hidden pipes and a concealed keyboard connecting organ pipes and a harpsichord enabled a single instrument to mimic wind and strings simultaneously, a kind of "one-man orchestra."[1]

Michele Todini (1616–1690) was both a musician and an instrument builder extraordinaire who founded the earliest museum devoted to musical instruments. Though the original house that held Todini's museum no longer exists, Todini described his Galleria Armonica in a book published in Rome in 1676.[2] Todini built his museum at the height of the seventeenth-century craze for collecting — the era of the "cabinet of curiosities" or the German *Wunderkammer* — a distinctly European phenomenon that fused art, nature, science, and economics and helped engender modern science and the modern museum.

The golden harpsichord, as a "one-man orchestra," reflects a time when collectors and musicians enjoyed elaborate assortments of a wide array of musical instrument families of all sizes, both wind and string. In fact, large musical groups performed both sacred and secular music for ardent musical patrons in the ducal courts of Austria and Germany. A rare, elaborately illustrated festival book prepared for a wedding feast records in great detail one of the most sumptuous and famous courtly festivals of the sixteenth century, the wedding of Wilhelm, Duke of Bavaria and son of Albert V, to Renée, daughter of Francis I, Duke of Lorraine and Christina, Princess of Denmark. The marriage took place on February 21, 1568, in Munich, but the celebrations continued for nearly two weeks, beginning with a well-documented seven-course musical feast.[3] The music for the fifth course alone included a piece for three choirs, six low viols, six recorders, and six voices with harpsichord. The sixth course featured a mixed ensemble composed of harpsichord, trombone, recorder, lute, cornamusa, mute cornett, viol, and small shawm. The seventh and last course featured three different choirs — a consort of four viols, another consort of four large recorders, and a mixed group composed of dolzaina, cornamusa, shawm, and mute cornett.[4]

During the Renaissance there were many consort families of string and wind instruments composed of instruments of many different sizes, each of small compass, corresponding to a range of the human voice, ranging from small high-treble instruments to gigantic basses.[5] Lowell Creitz, former cellist of the Pro Arte Quartet, conducted a study of the organological roots of musical instrumental families. He toured thirty musical instrument collections and consulted with approximately twenty violin experts to study the period of conformation when families of instruments were pared down to those most useful for concertos or solos. Creitz reported: "I deliberately selected Old Family examples from a 350 year span to demonstrate that various sizes were in existence for many years. . . . Once the conformation was stabilized, the several sizes continued to be made well into the 18th century. L. Mozart refers to 13 sizes and types of bowed chordophones."[6] Thus, in a very real sense, the creation of a new violin family is an old idea harkening back to the Renaissance, when an extravagant rainbow of sizes and tonalities characterized many families of musical instruments, from lutes and recorders to viols and violins.

The "cabinet of curiosities" fervor spurred collectors to accrue musical instruments as art artifacts. Collecting instruments was one way to study them. But the field of musicology — the formal study of music — is its own paradox because music is ever disappearing, anchored to the invisible thread of the present moment. Beyond studying the musical instrument, one can only study images in paintings or on artifacts and in sculpture to get a mental picture of musical performance and practice. Because music is the most invisible of all the arts — the way we *think* and write about music is also its story, a story that has fundamentally shaped musical practice and influenced the value a culture places on music as well. The only other way to study music is to study those who wrote about it.

The most influential medieval writer on music was Anicius Manlius Severinus Boethius (AD 480–525). Though Boethius wrote treatises on the four mathematical disciplines of arithmetic, geometry, astronomy, and music, only the one on arithmetic and part of the one on music survive. Yet his *De Musica* was the most copied treatise of the ninth-century Carolingian Renaissance and was reproduced continually for seven hundred years. So when Boethius intentionally set music apart—and above—the other three mathematical disciplines of the quadrivium, medieval readers took notice. The reason why Boethius ascribed such importance to music was because of its powerful, invisible influence on the body, mind, and spirit. He wrote: "[D]iscipline has no more open pathway to the mind than through the ear. When by this path rhythms and modes have reached the mind, it is evident that they also affect it and conform to their nature."[7]

While plainchant represented perhaps the purest expression of the inner harmony inherent in music, its apparent simplicity actually fostered endless opportunities for variations, necessitating that monks memorize a voluminous amount of sacred music. Enter the eleventh-century monk Guido of Arezzo (991–1033), who applied himself to the "science of singing" through two great inventions. First, he developed a four-line staff with fixed rows and a systematic musical notation that made it possible for the first time to make melody visible. Second, he created the first version of a stepwise rising melody that we know today as: do-re-mi-fa-so-la-ti-do, a mnemonic device that allowed singers to pick out and sing melodies they had never heard before. With his innovative system, Guido inadvertently made improvisation and originality possible.

In 1492, music theorist Franchinus Gaffurius published his *Theorica musicae*, the first printed book on music with illustrations and discussion of vocal music theory. His *Practica musicae* (1496) included subjects like ancient Greek notation, plainchant, counterpoint, and tempo and provided an overview for musicians and composers alike. In 1511, German composer Sebastian Virdung wrote the first treatise devoted entirely to musical instruments—*Musica Getutscht*. In 1528, Martin Agricola, a German self-taught teacher, musician, and theorist, wrote his *Musica instrumentalis deudsch*, the earliest work that included illustrations of musical instruments.

In 1619, in his celebrated treatise *Syntagma Musicum*, German musicologist Michael Praetorius made the greatest contribution to Western European musicology by adding exact measurements and tunings of nearly all the musical instruments of his time to his 188 detailed woodcut illustrations. Attention to number proved crucial to illuminating seventeenth-century musical practices. As a result, the two-volume, five-hundred-page treatise became the unofficial bible of musicologists, as they could finally measure and replicate old instruments with the correct dimensions and tunings.

Music and number are inseparable concepts — and science emerged from them both. In fact, it is no accident that the study of music and musical acoustics coincided with the scientific revolution — it was, in fact, central to it. The perception of music pervaded nearly all aspects of society prior to the Renaissance. Since Pythagoras, the study of music and musical instruments focused on the central theme of music as number. Then around 1600, experimentation and the empirical investigation of sound and music resulted in a major shift in focus from the perception of music as number to the idea of music as sound. The shift in the perception of music is central to understanding how music helped to focus the scientific revolution and then, for a century or two, was left behind by a reductionist view of music that attempted to separate the art and science of music, relegating music to the realm of the arts alone.

In 1636, French Franciscan Friar Marin Mersenne published *Harmonie universelle*, a 1,500-page compendium that constituted the first extensive treatise on sound and music. In 1638, in his treatise *Two New Sciences*, Galileo provided the first "scientific" discussion of the nature of sound. He demonstrated that pitch depends on frequency; showed the ratios of frequencies for various musical intervals; and explained resonance, sympathetic vibration, and the causes of consonance and dissonance.[8]

In 1650, German Jesuit scholar Athanasius Kircher published his two-volume, lavishly illustrated, 1,100-page book *Musurgia Universalis* — a title signifying its scope as an encyclopedia of the knowledge of sound in the seventeenth century. Galileo, Descartes (1618), Mersenne (1636) and Kircher (1650) all discussed sympathetic vibrations. In the *Philosophical Transactions of the Royal Society* for 1677, a Dr. Wallis published "On the Trembling of Consonant Strings, a New Musical Discovery."[9]

Sir Isaac Newton (1642–1727) was the first to note correlations between color and sound.[10] In his book *Measure for Measure*, Thomas Levenson highlights the strong parallels between Sir Isaac Newton and Johann Sebastian Bach.

> Newton may have listened to the harmony of the spheres, but we perhaps come closest to hearing its strains in a piece Bach wrote around 1715, the Fantasia and Fugue in G minor styled "The Great."
>
> The fugue is a technique rather than a fixed form. In the G-minor piece, one theme (the subject), its response (the countersubject), the theme again, another response, are each taken up by a separate voice of the organ. The lines speak to one another, variation succeeding variation to build an increasingly complex weave of all the elements. The melodies move in and out, until the pattern closes at the end, coming to rest on the original theme. As it unfolds, the piece creates an astoundingly vivid sense of an inevitable logic, combined with an exalting, soaring quality that evokes an older image, the sudden height of a gothic cathedral. It is an artistic effect born of the same aesthetic that animates the search for the ideal form in nature; Bach's "Great" fugue matches any of Newton's mathematical arguments in its logic and formal elegance.[11]

In fact, throughout his career, Bach continued to pursue the connections between music and the methodology and mindset espoused by the initiators of the scientific revolution. In 1747, three years before he died, Bach joined the composers Telemann and Handel as a member of an organization calling itself the Corresponding Society for Musical Sciences, "dedicated to rationalism in art and thought."[12] In order to qualify for membership, each had to compose a piece that would demonstrate the "expression of reason in music." Bach constructed an organ piece in which a pattern of melody in movements became increasingly complex — "the music of the spheres compressed into the compass of an organ's pipes."[13]

While the idea of celestial music has become a metaphor, one can argue that Bach perhaps most closely demonstrated the metaphor. Levenson explains: "Bach's works create a bridge between the language of poets and the language of modern science. The glory of his great organ pieces is that they feel 'true' — they are mathematically precise, complete, coherent — while remaining pleasing, to say the least, to the ear. They provide the experience, that is, that Bach clearly intended for his audience: they allow us to hear what Heisenberg meant when he spoke of the bond between beauty and truth and science."[14]

The full musical "exhibit" that composed Todini's Golden Harpsichord was apparently broken up in 1796, when it passed through several owners. In 1902, it was donated to the Metropolitan Museum of Art as part of the Crosby Brown Collection of Musical Instruments. As it sits in its place of prominence, lighting up the Met galleries, the gilded harpsichord reminds us of the potential within every musical instrument to be more than itself.[15]

11 ∫ Editor

Music is defined by measure, and instrument makers are the measurers of music. From long before the time of Pythagoras, craft has demonstrated the science of music. The fact that Carleen Hutchins was first and foremost a craftsperson proved essential to her role as an editor caught in the middle of the world of violin acoustics.

The door was always open at 112 Essex Avenue, and Hutchins was always ready to invite a stranger into her living room. The personal and the professional often merged over the kitchen table, or downstairs at the vibration table, or in the sound chamber-closets, or on violin plates vibrating black sand into stunning geometric patterns. So no one in the violin world—maker, acoustician, collector, dealer, or player—who knew anything about Carleen Maley Hutchins would be surprised by the photograph on the cover of the most important set of books devoted to violin acoustics. On the covers of both volumes 1 and 2 of *The Research Papers in Violin Acoustics, 1975–1993* is a photograph of the living room at 112 Essex Avenue. But it is not just Carleen's living room. Taking the place of furniture, leaning against dark wainscoting and the built-in corner bench nearest the tall red brick hearth are all eight members of the Hutchins Violin Octet—from left to right: baritone, small bass, and contrabass lean into the corner; tenor and alto sit on the corner bench; mezzo, soprano, and, treble are perched together on the floor.

This tableau of fiddles consumes the room much as the ensemble of violins consumed Carleen's life. But this photograph is exactly where it belongs —not because of the ego of Carleen Maley Hutchins—although her critics might argue this point. The photograph is appropriate because, as editor of the series, Hutchins gave her blood, sweat, and tears to the creation of the four most important volumes on violin acoustics—*Benchmark Papers in Acoustics*, vol. 5, *Musical Acoustics, Part I: Violin Family Components* (1975) and vol. 6, *Musical Acoustics, Part II: Violin Family Functions* (1976) and *The Research Papers in Violin Acoustics, 1975–1993*, two volumes, published by the Acoustical Society of America through the American Institute of Physics (1997). The photograph also legitimately belongs on the cover because the Hutchins new violin family was at the time, and remains, the most revolutionary, newsworthy "event" to happen in the violin world over the past four centuries — since Amati hit upon the optimal design for the violin and Stradivari perfected it. No other luthier has made as large a contribution to her field — bar none.

In addition to her work thus far — her experiments with Saunders, the completion of the first violin octet, the creation of the Catgut Acoustical Society, and her ongoing violinmaking — Carleen Hutchins was drawing attention from many different directions, primarily in the field of musical acoustics, a field that, at the time, was in its infancy.

On March 15, 1964, Mary L. Harbold, associate professor of physics at Temple University, presented a paper, "Summary of Current Developments in Musical Acoustics," at the Music Educators National Conference in Philadelphia. Though she provided a précis that included woodwinds and brass; organ, voice, and piano; and psychoacoustics, nearly a third of her report was devoted to strings and, primarily, the work of Carleen Hutchins. Harbold described the Montclair, New Jersey, housewife, mother, skilled woodworker, and former science teacher featured most recently in the Kennedy issue of *Life* magazine: "Her home has become the Mecca for a group of scientists, musicians, and miscellaneous people . . . pooling their contributions to study . . . the art of violin making and to produce new and improved instruments." The fact that her instruments have been "played and declared excellent" by musicians such as Mischa Schneider of the Budapest String Quartet, Kroll of the Kroll Quartet, Leopold Stokowski, and many string performers in major symphony orchestras "is the acid test of an instrument."[1]

Harbold further explained what distinguished Hutchins from all other researchers in violin acoustics around the world. "There has been no instrument-maker who had the broad woodworking background[,] . . . and the ability and training to do the scientific tests necessary to convert knowledge into real, improved instruments. . . . [She] has developed as scientist and instrument maker through her association with Saunders."[2] Harbold highlighted Hutchins's experiment in which she deliberately left a cello in "incorrect" form, according to her research, and then gave it to players to see their reactions. After it was handed back "with embarrassment" by all who played it, Hutchins took it apart and removed ten grams of wood (less mass than a piece of paper), then reassembled it and lent it to Mischa Schneider of the Budapest Quartet who pronounced it "Magnifico!"[3]

By August 1965, Carleen had begun searching for funding to further develop her electronic testing facility. When her application to the Radcliff Special Funding for Projects was declined, it was suggested that Hutchins consider applying to the Martha Baird Rockefeller Fund for Music. In her grant application, Hutchins summarized the scope of the violin acoustics field and the aims of the Catgut Acoustical Society, still in its infancy, from 1963 to 1965. Among the projects she proposed were a psychoacoustics experiment with luthiers and their audio perception of the tap tones of free plates, a reexamination of the baroque violin before it was modified, and a publishing plan for collecting papers in violin acoustics. It worked like a charm; in the spring of 1966, Carleen was awarded the first of two grants from the Martha Baird Rockefeller Fund for Music.

With these funds, and advice from longtime friend and CAS member Frank Fielding, Hutchins was able to purchase $10,000–$12,000 worth of electronic equipment and turn her father's basement wine cellar underneath the sun porch into a multifaceted test lab, including the pouring of six-inch-thick acoustic concrete walls on which Hutchins and Petie Evans installed two banks of heavy curtains to maximize sound absorption. Still, outside neighborhood noises sometimes made instrument testing difficult. Hutchins finally settled on testing instruments in the wee hours of the morning, when most everyone was asleep. She recalled: "At first, we had no way of filtering out the ambient noise, so for at least two years, I would wait until early in the morning, like 2:00–3:00 a.m., when it was quiet around here. Even then, when an airplane went over or my husband turned over in bed upstairs, I would get a blip on my strip chart." To add to the early morning acoustics problems, a policeman parked his car at the corner of Essex and Frederick Street and kept his engine running. When Carleen asked the sergeant not to park there, he asked what was going on at 2 a.m. "When I explained that I was doing some acoustical testing, he looked at me as if I had holes in my head. But never mind, they took the car off the corner so I could do a better job."[4]

In April 1967, when a violin octet was already on display at the ASA meeting in New York City, Nicholas Bessaraboff, musicologist and author of *Ancient European Musical Instruments*, invited Hutchins to bring the octet to his apartment. So in the mid-afternoon of April 26, Marjorie Bram, Ellery Lewis Wilson, Vincent O'Brien, and Carleen Hutchins took all eight new violins to Bessaraboff's apartment. As he watched and listened to Wilson play the contrabass, Bessaraboff exclaimed: "Lewis, it's a difficult thing. It's a new technique AND a new instrument. Absolutely, we are getting something entirely different. In the first place, consistent, beautiful. . . . [O]h, where is Pablo? Pablo Casals, where is he? What would he say?!"

Wilson said: It's even more forceful in a large auditorium — simply amazing!

Bessaraboff: I am simply put out to know what to say, I am so enthusiastic about it. Where are the geniuses we are going to need to write the music? What makes me think the path you are pursuing is correct, is the uniformity — it is a family, not just a conglomeration of instruments in the violin section.

Bram: You mean there is a "family resemblance"?

Bessaraboff: Yes! And it's so consistent.

Hutchins: This is what we've been working for. If we've got it, I'm deeply grateful.

B: The string section of my book, so far as the violin is concerned, has to be absolutely revamped [because of the Hutchins instruments].

H: That's exciting! It seems there is an effort to improve all instruments these days, but there has been so little effort that has succeeded in improving the string family, until this research was available. This is the result of 45 years of acoustical research.

B: That's precisely it. Some people think that orchestras should be revamped.

Bram: Stokowski says that too, doesn't he?

H: He feels there is a real place for these in the orchestra, but it's going to be slow. The tone was what got him excited. He's had one of our big violas for two years now. He heard it and went on from there.

B: The next subject — how should these instruments be arranged in an orchestra?

H: I wish there were enough to arrange!

Then Bram, and others said: "There will be, some day!"

B: Why heavens, yes. No question about it! I'd love to hear all of them

> played sometime, in a real string section. I was absolutely astounded. . . . It is so consistent; then you are the master of your trade, and you're controlling it. Scientific instruments do help, but you have already acquired the skill!!![5]

By the fall of 1968, Hutchins had gained such renown in violin acoustics that the ASA Technical Committee on Musical Acoustics asked her to lead a symposium devoted to violin acoustics during the 77th meeting of the ASA to take place April 1969 in Philadelphia. This symposium was a joint effort between the ASA and CAS. On April 11, Hutchins presided as chair of the Violin Acoustics Symposium. Sometime during this ASA meeting, Bruce Lindsay, editor at the ASA, cornered Carleen and told her that the Society was trying to get the *Benchmark* series going and it needed someone to edit a book on violin acoustics. He asked if she would be interested. "That's all it took," Hutchins remembered. "I was sure interested and it ended up in two books and a lot more than he ever expected — which was kind of exciting and nice." In fact, Carleen, without being conscious of it, had already indirectly put her hat in the ring back in 1963 when Saunders died and Mrs. Saunders sent her all of his reprints. At the time, Hutchins started to organize his correspondence and had begun contacting researchers who had written to Saunders. "I began writing to these guys to get information on their papers — and I just kept collecting these things. This was long before Bruce Lindsay, the editor of JASA asked me to do this."[6]

Hutchins was indeed already totally immersed in the field of violin acoustics. In the spring of 1970, a WNYC-FM radio program called *Men of Hi-Fi* featured an "informal bull session of experts" about violin acoustics. The lively discussion, taped on April 19, included A. Stewart Hegeman, president of Hegeman Laboratories, a foremost designer of loudspeakers; William Kroll, violinist, teacher and leader of the Kroll Quartet; composer Frank Lewin — and Carleen Hutchins.[7]

To be asked to edit the *Benchmark* volumes was a challenge and a great honor for Hutchins, and it validated not only her own experimental work on violins but her intense work developing a community in violin acoustics that included musicians, lawyers, artists, engineers, translators, editors, photographers, chemists, physicists, violin experts, composers, and conductors — such was the wonderfully bizarre Catgut Acoustical Society. The

Benchmark series, in its first edition, took Hutchins five years, from 1969 to 1974. "During the five years I worked to assemble these papers, getting permissions from each researcher—hundreds of letters back and forth—John Schelleng was always there to help criticize or point out definitive aspects of certain work. . . . [T]hese volumes are a tribute to him as well as the five years of my hard work."[8] By June 5, 1974, Hutchins had mailed the next volumes in the series to the publisher. The *Benchmark Papers in Acoustics,* vol. 5, *Musical Acoustics, Part I* was published in 1975; *Part II,* in 1976.

And the work was not complete. In the spring of 1990, by the time Virginia Benade asked Carleen to edit an updated version, Carleen had contracted a "creeping kind of slow polio" that struck her legs and back. She recalled: "I couldn't walk, but I could sit and work. I had to do something—that book sort of saved my sanity."[9] Carleen worked on the next series from 1990 to 1995. The subsequent two-volume edition of *Research Papers in Violin Acoustics, 1975–1993* was published by the ASA in 1997.

How do these books contribute to the field? Luthier David Brownell noted: "[T]hese papers contain acoustic relationships and much useful data that can improve our instruments. The books are worth, not just their cost, but the time we spend in careful study of how violins work and can be better made."[10]

The attempt to build a bridge between the art and science of making a better fiddle began with Savart and Vuillaume, then was buried for a century, and finally resurfaced in the work of the Sirs, Dautrich, Saunders, and Hutchins. A major catalyst for this paradigm shift had its beginnings in the living room at 112 Essex Avenue with a housewife-violinmaker willing to build bridges where there had been only walls.

12 ∫ *Lecturer*

Given her passion for both acoustics and fiddles, it was inevitable that Hutchins would become a troubadour touring with her fiddles — and she lectured all over the world to a wide range of audiences for thirty years. Like a Chladni pattern — that beautiful, vivid, geometric shape that forms suddenly from a disorganized pile of sand at a particular frequency — Hutchins was most comfortable and vibrant at the lectern, where, as a former science teacher who saw science everywhere in everyday life, she was sharing her passion. In doing so, she combined all of her best traits — spontaneity, cleverness, wit, generosity, humor, zeal — in one beautiful geometric pattern that everyone from any discipline or inclination could understand and appreciate.

Whether she and Mort were packing crates and loading instrument cases into the 1971 Chevy to drive to a lecture-demonstration or carting the four large crates — weighing eight hundred pounds and insured for $20,000 — to the airport, in these moments, Carleen was her most focused self. Each lecture, instead of having the same outcome, seemed to have its own distinct ripple effect, because Hutchins did not merely tell her story; she fanned each and every spark of interest she saw in her audience, inviting her listeners in, allowing them to reimagine their own connections to her work.

In late April, at the invitation of Dr. John Sarratt and Dr. Lawrence Slifkin, Hutchins took her octet down to North Carolina to the 1969 Fine Arts Festival at the University of North Carolina at Chapel Hill for a symposium sponsored jointly by the music and physics departments. Hutchins conducted a colloquium on April 23, in Phillips Hall, room 215. Following the lecture, the North Carolina String Quartet gave a concert featuring "Miss Hutchins' 'first family of fiddles.'" The program noted that Hutchins and CAS were "lending artistry a hand by debunking the many peculiar superstitions which plagued violin artisans since Stradivari."[1]

Richard Eckberg, a bass player and a chemistry doctoral student, was in the right place at the right time. Eckberg had studied bass with Oscar Zimmerman at Eastman School of Music and at Hamilton College, and he had joined the UNC Symphony Orchestra as principal bassist. When Eckberg learned Hutchins was staying for the weekend in Chapel Hill, he asked if he might play the contrabass for a Friday night rehearsal and Saturday concert with the UNC Symphony, which was performing Carl Orff's *Carmina Burana* and Gian Carlo Menotti's *Death of the Bishop of Brindisi*. When asked to recall his experience, Eckberg wrote: "These are large bombastic works requiring a big orchestral sound. It occurred to me that the big Hutchins Bass would be a great addition to the orchestra and I really wanted to play it!" Carleen agreed, excited by the prospect of a debut for her contrabass in a professional orchestra. Eckberg recalled his first impression of playing the contrabass: "Despite the girth and depth of the sound box, it played easily, with even response and light action. . . . It had an amazing huge sound that blew everyone away. Compared to my run-of-the-mill laminate bass, the Hutchins 'Uber-Bass' sounded like a cannon. Playing [it] . . . required a lot of control lest it overwhelm the ensemble."[2]

In the Friday night dress rehearsal at Memorial Hall, preparing to play *Carmina Burana*, Eckberg tuned the contrabass's low E string to a low D, put extra rosin on his bow, and waited for the opening movement. "The piece starts with a big *fff* D minor chord in orchestra and chorus, and I whaled way on the low open D. . . . The conductor startled at the thunderous sound coming from the lower strings. Half the orchestra turned around in their chairs to stare at the bass," recalled Eckberg who glanced at the audience and "spotted Carleen sitting there just beaming. . . . There was no doubt about how effective the Hutchins Bass was in underpinning these big colossal pieces." He continued: "That bass is a one-of-a-kind miracle and there is nothing like it on the planet. I am happy to know that it along with the other violins are delighting new audiences." Eckberg currently plays with the Durham Symphony.[3]

The highlight for Hutchins of a fall 1970 trip to California was the day she crashed a master class. She had finished her lecture-demonstration and was about to leave the music department at UCLA, when she walked into the foyer and stopped short at the sound of music coming from the auditorium stage — a Piatigorsky master class. On stage, with bows in hand, were five gifted young cellists: Paul Tobias, Jeffrey Solow, Nathaniel Rosen, Terry King, and Myung Wha Chung — listening to Piatigorsky in the deserted auditorium. "What would happen if I stuck my head in there?" asked Carleen of the receptionist seated near the auditorium. She said: "You'd get your head chopped off!" Carleen promptly went out to her van, grabbed the tenor and baritone violins and came back to the foyer. Without a word to the receptionist, she walked up to the door of the auditorium, opened it and stuck one of her violins in the door—just her arm and the violin showing in the doorway—and waited, wincing at the risk she had taken by interrupting the maestro. Gregor Piatigorsky looked up and shouted to the back of the auditorium: "What's this?"

"Try it, Maestro!" cried Hutchins as she made her way down the aisle to where Piatigorsky was poised in front of his students. What Carleen recalled most vividly was that the maestro was as curious about how his students would react as he was about the new instrument. When one of his students began to bear down on the strings, the maestro cautioned: "You must first listen to the instrument—go gently so you can discover what it can do." Piatigorsky then spent the next two hours, demonstrating, discussing, and having his students try the tenor and baritone. Then the maestro let loose on the baritone. Hutchins recalled: "Piatigorsky played the baritone for nearly half an hour, giving it a tremendous workout. He then lectured on how to approach a new instrument, to try and exploit its real potential without imposing preconceived techniques or ideas on it." Then one of the students played the baritone as the lowest voice in a cello quartet. "Unanimous opinion of the group was that the full low range of the baritone [added] new depths and meanings to the entire composition. At the end of the session, Piatigorsky handed Mrs. Hutchins the two instruments and said one word, 'Bravo!'"[4]

Many years later, Paul Tobias recalled: "It would have certainly taken some guts and resolve to walk into that master class cold." Tobias said that the new violins were viewed by most musicians at the time as "outer edge," and that given the spirit of the times, Carleen was met with more than a "good measure of skepticism—something radically different from the norm was seen as gimmicky."[5]

In March 1980, through the auspices of composer Frank Lewin, the new violin family presented its own interactive "lecture" to eighty-five thousand spectators during the Leipzig Trade Fair, one of the largest in Europe, where five octet violins were on display for eight days. The invitation had arrived in a letter from David Paul, senior project director of the Exhibits Service of the International Communication Agency in Washington, DC, who recalled the 1962 *Scientific American* article. Hutchins asked composer Frank Lewin to coordinate the interactive display of five instruments. The original plan was to demonstrate the mezzo and alto violins only. Lewin recalled: "However, the young musicians were eager to try them all, and at one time or another gave a workout to each of the five. A few visitors were given a chance to step onto the stand and play the instruments; their response, invariably, was one of astonishment and delight."[6]

In July 1980, Carleen and Mort traveled to Australia to attend the Fifth CAS Technical Meeting, held July 5–8, in the physics department of the University of Wollongong, New South Wales, preceding the Tenth International Congress on Acoustics in Sydney. This was the first time that Australian CAS members had come together in one place, and the gathering also included members and visitors from Yugoslavia, Belgium, Sweden, Japan, England, the United States, New Zealand, and other Australian states.

The musical highlight came with the arrival of a celebrity violinist—Harry Kirby, first violinist of the famous Sydney String Quartet. On short notice, Kirby had agreed to participate in a recital featuring Australian-made violins. Kirby performed excerpts from virtuoso violin music on eighteen instruments before an audience of about two hundred people. While all the instruments appeared to be of generally good construction and a high standard aesthetically, acoustic quality varied greatly. "The most successful instrument acoustically from the viewpoint of the player and the audience was an instrument made by Mrs. Hutchins that she had brought with her."[7] Through the efforts of David Strahle, Robin Williams of Australian Radio ABC in Sydney interviewed Hutchins for a half-hour show on violin acoustics.[8]

Most likely because of the international response to her October 1981 *Scientific American* article, forever memorialized by the front cover image of Chladni patterns on six violin plates, Hutchins received an invitation to visit Japan and China the following year to give lecture-demonstrations of her plate-tuning techniques. The trip was planned at the invitation of Professor Wang Xiang of the Institute for Theater, Science, and Technology in Beijing. During their weeklong stay in Japan, hosted by Professor Isao Nakamura, Carleen gave a lecture to that country's chapter of the ASA. Carleen and Mort also visited "a department store exhibit-sale" of violins, including a dozen or more Strads, Guarnerius, and other early instruments, along with contemporary ones from all over the world.[9]

In Beijing, Hutchins presented seminars on testing violin plates in the Laboratory of Acoustics.[10] Carleen's morning work sessions were attended by an impressive array of acousticians, including Maa Dah-you, president of the Acoustical Society of China and fellow of the Acoustical Society of America; Chen Tong and Guan Dingua, both deputy directors of the Institute of Acoustics; and Liu Xu, director of the Institute for Theater, Science, and Technology.[11]

Her afternoon sessions had an equally diverse audience — seventy members from the Beijing Film Institute, the Central Conservatory of Music, and two violin factories, with several independent violinmakers coming from distant parts of China. Hutchins recalled: "To watch their faces and their long sensitive fingers as they felt the vibrations in the violin plates on the shaker table was an experience in itself. Lecturing through an interpreter was also an experience but we made it work. When the lady interpreter, Xu Wei Fang, got confused, Maa Dah-you, a Harvard graduate and fluent in English, would help out. Along with all this our taxi with interpreter and lady guide took us to several temples, palaces, the Ming tombs and the Great Wall."[12]

In Shanghai and Canton, hosted by Professors Wang and Yan, Mort and Carleen toured violin factories and conducted demonstrations and discussions for workers there. Hutchins recalled:

> In each factory there were eight or ten master violin makers doing excellent work, some of whom have won prizes at the Violin Society of America competitions. Then there are two or three hundred workers dealing with violin parts on a partly mechanized basis all the way from cutting the big spruce logs coming in from northwest China to making the purfling, assembling ribs into forms, planing and sanding the archings for either the 'art' or the inexpensive student instruments — piles of violins of all sizes, even cellos and basses! Each place had a specialist for varnishing the fine instruments. One lady could varnish 30 a month and they really looked lovely.[13]

From Gaungchou, the Hutchinses took a train to Hong Kong with Sie Anton and were met by Dr. Shih-yu Fent, who had arranged lectures at the Chinese University of Hong Kong in the music and physics departments of Chung Chi College — "a beautiful campus nestled into the hills north of the city where we enjoyed the guest house with breakfast on the terrace overlooking miles . . . of water, islands and mountains."[14]

On March 2, 1999, Carleen Maley Hutchins gave her last public lecture to 150 acoustical physicists at the NASA Langley Research Center in Hampton, Virginia. Over the past three decades, she had traveled two hundred thousand miles to give lecture-demonstrations to audiences in music and science circles. Carleen waited backstage, ready to give a lecture and slide presentation titled "Acoustics and the Violin — Past, Present, and Future" at the H. J. Reid Conference Center as part of the center's colloquium "What Is Music?." NASA physicist Dr. George Brooks stepped up to the podium to set the tone for Hutchins's presentation: "Just like a fine painting, acoustics brings unbelievable complexity, unbelievable density of information to us and to instruments that can measure acoustics, not too different from a beautiful painting. . . . With regard to musical instruments, acoustics, of course, plays the instrument."[15] Peering out at the audience and then at the eight octet violins poised on the stage floor, Hutchins, now eighty-seven, felt sad at the thought that this would be her last lecture — the tour de force in a long line of lecture-demonstrations she had brought to colleges and universities, as well as International Congress on Acoustics and ASA meetings throughout the United States and abroad.

Later that day, Hutchins gave a modified evening lecture, "Science for the Violin Maker and the Violin Player," for the general public at the Virginia Air and Space Center. Following her lecture, three Williamsburg Symphonia players demonstrated the seven of eight octet violins. As the large contrabass stood dormant on stage, Hutchins turned to her audience: "Is there a bassist in the house?" One young man's hand shot up. He was out of his seat before Hutchins could respond, bounded up on stage, and took up the bass with a passion, performing an improvisational jazz piece that brought the house down. He turned to Hutchins as the applause subsided, and asked, "Can I take it home?" Hutchins laughed and thanked him for the "best demonstration of the evening."

In a post-concert interview, David Nicholson, reporter for Tidewater, Virginia's *Daily Press*, observed that Hutchins insists her violins sound "pretty close" to the heavenly tones of a Stradivarius or Guarnerius. She boasts: "After my instruments have been played for 150 to 200 years, they may sound better!" In answer to the complaint from other luthiers about putting numbers on the violin's mystique, Hutchins just laughed, saying, "What they forget is that there are so many mysteries still to solve in understanding how a violin makes sound — it's all mystique!"[16]

Inversion

Statement of a motive where interval directions move in the opposite direction of the original motive

Timothy A. Smith, "Anatomy of a Fugue"

13 *Fiddles and Guitars*

SYMPATHETIC STRINGS

Like minds reverberate with each other and resonate in all kinds of ways, like the strings of a violin or the Chladni sand patterns that form on a vibrating violin plate at certain unique frequencies. This was never truer than in the synergistic relationship between the Catgut Acoustical Society and the Guild of American Luthiers. In fact, the formation of Catgut in 1963 inspired Tim Olsen to found GAL a decade later, directly inspired by the "no secrets" open forum model of CAS.

So on June 24, 1992, it seemed supremely natural when CAS and GAL held their first joint meeting at the Shrine to Music Museum at the University of South Dakota, in Vermillion. Later renamed the National Music Museum, the museum began in 1966, when Arne B. Larson, a Minnesota farm boy and bandleader, donated his collection of 2,500 musical instruments to the University of South Dakota. Officially founded in 1973, the National Music Museum—though a relative newcomer among musical instruments museums—is now the largest museum of its kind, housing fifteen thousand musical instruments, making it the most extensive global archival research center for musical instruments in the world.

Carleen's connections to guitars began in 1967, the year she visited the C. F. Martin Guitar factory in Nazareth, Pennsylvania, celebrated manufacturers of guitars for more than 150 years, ever since 1833, when Christian Friedrich Martin first emigrated from Germany to New York City, where he made guitars for five years before moving his shop to Pennsylvania. After reading the 1962 *Scientific American* article, John Huber, who first went to work for C. F. Martin in the company's repair shop, paid a visit to Hutchins in Montclair. Hutchins and Huber got to know each other while sharing their different methods in carving top plates. On the recommendation of Huber, C. F. Martin III then approached Hutchins with an interest in the acoustical testing of guitars and parts thereof, following the idea that methods used in violin testing might be adapted and made useful in the construction of plucked stringed instruments such as guitars, mandolins, and ukuleles. In keeping with Hutchins's philosophy and that of CAS, the

Martin Company agreed in writing that any information resulting from this collaboration would be open and available for publication and discussion without concern for patent rights.[1]

Conferences were set up with John Huber and Donald Thompson of the Martin Company and members of the CAS: John Schelleng, Robert Scanlan, Arthur Benade, Frank Fielding, Stuart Hegeman, Eugen Skudzryk, Karl Stetson, and Carleen Hutchins. In 1969, Huber went to Sweden for the summer, where he met an American—Karl Stetson—doing his thesis on laser holography. Huber described holographic interferometry: "You divide coherent light so it makes interference patterns. . . . Any changes in vibration makes an interference in the light, producing a pattern of vibration. You can actually see stress patterns. . . . When you tighten a string, you can see the area where the wood is stressed—that was very interesting."[2]

So Huber took a lot of these holographic images of guitar and violin plates—and brought them to Carleen. Huber recalled how this "new" method of holography impacted CAS members in the fall of 1969 when they were meeting at Carleen's home and Art Benade was a houseguest of Hutchins: "It was earth-shaking—a new world. We had several meetings, and no one knew how to interpret these images. Art Benade took all of these things up to his room at 112 Essex—and he put them on a wall. Then he came down the next morning and he knew all about it. He could explain the ring mode." Meanwhile, Huber continued to apply relevant elements of violin acoustics to guitarmaking. He recalled: "Then from there, we developed our own lab and studied guitars. We had some practical problems we had to solve—for example, how to make guitars to play in tune. We had to study strings, fret location, bridge problems.[3]

This kind of collaboration was as important to Hutchins as innovation. For her, they went hand in hand. In a letter written on April 23, 1971, C. F. Martin III wrote to Hutchins:

> Without reference to a specific occasion, it seems generally appropriate to thank you for the many times your guidance and cooperation with our research department has helped to place our art of guitar making on a scientific foundation. Also, through your *liaison* between us and the scientific and academic communities, we now have well-established and productive relationships with a number of extremely well-qualified consultants.

As you know, we are active participants in the Catgut Acoustical Society and strongly support its growth and interests. We hope that our mutual interests will continue to contribute to increasing our understanding and the quality of stringed instruments everywhere.

Sincerely and again with thanks,

C. F. Martin.[4]

In the early 1970s, CAS member Dr. Daniel Haines of the Department of Engineering at the University of South Carolina and his student Nagyoung Chang had begun to experiment with developing an alternative material to replace the spruce top plates in violins and guitars. Haines and Chang laminated a piece of fiberboard between two layers of graphite-epoxy, creating a laminate composite. Carleen collaborated with Haines by attempting to make a similar laminate for a violin top. Morton Hutchins used technology at Hercules, Inc., to form the plate over a solid mold of a violin top in a 350-degree Fahrenheit oven, producing a top plate that displayed a clear tap-tone.

Carleen collaborated with Haines by attempting to make a similar laminate for a violin top. Morton Hutchins used technology at Hercules, Inc., to form the plate over a solid mold of a violin top in a 350-degree Fahrenheit oven, producing a top plate that displayed a clear tap-tone. Carleen continued to collaborate with Haines — on work that soon caught the interest of *Scientific American* editor Dennis Flanagan. On the morning of January 28, 1975, Carleen, with the help of Mort to load up fiddles and equipment, gave a "Physics of Everyday Experience" lecture-demonstration in New York at an American Association for the Advancement of Science meeting. That afternoon, at a recording studio on West 75th Street, WOR radio host Jonathan Peale taped Flanagan interviewing Haines and Hutchins about their recent work.[5]

Several months later, on March 11, Bud DiFluri, district sales manager of the Selmer Division of Magnavox, and Bob Hackett, part of the Ampeg Division of Selmer, visited Montclair to discuss the graphite-epoxy violin work with Carleen and tour the facilities at 112 Essex.[6] Hutchins and Haines found that modal analysis of the graphite epoxy "sandwich" top plate displayed characteristics similar to traditional violin tops and reported in the November 1975 *CAS Newsletter*: "Two stringed instruments, a violin and a guitar, have been constructed with graphite-epoxy composite tops plates instead of the usual spruce. Tests indicate that these instruments are very successful. Unlike wood, the new composite is reproducible and stable. Since the replacement of spruce soundboards has been regarded as perhaps the most challenging problem in the development of non-wood instruments, we feel this work represents an important step toward the ultimate goal." Most important, the graphite-epoxy guitar and violin had passed musical muster, gaining favorable reactions from musicians and luthiers who found their sound to be "indistinguishable from that of fine instruments made with conventional materials."[7] Nevertheless, solving the challenges of handling the graphite material had delayed the work of Haines and Hutchins, during which time a competing firm secured a patent on a similar product. While few violinmakers experimented with the new material, some commercial guitar companies did adapt it to production methods. Today graphite-epoxy guitar tops are relatively common.[8]

In the spring of 1976, Donald J. Thompson of the C. F. Martin Company, sponsored the Third CAS Technical Conference at 112 Essex Avenue—a two-day meeting on April 3–4, held on the weekend prior to the ninety-first meeting of the ASA in Washington, DC.[9] That evening, a session of folk music started up with Don Thompson playing the graphite-epoxy top guitar, Ann Janerone on the graphite-epoxy top violin, with Mary Lee Esty on the mezzo violin. The whole group joined in—the highlight being a rendition of "Waltzing Matilda" sung by Australian Neville Fletcher and the CAS chorus.[10]

Meanwhile, Carleen continued her research using Chladni patterns on free violin plates in an attempt to find the optimal relationship between modes for the best instruments. Once again, to her surprise, she made the October 1981 cover of *Scientific American*. This time it featured a painting by Marvin Mattelson of Chladni sand patterns on six violin plates displaying modes 1, 2, and 5. In the lead article, Hutchins explained the variables involved in the analysis of free plates: "The process of tracing the evolution of the eigenmode characteristics from a pair of free violin plates to the assembled instrument in playing condition is extremely complicated and not yet clearly understood. The theoretical analysis of even one free plate must take into account at least nine parameters, the calculation of which would take a great deal of technical skill, to say nothing of more time and money than are currently available."[11]

The last experimental violin that Carleen Hutchins created was the most dramatic and memorable. Sometime in the early 1980s, inspired by consultations with acousticians Edgar A. G. Shaw and Arthur H. Benade, Hutchins built the "swiss cheese" violin. Carleen drilled sixty-five holes five millimeters apart in the ribs around the entire perimeter of a Stradivari-model violin. She then plugged the holes with corks to test the air resonance inside the cavity. Experiments with this violin spanned eighteen years.

In 1982, "Le Gruyère" made quite a sensation at the Eleventh Annual Conference on Acoustics in Paris when Hutchins persuaded the German physicist Jürgen Meyer, a fine violinist, to play the violin as she removed the corks one by one. But soon Meyer's skepticism turned to amazement as the sound changed. Hutchins explained: "The relationship of the body cavity resonances to the openings of the ff-holes is so sensitive that removing just one or two corks makes the violin sound thin and scratchy. When all the holes are plugged, which loads the ribs with the mass of 65 corks, the violin still has a good sound."[12]

On June 24–28, 1992, when the Catgut Acoustical Society joined the Guild of American Luthiers for its twentieth anniversary meeting at the Shrine to Music Museum in South Dakota, it was the largest meeting ever for both groups, hosting four hundred instrument builders from the United States, Canada, Europe, Australia, Brazil, and Asia. In celebration, André Larson, director of the museum, invited Hutchins to bring her violin octet to be played and displayed at the meeting. Evidently, Hutchins and the new violin family did make an impression on the staff. Just a week after the convention, on July 6, Larson wrote to Hutchins to ask if the octet could be loaned to the museum, proposing the idea of starting a CAS archives. It was, in fact, auspicious timing, because Hutchins and CAS had been researching several different options for creating a CAS archives.

The first idea about a violin acoustics archives had come in 1963 with Wurlitzer's proposal to start such a center at Lincoln Center, but the plan died the same year with the passing of Saunders and Wurlitzer. The idea resurfaced in 1973 when there was a discussion about possible affiliation with the Research Library at Lincoln Center, but nothing ever came of it.[13] Next, because of its early interest in the violin octet in the 1960s, when Frank Lewin and Broadus Erle were on the faculty, Yale University had shown a sporadic interest in housing the CAS archives. In addition, Hutchins had already developed a working relationship with Stevens Tech in Hoboken, New Jersey, just a short distance from Montclair. In fact, on May 26, 1977, Stevens had awarded Hutchins an honorary degree of doctor of engineering.[14] From 1977 to 1990, Stevens Tech retained close ties with Hutchins and even stored octet violins during the summers of 1988, and again in 1989. But by November 1990, Stevens was having its own problems with mold, so Hutchins retrieved the violins.

Just three days later, the total direction of the CAS archives shifted once again—this time to the West Coast. On November 17, at least one CAS member—most likely Max Matthews—suggested that the musical acoustics archives at Stanford University would be an auspicious place for the Hutchins and CAS archives. On Valentine's Day, 1991, Max Matthews came east to visit Carleen at 112 Essex to discuss space requirements. By 1992, the slow process of moving files to Stanford began. Today, a significant number of CAS files reside at the Center for Computer Research in Musical Acoustics at Stanford.

Meanwhile, in May 1994, André Larson wrote to Hutchins to ask if she would consider donating her violin octet currently on loan. On April 23, 1999, Hutchins and Larson reached a final agreement for the violin octet to join the permanent collection at the National Music Museum. In May 2004, the National Museum hosted a special exhibit of three of Hutchins's most important experimental instruments now held in the museum's permanent collection—The "Flat-Top" Viola, SUS #13; the "Black-Top" Violin; and "Le Gruyère."

14 Fiddles in the Conservatory

ENGLAND, WALES, SCOTLAND

The first overseas octet came about because of an unlikely concentration of four musically minded scientists in England, Wales, and Scotland who linked up with one versatile violin virtuoso who also happened to be an avid early music performer. The first link in the chain was the English physicist-bassist-conductor Bernard Robinson, a passionate amateur chamber music enthusiast. For three decades, Robinson had run a summer chamber music camp in the English countryside at Pigotts, a farmhouse perched atop a hill surrounded by a ring of beech trees near High Wycombe, just outside of London. The other connections were forged by the university physicist and musical acoustician Charles Taylor in Cardiff, Wales; the English physicist-violinist Michael McIntyre in Cambridge; the acoustical engineer Peter Fellgett in Wales; and the London violinist, *viola da gamba* virtuoso, and composer Roderick Skeaping. The setting of the stage for the first overseas octet took more than a decade.

In 1960, these lines of interest began to converge. On March 18, Saunders wrote to Hutchins that she ought to meet the physicist Bernard Robinson, visiting from London, who would be playing chamber music with Helen Rice at her apartment. Hutchins showed up the next day with eight violas, a cello, and the Apgar violin and viola. Robinson and Hutchins hit it off so well that Robinson visited 112 Essex the next day. As Robinson had no car and wished to visit Saunders and Rice in South Hadley and Stockbridge, Hutchins offered to drive him. Robinson and Hutchins got along famously. By their fourth meeting in six weeks, which took place at the Café des Artistes in New York City, Robinson offered Carleen the opportunity to come to England to use the testing equipment at the Bureau of Standards. Carleen could only voice regret in the family log: "Very successful dinner with Robinson — made plans to work by mail, since at present I cannot spend six months in England — as he suggests, using practically any equipment I needed for testing."[1]

On October 26, 1961, Robinson wrote to Hutchins: "I knew you were a most accomplished person — who could manage to bring up a family, pacify a husband, become a skilled craftsman, and an expert applied scientist all at the same time—but I didn't know you were also a biologist, a skilled teacher and a most able expositor! Your DNA book is most interesting. . . . How are the violas?"[2] In January 1964, Robinson visited Carleen again.

Meanwhile, in Wales, on October 10, 1966, Charles Taylor, newly appointed chair of the Physics Department at University College Cardiff, recalled the 1962 *Scientific American* article and had written to Hutchins about CAS membership. Five years later, in late 1971, Taylor gave his first "Christmas Lectures" at the Royal Institution—an extremely popular BBC series called "Exploring Music," in which Taylor discussed Hutchins's new violin family. In the spring of 1972, to Carleen's amazement, BBC producer Alan Sleath wrote to her about the great success of Taylor's Christmas Lectures. His enthusiasm sparked an idea in Carleen. Why not fan the flame of enthusiasm in Britain by bringing an octet to London for the July 1974 International Congress on Acoustics (ICA) meeting?

By August 1972, Carleen had already written her idea to Sleath and then asked Taylor about shipping and the fact that customs required her to obtain an "official" invitation in writing. The appeal to Taylor worked like a charm—so well that by late September, Taylor and Sleath began working on bringing the violin octet to England.[3] Meanwhile, Carleen reached out to Robinson—could he find players to play the first overseas octet? By May 1973, Taylor wrote back to Hutchins that he had met with Sleath, Sandy Brown (the person in charge of ICA social events), and Robinson and that all were enthusiastic about collecting together a group of accomplished amateur players. Then, in July 1973, Michael McIntyre, a lecturer in applied mathematics at the University of Cambridge and a professional violinist, caught wind of the plans to bring a violin octet to England and asked about participating as a performer so that he might use his "musician's ear and physicist's eye, so to speak."[4]

Meanwhile, Carleen hatched a plan to coordinate a small CAS meeting in conjunction with the 1974 ICA meeting. As a result, in the fall of 1973, Virginia Apgar, acting on behalf of Carleen and CAS, met with Professor Lothar Cremer in Berlin to discuss the possibility of planning a CAS Technical Meeting on July 15–19 at the Mittenwald School of Violinmaking, in Mittenwald, Germany, the Bavarian capital of German lutherie, prior to the July 23–31 ICA meeting in London.

In early March 1974, the stars had aligned for the first Hutchins violin octet to travel overseas. Packing, crating, and trucking the violins to Newark airport and passing them through customs took Carleen and Mort three days, with one day spent on the TWA air-freight loading platform—where to pass the time, Carleen entertained customs and air freight crew by playing her violins.[5]

Finally the announcement came from Robinson at the music camp at Pigotts in a letter dated March 11: "Well, the instruments are safely here, and we have had our first rehearsal!"[6] By early April, Robinson had been asked to present the new violins at the London College of Furniture, the only place in England where violinmaking was seriously taught; at the Triad Arts Center at Bishops Stortford; and at a soiree at the Imperial College.

On July 15, 1974, Carleen and Mort flew from New York to Munich and found their way to Mittenwald, joining CAS members from the United Kingdom, Sweden, Germany, France, Hungary, Poland, and Russia. At Mittenwald, Hutchins met Michael McIntyre and James Woodhouse, a physics graduate student and amateur luthier studying with McIntyre. As it rained most of the four days, with sightseeing in the Alps confined to a few hours, thirty CAS members gathered in the marbled hall of the Geigenbauschule overlooking the alpine lake, discussing everything from highly technical problems about varnish and wood to making and playing instruments. On July 22, when Mort and Carleen returned to London, the Robinsons welcomed them at their home outside London, at 366 Goldhawk Road. Shortly thereafter, the Robinsons left for music camp at Pigotts, allowing Carleen and Mort to set up a temporary CAS headquarters for the next ten days—mimicking the "open door" policy that had been stock and trade at 112 Essex Avenue.

The highlight of their ten-day stint in London was a three-day series of events on July 27–29—a public recital at Imperial College, a concert-demonstration at Pigotts, and an informal CAS meeting. On July 27, Hutchins gave a lecture, followed by a public recital featuring a group of talented amateurs and professional players conducted by Robinson at Imperial College for an enthusiastic audience of more than three hundred. One reviewer wrote that from an acoustic perspective, the octet violins were "hi-fi" in comparison with the traditional ones, particularly in the Corelli, in which listeners could make a direct comparison between old and new violins.[7] The following day, Carleen and Mort traveled to Pigotts to hear Robinson lead a music camp concert featuring the violin octet. Even as Mort and Carleen returned home from London at the close of the ICA meeting, Carleen knew that promoting the new violin family in Britain would be slow going, but McIntyre did not give up. In the face of apathy about the violin octet from symphony players, McIntyre had now switched his tactics and began promoting the new violin family as a consort to early music viol players—but he had not yet found the right situation.[8]

By May 1, 1975, when customs issues proved difficult, Hutchins faced the possibility that the instruments would soon need to be returned to her, but she did not give up hope even as she wrote to McIntyre in capital letters: "IF AND WHEN YOU AND BERNARD DECIDE TO SEND THE NEW INSTRUMENTS BACK, I MUST HAVE AT LEAST THREE WEEKS NOTICE BEFORE YOU SHIP THEM."[9] With so little news coming from Robinson and McIntyre, in England, Carleen looked to Taylor, in Wales. Would there be any interest in Wales to purchase the full set of eight instruments? Carleen offered the set for the present customs valuation of $10,000, though they cost far more than that to produce.[10]

Quite unbeknownst to Hutchins, Taylor had already taken the situation to heart. On May 12, 1975, when an appeal to the Welsh Arts Council proved futile, Taylor had found a solution in his discussions with Sir Brian Flowers, president of the Institute of Physics, who had heard the new violins at the ICA meeting in London. Flowers, also the director of the Imperial College, had close connections to the Royal College of Music in London, and he thought the necessary $10,000 might be raised by Imperial. So in two weeks' time, the situation reversed itself—from shipping the violins home—to selling them! By early June 1975, though the CAS consensus was that $10,000 amounted to "giving them away," the sale would keep the first overseas octet afloat—thanks to Taylor and the funds of a mysterious benefactor who agreed to purchase the octet on the condition of anonymity.

Meanwhile, through the efforts of McIntyre and the influence of Flowers, Carleen received even greater news from the Royal College of Music. On July 2, 1976, an airmail message from McIntyre notified Carleen of a three-year Leverhulme Trust grant of £21,000, payable over three years to the Royal College of Music, with the stipulation that the instruments also be loaned for scientific research at the University College Cardiff. Mort wrote in the family log: "This is the crowning recognition of Carleen's 20 years of work on these instruments. Represents official acceptance of the whole idea of the NVF [new violin family]!!!"[11]

By this time, the London violinist Roderick Skeaping had heard of the violin octet from his father, Kenneth Skeaping, who had also been present at the debut concert in London. A renowned *viola da gamba* player, professor at the Royal Academy, and specialist in baroque music, Kenneth Skeaping had known and had performed with both Arnold Dolmetsch (founder of the early music movement in England) and Robinson. In the 1950s, Skeaping became a key early music enthusiast, promoting ideas of authenticity in baroque performance in England. Consequently, Roderick Skeaping had grown up surrounded by early music, and the musical virtuosity and versatility of his father. "Roddy" began performing Elizabethan music in a consort of viols — two trebles, two tenors, two basses — at the age of sixteen, when as Skeaping recalled, no one else his age was doing it. Though Roddy had not witnessed any of the previous London events, his father's enthusiasm proved contagious. Roddy Skeaping recalled: "I liked the spirit of the thing because as a fan of early music, one remembers, after all, that the violin started with lots of different sizes." Skeaping was right at home with a family of strings: "I've always liked the things you can do with a matched family."[12]

On December 7, 1976, just a few months after the news of the Leverhulme Trust grant, Taylor wrote to Hutchins about their unanimous consensus that Roddy Skeaping was "the man for the job," the person who would best serve as key advocate for the new violin octet in Britain. In fact, Skeaping had essentially selected himself. Skeaping performed regularly as a professional member of the Academy of St. Martin-in-the-Fields, Musica Reservata, and the Early Music Consort, among others — and he taught *viola da gamba* at the Royal College of Music. As a player, he could switch from the rebec to the *viola da gamba* and other viols, and he was a composer and an improviser in jazz and folk groups. He was also very enthusiastic about the new violin family.[13]

In the summer of 1977, McIntyre and James Woodhouse hosted the Second CAS Technical Conference, June 27–July 1, at the Department of Applied Mathematics and Theoretical Physics at the University of Cambridge — prior to the Ninth ISMA (International Symposium on Musical

Acoustics) Meeting in Madrid. The musical highlight of the weekend was the British octet's Cambridge debut at Queens College Chapel on Tuesday evening, June 28. In his article "Catgut in Cambridge," in the July 21, 1977, issue of *New Scientist*, Dr. Jon Darius, Royal Society Radcliffe Lecturer in the Department of Physics and Astronomy, University College, cited the "revolutionary principles embodied in the New Violin family" and called the octet performance a "show stealer."[14]

On April 12, 1978, thanks to the persistence of Skeaping, internationally known violin virtuoso Yehudi Menuhin visited the Royal College of Music to see and hear the new violin family. Taylor reported that Menuhin was intrigued, especially by the noticeable uniformity of tone. When the idea of a possible television program came up, Menuhin volunteered to participate as a player in a demonstration and discussion that might include a composer, luthier, music educator, and scientist.[15]

But by this time, Skeaping had found acoustical problems with the tone quality of the baritone not matching the rest of the NVF instruments, which had to do with a mistake Hutchins and Schelleng made in their calculations of the proper air resonances of the baritone as it related to the cello. Shortly thereafter, Skeaping noticed other resonance problems with several of the lowest violins, acoustical problems that seemed insurmountable. On October 9, 1978, McIntyre wrote to Hutchins: "I'll do anything I can to save the project but the odds are now stacked heartily against. Obviously, it can be remedied by changing rib heights but only after long delay and expense—and besides it's quite possible the instruments sound better as they are, which is the real irony. My heart is with you."[16] Two weeks later, Hutchins wrote to Skeaping: "We are all working on the interface between art and science where compromises . . . are the order of the day. In . . . violin making and playing where art is 300 years ahead of science, science needs make most of the adjustments—at least until we know more about the constraints."[17]

In truth, Roddy Skeaping turned out to be the Don Quixote of the first overseas octet. Throughout the entire project, he remained enthusiastic about the new violin family, but remained uncertain about how to address the acoustical discrepancies. Still, Hutchins had only praise for Skeaping, declaring that it was not yet possible for a violin octet to be played in any American music conservatory, and that the NVF project at the Royal College of Music was way ahead of its time.[18] But by the end of 1978, the project looked as if it was in danger once again.

Then, out of the blue, Charles Taylor came to the rescue. In his letter of November 13, 1978, to Dr. R. C. Tress, director of the Leverhulme Trust Fund, Taylor turned lemons into lemonade, claiming that the current problems with the octet were a natural result of the discrepancy between theory and practice — the very nature of scientific inquiry. Taylor argued that the extra power and increased resonances of the new violins made the problem of placing resonances more critical. He not only described the mountain that Hutchins and her colleagues had attempted to climb; he managed to see the aerial view from the top of the mountain, focusing on what had been accomplished. After all, the British octet had been the first octet to be tested as a whole, and the first to be tested musically as an ensemble. Taylor reasoned: "This is *not* as a result of 'mistakes' in construction but stems from the fact that still further modification from strict scaling is necessary. The human ear-brain system is so complex that judgments by players and listeners only become reliable after a lengthy period of time." What's more, Taylor argued, the project, from the standpoint of the Leverhulme Trust, was not only *not* a failure; it remained fully on target. "In my view, this means that the energetic efforts of Mr. Skeaping and the enthusiasm of students and others involved have given us precisely the information we sought."[19] Taylor's arguments were so persuasive that Tress responded that the proposal for the third year was "entirely within the spirit of the trustees' grant and I am sure they will find it [as] exciting as you do."[20]

In early 1980, in his summary to the Leverhulme Trust, Skeaping cited the challenges facing the British octet, chief among them, a lack of funds to pay professionals, which necessitated the use of student musicians whose mindset, shaped by the competitive nature of a music conservatory, worked against innovation. Skeaping remembered: "Throughout the three years of the project the New Violin Octet never lost its power to excite extremes of reaction. Whilst the sound thrilled composers, many players perceived it almost as a threat to the status quo. But it is the change in the pattern of reaction during the project that seems to hold the key to their successful future."[21]

In April of that year, Hutchins signed an agreement for the official transfer of the octet from London to Cardiff. But between 1980 and 1986, momentum slowed and shifted. Taylor had retired, and his successors were more interested in doing acoustical testing of conventional instruments rather than the new violin family. With the end of the Leverhulme Trust grant, and interest in the new violins waning, the British violin octet remained in question, as its owner was still anonymous and there was no permanent home for it in England or in Wales. Carleen knew if she did not find a permanent home there for her fiddles, they would be coming home. Suddenly, Peter Fellgett stepped in, offering to take charge of the octet instruments temporarily until the anonymous purchaser could locate a home.

Meanwhile, on February 21, 1987, Arnold Myers, honorary curator for the Collection of Historic Musical Instruments, Edinburgh, wrote to Maurice Hancock, the current CAS-UK vice president, about acquiring "the full matched set" of the new violin family instruments. Edinburgh was the perfect place for the violin octet. The Scottish musicologist John Donaldson (1858–1940) had founded the museum because of his great fascination with musical acoustics, inspired by the musically inclined physicists of his time — Chladni, Biot, Savart, Wheatstone, and others investigating the science of music. Though Donaldson was gone, his spirit lived on in Edinburgh — in the close collaboration between the musical instruments collection, the music faculty, a very active acoustics laboratory, and a public museum. As Myers wrote Hancock: "We are thus well placed to promote the use of the octet in performances, teaching and research on a long-term basis."[22]

Hutchins grabbed hold of the idea and appealed to the person she thought was the anonymous donor — Bernard Robinson — asking for his help in promoting the move of the violin octet from Cardiff to Edinburgh. Robinson replied that he was *not* the mysterious donor and could not help with the transfer, though he felt it was a good move.[23] By October 25, 1988, the British octet had taken residence up in Edinburgh for the time being, on loan from the anonymous purchaser. Meanwhile Myers, music professor Christopher Field, and physics professor–*viola da gamba* player Murray Campbell began working on a violin octet demonstration for a combined meeting of the Musical Acoustics and History of Instruments classes.[24] The next summer, at the Galpin Society annual meeting, June 16–19, 1989, a demonstration recital of the new violin family took place in the Reid Concert Hall at the University of Edinburgh.

In early April 1993, Carleen finally discovered that the anonymous donor was none other than Peter Fellgett himself. In his work developing ambisonic technology for surround sound, Fellgett had relied on the generosity of musicians he could not afford to pay, and he did not want to alienate them. He explained: "Some, like Roddy, were keen on the violin octet but others, bitterly hostile to it, so I felt I had to remain anonymous."[25]

In December 1994, Skeaping traveled to St. Petersburg to hear the second concert of the Russian octet. Ever optimistic, Skeaping later wrote Hutchins: "I am delighted how *different* the response seems to be this second time around — so much more positive and enthusiastic. I sense a genuine excitement about the new possibilities the Violin Octet has created for string sound. . . . I no longer feel the need to constantly justify their development and existence, since the jaded professionals that I had to contend with at the Royal College back in the seventies are being replaced by a much more positive brand of player. I feel the world may be ready for this now if I can only push a few of the right buttons!"[26]

15 ∫ *Fiddles in the Bakery*

SWEDEN

The journey from a new music festival in Hanover, New Hampshire, to a musical instruments graveyard outside Stockholm, Sweden, was a circuitous one that began auspiciously enough when Carleen Hutchins met another inventor like herself — Hans Olaf Hansson. The Swedish connection for Hutchins and her violin octet began with the tale of two experimental violas — one designed after the viol — Hansson's *violino grande* — and the other designed after the violin — Hutchins's alto violin SUS #69, a "vertical viola." While it wasn't easy to surprise Carleen Hutchins with much of anything truly "new" in the violin world, she would forever recall attending the Webern Festival for New Music at Dartmouth College in July 1968, where the *violino grande* immediately caught her fancy.

Collaborating with the professional violinist Bronislaw Eichenholz, Hansson had modeled his instrument after the viol because he surmised that the viol-shaped instrument, with its simpler outline and inner architecture, would possess a larger air volume in relation to its size than a violin-shaped instrument. Keeping these aspects in mind, Hansson reasoned that he should take the simpler outline and construction of the viol and combine it with the arched back of the violin. In this way, the *violino grande* became a true hybrid of viol and violin — a five-string instrument the size of a viola tuned in fifths like the violin family instruments. The viol-shaped five-string instrument encompassed the range of a violin and viola together, with its bottom string the viola's C; and its top string, the violin's E. Because the *violino grande* had a viol shape, its plates were larger than the conventional viola, and its sloping, viol-like shoulders ostensibly made it conveniently playable in the highest positions, like the violin.[1] The *violino grande* had no direct predecessors except perhaps the five-string viola that Bach commissioned to be built in the 1720s that he called a *viola pomposa*.

In April 1969, the 77th meeting of the Acoustical Society of America, held in Philadelphia, marked the first time CAS held a meeting in conjunction with the ASA. On April 9, in response to an invitation from Hutchins, Bronislaw Eichenholz, gave a concert on the *violino grande*. Hansson, a luthier, musician, chemist, engineer, and manager of materials research at Sieverts Cable Works, presented a paper on his new instrument.[2] On October 31, 1969, Hutchins wrote to Hansson again, congratulating him on the creation of the *violino grande*, remarking that she would look forward to seeing the other violins in the *violino grande* family.[3] But as it happened, nothing ever came of this idea. Work and health difficulties kept Hansson from ever making another instrument.

Nevertheless, the Swedish connections strengthened in 1971 at the International Congress on Musical Acoustics in Budapest, August 18–26. There, Hutchins met Stockholm Symphony violinist Semmy Lazaroff and Swedish musicologist-acoustician Johan Sundberg, who came to visit her in Montclair the following December. A year later, in November 1972, Hutchins hosted a two-day CAS Technical Conference at 112 Essex Avenue, where two Swedes, Erik Jansson and Karl Stetson, presented papers on violin air resonances and hologram interferometry, respectively.[4]

As if to highlight the Swedish connection, the November 1972, issue of the *CAS Newsletter* presented a one-page summary of musical acoustics research in Sweden, describing GRAM—the Group for Research in the Acoustics of Music located in the Department of Speech Music Hearing at the Royal Institute of Technology (KTH), Stockholm. GRAM members included Sundberg, Jansson, and Anders Askenfelt, KTH professor of music acoustics. The *CAS Newsletter* also carried a ten-page article featuring the *violino grande*.[5]

In the summer of 1974, in anticipation of her trip to England, Germany, and Sweden, Hutchins prepared for the unexpected by building the "black box," a special container to transport four instruments—three octet violins (Alto SUS #69, a mezzo, and a soprano) and a seventeen-inch conventional viola—plus room for some free plates and black glitter to demonstrate Chladni patterns. Hutchins recalled: "Heathrow Airport security guards thought the black stuff looked like gunpowder and very nearly confiscated it."[6] Carleen and Mort Hutchins arrived in Stockholm on August 2, 1974, and toured various places in Scandinavia until August 11.

In Uppsala, Sweden, Hutchins lectured to thirty-five members of the Physics Department at Uppsala University and planned further research on violin wood and varnish with Swedish conductor and music professor Arne Tove. The Toves hosted Carleen and Mort for three days, including informal acoustics talks and an evening demonstration of the traditional Swedish folk instrument, the *nyckelharpa*, and a "keyed-violin."[7] Professor Tove contacted Semmy Lazaroff specifically to invite him to come see and hear the Hutchins Alto SUS #69, the "vertical viola." Lazaroff recalled: "I wanted to borrow it. . . . It is a marvelous instrument. I was thrilled because it sounded more bass than a normal viola — more resonant."[8]

After taking the black box to Trondheim, Norway, on August 19–21 to present a three-day symposium, Hutchins, taking a cue from the enthusiasm of Tove and Lazaroff, decided to leave the black box in Uppsala for the next year to give players ample time to explore the instruments. A year later, in early December 1975, five members of the Stockholm Symphony visited 112 Essex. Hutchins saw more Swedish CAS colleagues at the 1977 CAS Technical Conference at Cambridge. A year later, in October 1978, she was invited to return to Sweden to lecture.[9]

Eventually, Hans Astrand became secretary of the Royal Swedish Academy of Music, a post he held for sixteen years.[10] In the spring of 1979, Astrand created a musical acoustics committee. In the interest of bringing nationally known figures in musical acoustics to Sweden, Astrand invited Max Matthews, Arthur Benade, and Carleen Hutchins to present their work at the first SMAC (Swedish Musical Acoustics Conference) meeting in November 1979.[11]

By this time, Sundberg had been promoting the violin octet to Astrand and his KTH colleagues. Astrand had the interest, influence, and power to orchestrate acquiring the octet, and he encouraged Hutchins to send her instruments to Stockholm in anticipation of the SMAC meeting. On June 7, 1979, five of the smallest octet violins — excluding the vertical viola and the two basses — were shipped to the Royal Institute of Technology in Stockholm: Treble SUS #120, Mezzo SUS #111, Soprano SUS #115, Tenor SUS #149, and Baritone SUS #165. (The Contrabass SUS #174 was shipped in April 1980 and the Small Bass SUS #171 in June.) In November 1979, Carleen and Mort returned to the Swedish Royal Academy of Music for a two-day SMAC Symposium. On November 11, Musikmuseet, housed in the splendid seventeenth-century former Crown Bakery, the oldest industrial building in Old Stockholm, hosted a violin octet concert. The very long, narrow building had performed a number of functions over the centuries — as bakery, weapons depot, and spirits store. Yet throughout its colorful history, from 1640 to 1958, it served consistently as a bakery for the armed services of Stockholm.[12] As circumstance would have it, the Swedish violin octet in concert — fiddles in the bakery — sealed the deal.

It was indeed a glorious Thanksgiving weekend for Hutchins. On November 29, 1979, Hutchins wrote Astrand: "The Catgut Acoustical Society is very pleased that you wish to purchase the full set of eight instruments of the New Violin Family. . . . [W]e are excited to see their musical potential being further developed."[13] By July 1, 1981, Gunnar Larsson at Musikmuseet had responded with full payment for the Swedish violin octet. "We thank you for your patience. . . . The instruments are a most valued addition to our collection and we are making an effort with the support of the Academy to see to it that the violin family is suitably used."[14] Meanwhile, on the afternoon of March 18, 1982, two gentlemen from Swedish Radio — Christian Ljunggrew and Bertil Olegren — arrived at 112 Essex to take a tour of the test facilities and interview Carleen for a radio program to be broadcast in Sweden.[15]

By 1983, CAS membership had grown to eight hundred, with members in twenty-seven countries.[16] The Stockholm Music Acoustics Conference, held July 28–August 1, 1983, was a joint meeting of CAS and the International Association of Experimental Research in Singing, organized by KTH, the Royal Institute of Technology, and the Swedish Acoustical Society; it attracted an international audience of 170 participants. One highlight for Hutchins was the evening concert in which instrumentalists from the Music Academy performed award-winning pieces from the violin octet new music competition. Semmy Lazaroff had the challenging task of finding, assembling, and training musicians to play the octet violins, conducted by Miklos Maros.[17]

By all external appearances, things seemed auspicious in Sweden. At Musikmuseet, museum curator Cary Karp planned an exhibition featuring the violin octet that ran from March 1985 to March 1986. The instruments were positioned center stage at the entrance to the main exhibition halls and attracted much attention. On August 8, 1986, Karp reported to Hutchins: "The lay public was clearly captivated. The exhibit generated as much feedback as we've ever gotten from an exhibition." Even though the exhibition ran for a year, a puzzling apathy among KTH scientists took the wind out of Karp's sails in his efforts to promote the Swedish octet. Karp lamented the fact that he could not generate interest among KTH scientists to collaborate on any sort of joint venture to present the violin octet in concert.

On May 20, 1990, Semmy Lazaroff visited Hutchins to test instruments and to discuss his hopes of planning a concert series by composing a letter appealing to the director of Musikmuseet to urge the release of the octet instruments from the museum to a group authorized and organized to give a series of concerts.[18] But it was too little, too late. The turn of events over the five years from 1985 to 1990 was the result of a change in museum policy about the use of the octet instruments — they had now become museum artifacts. Karp, who had promoted the 1985 octet exhibit, now declared that the museum could no longer lend the octet violins to anyone, and that anyone interested in playing them had to do so on museum premises.[19]

By November 1990, despite the fact that Semmy Lazaroff was still striving to gain access to the violins, the cultural climate had reversed itself about performance versus preservation.[20] The state became increasingly involved in the governance of the museum. Two new curators were more concerned about public access and interactive exhibits aimed at younger audiences and less interested in history and collections. The last concert featuring the violin octet took place on July 29, 1993, in connection with SMAC 1993 meeting. But from the standpoint of professional players like Semmy and Kristen Lazaroff and any other interested members of the Stockholm Symphony, the Swedish violin octet had essentially been locked up. Lazaroff recalled: "Musikmuseet — a problem, rules. We got the violin octet out for two concerts — 1983 and 1993."[21]

Musikmuseet is now primarily focused on interactive exhibits for preschool children. Consequently, the Swedish violin octet has joined the ranks of thousands of other musical instruments in a warehouse thirteen kilometers outside of Old Stockholm. For all intents and purposes, the Swedish violin octet remains invisible. In 2004, Hans Riben, a Musikmuseet curator for seven years, had never even heard of it. He commented: "I read about Carleen Hutchins when I was a schoolboy; I was shocked to know we had an octet in Sweden — I had only read about it in books."[22]

Hans Astrand was more philosophical. "Things go like this, things go in cycles — somehow Carleen is in the same boat as composers. Usually, it takes fifty years after they die before people really come to think about their value. What is amazing? She has really gone through the history of the violin — of string instruments," said Astrand. "The violin octet would be a success if it were widely known and recorded often. But today, nothing but the standard stays — a symphony orchestra, or a string quartet. That's what happens to everything that is new. No music survives on its first hearing. Never. We had money in the '80s, and we bought the octet because nobody else would and because we could. Of the eight violin octets, one is being played. This is what happens. On the other hand, if you don't do anything, then nothing will happen. Her time may come — and even if it doesn't come, she has done her job — it's brilliant! It's amazing!"[23]

Intermezzo

Innovation – Virtuosos and Inventors

To raise questions, new possibilities, to regard
old problems from a new angle requires
creative imagination and makes
real advances in science.
— Albert Einstein

Musical virtuosos are, by nature, innovators. Likewise, innovative musical instrument makers need virtuosos — those players who are not only open to new ideas but seek to stretch limits and envision new frontiers.

The second-most-famous fiddle in the world sits in a display case in the Town Hall of the Palazzo Doria Tursi in the heart of Italy's "Old Town" Genoa: "Il Cannone" of Niccolò Paganini, the city's native son and the most famous violin virtuoso who ever lived. The violin, made by Guarneri del Gesù in 1743, hangs in a narrow, circular case that allows visitors to view it from all sides. But it is not just the instrument that hangs in this case — the stories of its owner hover there, too, forever changing our view of what is possible with a violin. Legend has it that Niccolò's father would deprive his son of food and water when he faltered in practicing. The young star had already been seasoned — at the age of fifteen — by the loss of his first violin, an Amati he relinquished to settle a gambling debt in 1797. But when a Monsieur Livron presented Paganini with a neglected Guarnerius del Gesù violin, this instrument stayed with Paganini for the rest of his life, named "Il Cannone" (the cannon) for its powerful sound.

The synergy between Paganini and his violin became his trademark. Paganini's reflexes, sensibilities, and intuition combined with the quick response and booming sound of the del Gesù became Paganini's "sound." The two defined each other.[1] Paganini, known for his mastery of the violin, his charisma, and personal mystique, created a benchmark for all virtuosos that would follow. Robert Schumann said: "Paganini is the turning-point in the history of virtuosity."[2] Most of Paganini's music, highly imaginative and well crafted, is seldom heard; his compositions require a hand that is both large and flexible, and few violinists can master them. Though he most likely composed his most famous *Caprices* as early as 1802, Paganini kept them secret, publishing them only in 1820, and dedicating them to "the artists"—those few virtuosos who were up to the task of playing them. Each caprice is a mini-masterpiece exploring a different aspect of violin technique so that, in total, the collection offers an almost complete compendium of works that focus on the violin's potentialities. In fact, the *Caprices* also inspired both Liszt and Schumann to write piano transcriptions. Brahms, Rachmaninoff, Lutosławski, and Andrew Lloyd Webber all used the theme of the final caprice as inspiration for other famous compositions.[3]

Paganini's most famous set of variations was based on a melody he heard from Süssmayr's *Le streghe* (The Witches). In the piece, Paganini teases the audience, introducing a minor theme as if it were the main theme, a gracious melody, after which he introduces the witches theme; then he takes the listener on a roller-coaster ride, demonstrating jaw-dropping techniques. Paganini left audiences incredulous upon hearing this work, spawning rumors that its composer must be in league with the devil.[4]

The role of the virtuoso in the history of music is legendary and powerful, for it shaped the very nature of the music performed and composed. In the early seventeenth century as opera soared in popularity, composers began to distinguish between vocal music and instrumental music. Up until this time, with the exception of dance music in the Renaissance era, music written for instruments had been essentially no different from music written for voice. But the sonorities of new instruments raised new musical ideas for composers, who began to realize that instruments—in the hands of the right players—could go way beyond what any singer could do with the voice. It followed naturally that virtuoso-composers would push the boundaries and create new frontiers for their instruments.

It was most fortuitous that three Italian violin virtuosos—all contemporaries of Stradivari—would bring the violin to its full expression in very different ways—Arcangelo Corelli (1653–1713), and his students Francesco Geminiani (1687–1762) and Antonio Vivaldi (1678–1741). Each of these extraordinary players was an innovator who pushed the boundaries to explore the violin's sonority. Corelli, born in Fusignano, propelled the violin into prominence through his popular concert tours throughout Europe, and his playing became famous for the "beautiful singing tone" that he drew forth from the instrument, called by some "the most remarkable in all of Europe."[5] Though his output as a composer was relatively small, Corelli's music was the most popular instrumental music of the day.

Geminiani, born in Lucca, in Tuscany, soon became recognized as a brilliant virtuoso violinist. In 1711, he moved to Naples to assume the position of leader of the Opera Orchestra. Records suggest that even the orchestra had difficulty following Geminiani's improvisational virtuosity, described as his "unexpected accelerations and relaxations of measure."[6] In 1714, he moved to London, where he and Handel, also a student of Corelli in Rome, brought the Italian music style to English audiences. Geminiani soon established himself as leading master of the violin, through concerts, composing, and his authorship of the first and most important theoretical treatise on his instrument, *The Art of Playing the Violin* (1731).[7]

Vivaldi, born in Venice, was ordained a priest but spent his life in music. A prolific composer, Vivaldi came to be violin teacher at the Ospedale della Pietà, one of several homes for orphaned girls, many of who were female offspring of dalliances between noblemen and their mistresses. It was most auspicious timing for the violin that three such celebrated Italian virtuoso-composers would bring the violin onto the stage and into the limelight.

Though necessity is the mother of invention, inventors—like virtuosos—are often ahead of their time. Whether it is a slip-action for a keyboard, pedals on a giant contrabass, a family of saxophones, or a family of fiddles, a new idea takes time to be absorbed. Consequently, the inventors are often like prophets in their own land, ignored for a time, and maybe heeded years later, when the "new," bizarre idea finally seems totally logical. A notable example is the piano.

More than a century after Amati invented the violin, Bartolomeo Cristofori (1655–1731) invented the piano. The oldest piano in existence, circa 1700, is a prized possession of the Metropolitan Museum of Art, made doubly valuable because it was also built by its inventor. An innovative harpsichord maker, Cristofori invented the hammer-action-mechanism that distinguishes the piano from its predecessors. In its day, the new keyboard instrument was named *gravicembalo col piano e forte* or "harpsichord that plays soft and loud."[8] By 1711, Cristofori had built three pianos; by 1726, he had made approximately twenty. Nevertheless, even though the first music written expressly for the piano appeared in 1732, throughout his life, Cristofori never witnessed significant interest in his invention — the piano was pronounced too difficult to master.

It was almost a century later that German composer Ludwig van Beethoven (1770–1827), the first celebrated composer who was also a virtuoso pianist, brought the piano out of the shadows in a dramatic way. A few decades later, the Polish pianist Frédéric Chopin (1810–49) elicited a quieter aspect of the piano with his reserved, polite style and his ability "to create inky and subtle colors . . . more a profound poet than a keyboard acrobat."[9] But it was the Hungarian pianist Franz Liszt (1813–86) who displayed on the piano what Paganini displayed on the violin. A dazzling virtuoso, Liszt was also a crowd pleaser — the first performer to hold solo piano recitals in which he would sit sideways to the audience so everyone could see his hands in action. Liszt forged new horizons in what was possible on the piano.[10]

Like Paganini, Liszt wrote music for the piano that was incredibly difficult to play, music that at the time only he was capable of performing.[11] Liszt was especially important because he championed other composers, like Wagner, Bartók, Debussy, Schubert, and Beethoven by transcribing works of these composers for piano and playing them in his recitals, bringing them to the attention of people who would otherwise never have heard them.[12]

The story of the saxophone is also instructive. The Belgian instrument builder Antoine-Joseph "Adolphe" Sax (1814–94) was an intuitive genius at his craft. At the Belgian Exposition in 1840, Adolphe, at age twenty-six, presented nine musical instruments of his own invention. Though his inventions were worthy of a gold medal, the committee awarded him second place because of his age and the fact that there would be nothing left to award him in future expositions. Sax rebelled, refused the second place award, and moved to Paris. In 1841, seeking an instrument to bridge the gap between woodwinds and brass — ideally creating the loudest woodwind instrument with the versatility of a brass instrument — Sax invented the instrument named after him — the saxophone. By 1846, Sax had already designed and patented the saxophone in two families, each containing seven different sizes, running the gamut from soprano sax to subcontrabass.

The composer Hector Berlioz championed the saxophone in a series of articles published in the 1842 *Journal des Débats* and then conducted its orchestra debut with a new choral work in 1844, the same year the saxophone was introduced at the Paris Industrial Exhibition. Nevertheless, orchestras still shunned the saxophone. In fact, Sax faced an uphill battle his entire life. Jealous instrument makers did everything they could to criticize Sax and his instruments, including slander in the press and contesting his patents in extensive court proceedings that caused Sax to declare bankruptcy three times. When Sax died in 1894, the saxophone had yet to reach its potential, primarily owing to the reluctance of composers to explore its possibilities.

Eventually, bandleaders embraced the saxophone. For several years, John Philip Sousa had a twelve-piece sax section, including the complete family ranging from soprano to contrabass. Sousa and Gilmore bands featured saxophone sections, thus introducing the new instrument to thousands. But it was not until 1910 and the dawn of the jazz age that the saxophone came into its own with two virtuosos—Charlie Parker and John Coltrane.[13] Now the saxophone is used in a wide range of repertoire from orchestral compositions to military band music to rock and roll.[14]

Four decades after the death of Paganini, another giant of a violin virtuoso would do more for the violin and the violin world as a pioneer on many fronts than anyone after her—the legendary American violinist Maud Powell (1867–1920), recent winner of the 2014 Grammy Lifetime Achievement Award. Powell, recognized as America's greatest violinist, ranks among the preeminent musicians in the world. She was a pioneer when she stepped into a recording studio in 1904 to play her violin into a recording horn, thereby launching "the science and art of recording the violin." Jascha Heifetz, Fritz Kreisler, and Yehudi Menuhin considered her one of their musical heroes.[15]

"Old Town" Genoa sits like a grand amphitheater, framed by a nearly perfect circle of coastline surrounding a secluded gulf, a strip of land on which a very old seaport sits nestled between saltwater and steep hills dropping to the sea. Just as circular are the pink and white curving palladiums surrounding the courtyard of the Palazzo Doria Tursi where serpentine archways reflect the curved "c-bouts" of a violin. Inside, another violin sits opposite the Cannone—the "Vuillaume," a copy of the Cannone made by Jean-Baptiste Vuillaume when Paganini brought his instrument to Vuillaume's shop to be repaired. Both violins hang side by side in Genoa's Town Hall. Legend has it that Paganini could not tell the difference between his violin and the copy until he played them.[16]

The Cannone still retains its original neck; its plates have never been re-graduated; its varnish was never polished.[17] Every two years, Genoa holds a Paganini competition for young players between the ages of sixteen and thirty. The winner gets to perform on the Cannone at the end of the competition.[18] As visitors view the Cannone and the Vuillaume, issues of comparison and value come into play in a world based on comparison and copying of old violins.

Just a few blocks away from the Palazzo Doria Tursi, the spacious workshop of the Genovese violinmaker Pio Montanari overlooks a small piazza near the docks on the edge of the Mediterranean Sea. As assistant violinmaker for the maintenance of the Historical Violins of Genoa, Montanari has been in charge of the maintenance and preservation of the Cannone since 1994.

Pio has never met Hutchins, but he feels as if he has. When interviewed in 2004, he recalled: "I was making guitars in 1981 when I saw her *Scientific American* article. I began plate-tuning because of this article and have never abandoned it." Since 1985, Montanari has made violins, cellos, and violas and credits Hutchins: "I do not think I would still be making violins if not for plate tuning and Carleen." As of 2004, Montanari was working to complete the first Italian violin octet, based on the blueprint designs of Hutchins. He and his partner Luigi Francesco Gazzolo had completed a treble, soprano, mezzo, and tenor — the alto was, as of that date, in process. "I am making this violin octet because I am thanking Carleen — it is my thank-you to her."[19]

16 ∫ *Fiddles in the Limelight*

VIRTUOSOS ON THE VERTICAL

For a luthier with a "new" family of fiddles, finding talented and dedicated players is a basic necessity. Finding a willing virtuoso can feel like finding a diamond in the rough. And for Hutchins, a diamond in the rough was a find, a gift outright—whether it was received through intermittent contact with a celebrated family of cellists, teaching violinmaking to an avid bassist, or responding to a cello superstar in search of a way to play viola repertoire. All three scenarios came to fruition. The friendship and synergy between Carleen Hutchins and Helen Rice made it possible for Carleen to meet a myriad of accomplished musicians whom she would never have met as an amateur violist or while carving fiddles in her kitchen. However, two exceptions were a couple of virtuosos who actually sought out Hutchins—indeed, neither could stay away—the cellist David Finckel and the bass player Diana Gannett.

The Finckel family of cellists—George Finckel, his sons Chris and Michael, and their cousin David Finckel—had all become aware of Hutchins and eventually would work with Carleen in various capacities; each played her octet violins at various times. But it was David Finckel, the virtuoso cellist of the Emerson Quartet for thirty-three years (he left in 2012), who as a young player had first taken a real shine to Hutchins, because her work fascinated him on so many levels. As the son of a conductor, composer, and pianist in a "do-it-yourself" family that built its own music camp in Vermont, David immediately identified with the craftswoman at 112 Essex. In the 1960s, when he learned of violin research she was conducting in her basement, he could not stay away.

"Somebody told me about CAS doing research on improving instruments—and I just took to it like a duck to water. I was very uninhibited, and I think I probably called her up and said, 'Can I come over?' She had that 'let's-get-down-to-work' attitude that I loved as soon as I came in the front door," recalled Finckel. "I remember we strung up my cello, tested it, and I remember these readouts coming out of the printer. I thought this was the greatest thing I ever had ever seen in my life!" He especially loved playing the tenor and baritone and marveled at the contrabass. "I loved playing on the tenor especially. I may have even made a recording on it." Actually, the whole operation at 112 Essex fascinated Finckel. "It was really the exploration of how and why instruments sound good, what they were actually doing that was so exciting. This is something that still fascinates me. . . . She treated instruments with respect to science and not in terms of mythology — or even art, to a certain extent."[1]

According to Finckel, it was not only lack of repertoire that made players less interested in the violin octet, but the playing adjustments that the different-sized violins require. "I always felt the octet's major challenge was repertoire and engaging top players to use the instruments — because they are all different sizes. I spend every waking minute with my cello, trying to get to play it better. To switch sizes, to reimagine how a Beethoven quartet is going to work on all these different instruments — that's a real chore!"[2]

Like Finckel, the bassist Diana Gannett discovered Carleen when she was a teenager learning to play bass. Gannett went on to study with Eldon Obrecht, Stuart Sankey, and Gary Karr and received the first Yale doctorate awarded in double bass. Gannett has played with the Guarneri, Emerson, Laurentian, and Stanford Quartets and the Borodin Trio. For many years she held the position of principal double bass at the Eastern Music Festival in Greensboro, North Carolina.

Gannett recalled the November 1963 *Life* magazine article on Carleen: "The image I have stuffed in my brain was that she was sitting inside the big bass template, as if she was scooping out the wood — and I said, I've got to meet and work with this woman — I was fourteen!" Eight years later, when Gannett was in graduate school at Yale, she found out about the violin-making classes at 112 Essex Avenue. "I couldn't get there fast enough — it was exactly one hundred miles from my door to hers. I did it every weekend for three or four years. It meant so much to me — the people and the workshop. It was a totally magical, wonderful place — I loved every second of it!"[3]

Years later, after the creation of the violin octet, when Gannett was teaching at Yale, Hutchins phoned her to ask if one of Gannett's students might be interested in buying a bass. "So I went to 112 Essex and I fell in love with the bass," said Gannet — who bought it. Then when Carleen asked if Diana knew anyone to help her make basses, Diana took the bait willingly. At the time Tom McLaughlin was helping Hutchins make basses. Gannett came down to Montclair on many weekends to work on basses in the Hutchinses' home.[4]

It was actually through the violinmaking classes at 112 Essex that the violin octet instruments eventually got the attention of Yo-Yo Ma. In 1983, Hutchins, along with three of her students — Alan Carruth, Daniel Foster, and Tom Knatt — attended a concert featuring Ma in a trio performance at Montclair High School. When Knatt heard a radio interview of Ma in which he said he would like to access the viola repertoire, Knatt contacted him about his "big viola" — the alto violin he had made while studying violinmaking at 112 Essex with Hutchins. Ma agreed to try it. Knatt recalled his visit with Ma: "He used his regular cello bow, and I had to caution him to lighten the pressure. The instrument responds best when the bow stroke is less forceful than a cello requires." Knatt left the alto with Ma but heard nothing more. "Then, at last, a postcard arrived. He wrote that he very much wanted to play it at Carnegie Hall, but couldn't muster the courage. 'Rats!' I exclaimed, thinking that the best chance had been lost for the instrument to be heard."[5]

A decade later on September 24, 1992, in another radio interview, Ma again stated he had always been interested in the viola repertoire but regretted he was unable to access it as a cellist. Shortly thereafter, CAS member Joan Miller sent a letter and supporting materials to Shoko Kashiyama, assistant to Yo-Yo Ma, including information about CAS and the vertical viola. On January 13, 1993, Ma performed Bartók's Viola Concerto on a Tom Knatt alto with the Baltimore Symphony in Toronto. When he decided to record the piece but was not entirely happy with the treble register on the Knatt instrument, Knatt suggested that Ma try an alto violin made by Hutchins. A few days later, Hutchins sent three altos and one tenor to Yo-Yo Ma — tenor violin SUS #192, insured at a value of $12,000; and three alto violins, SUS #130, #137, and #144, each valued for insurance purposes at $10,000 each.

The real miracle, as Carleen thought about it months later, while sitting in the audience in Baltimore watching rehearsals, was that Yo-Yo Ma showed up at all, given the negative press coverage of his "experiment." In Toronto, the Canadian music critic Tamara Bernstein clearly meant to punish Ma for trying something new in her January 16, 1993, *Globe and Mail* article "Yo-Yo Ma's Performance a Musical Disaster." Bernstein described the new viola as having a "colourless, dull sound, devoid of the richness and colours of a good viola. . . . The playing was technically polished, but Ma hadn't yet gotten around to finding an interpretation. . . . In all, I wish that Ma had simply left the piece to violists."[6]

In her February 17, 1993, review titled "The Yo-Yola: Mr. Ma's Experiment," *Wall Street Journal* music critic Heidi Waleson started her piece by reciting a litany of viola jokes, mimicking the bantering between conductor and cellist that had occurred when Ma had walked on stage with the "shrunken" cello. Ma explained to Waleson: "The cello sounds almost too cultured. . . . The piece is about death, it's lonely; you need a suffocating kind of cry. The viola sound is more appropriate, but I can't play the viola." And when Ma decided to use the vertical viola to play the Bartók, members of the Toronto press quickly dubbed the instrument the "Yo-Yola." Waleson offered her closing viola joke: "Could this be the ultimate viola joke—in order to play the viola properly, you have to be a cellist!"[7]

A few days later, on February 28, Stephen Wigler, music critic for the *Baltimore Sun*, interviewed Yo-Yo Ma and the Baltimore Symphony music director and conductor David Zinman, and called the vertical viola "an overgrown viola." Wigler wrote that Yo-Yo Ma "does not believe in making things easy on himself. . . . [W]hen Ma walks on stage . . . to play the Bartók . . . Ma will not be carrying the 250-year-old Stradivarius [but] . . . a miniature cello that suffered an accident at the dry cleaner's. It will be, in fact, a huge viola . . . that can be planted, cello-like, on the floor."

Ma explained that he wanted to try something that would approximate the viola. "It's part of being a musician to explore. Some people do it by inventing new instruments and new material. I'm trying to figure out if it's possible to do that by finding another expressive medium." To find new repertoire, one had to be creative and look in many different directions. Ma continued: "Many of the works cellists play today, such as Schubert's 'Arpeggione' Sonata and the Bach Sixth Cello Suite, were not written for the cello, but for instruments that became extinct. People have always tried to do things better."

Wigler credited Ma for pursuing the "new" vertical viola as a demonstration of his willingness to push boundaries and take risks to widen the cello repertory—a move similar to experimenting with electronic instruments like the "hyper cello" designed by MIT composer Todd Machover. Wigler concluded: "Ma's become the Ancient Mariner or the Don Quixote of the cello world, pigeon-holing composers and conductors to try new things.... He's been telling composers, 'Write whatever you can, as high ... or as hard as possible, and I'll find a way to play it.'"[8]

On March 4–5, 1993, Carleen found herself in the audience in Baltimore for the concert of a lifetime—watching Yo-Yo Ma rehearse and then perform Bela Bartók's Viola Concerto on her alto violin. In his March 11 *Baltimore Sun* review, music critic Stephen Wigler concluded that Ma's risk with the vertical viola was ultimately a mistake. "If he [Yo-Yo Ma] wants to expand the cello's scope, he would be wise to look elsewhere, leaving the viola to the violists."[9]

On March 18—just shy of two weeks after the Baltimore debut concerts featuring the alto violin, Yo-Yo Ma returned alto violins SUS #144 and SUS #137, keeping on loan SUS #130, the one he had played in the Baltimore concerts. The recording of this Baltimore concert that Hutchins witnessed featured the Bartók (alto), alongside pieces by Stephen Albert and Ernest Bloch (cello) and eventually became Yo-Yo Ma's *New York Album*.

In March 1995, Yo-Yo Ma and the Baltimore Symphony won two Grammys for the Sony Classics recording *The New York Album*—one for the category of Classical Contemporary Composition (the Albert), and the other for the category of Classical Instrumental Soloist with Orchestra. On March 23—just three weeks after the Grammy announcement, Hutchins wrote a letter to Yo-Yo Ma congratulating him on the Grammy and inviting him to be a member of the CAS Advisory Board. On April 5, on behalf of Yo-Yo Ma, assistant Sara Stackhouse wrote to Hutchins to decline her invitation, "due to the volume of requests of this kind and the large number of organizations with which he is already affiliated." But she added: "However, he asked me to pass along to you his congratulations for your contributions to *The New York Album*. He certainly enjoyed playing the Alto Violin!"[10]

In a phone interview in December 2014, Yo-Yo Ma recalled the thrill of playing the Bartók on the Hutchins alto violin: "It was fascinating to be able to go into a different sonic range without having to spend years trying to master another instrument."[11] Talking about the difficulty of switching instruments, he said: "If you ever travel in the world of folk musicians, they play half a dozen instruments. So it's kind of more the anomaly [in the classical music world], the idea that people just play one instrument. It's the idea that I play the piano, but I would never touch the harpsichord—yet the harpsichord is a keyboard instrument."

When asked if there was more resistance to change in the classical music world, Ma said: "The classical music cultural world has changed, shifted. Many more things are possible today. There's possibly much less resistance because the culture around us has changed so much. I think people realize change is inevitable, whereas before I think there was a certain idea that change happened more slowly and was more static." Regarding the role of the virtuoso, Ma remarked: "The virtuoso is by nature one individual, so you cannot make a generalization. But if you look historically at the virtuoso, Mozart was a virtuoso; Beethoven was a virtuoso; Liszt was a virtuoso. They were all big into change."

With respect to how a "new" instrument can be promoted or accepted, Ma said: "It's one thing to do what you think is the right thing and to invent something. But it's a completely different thing to look at markets and needs and packaging or repertoire. Does it benefit? So beyond that person who is really curious to invent something, how does it help a cellist in his or her life?" What factors inhibit innovation? Ma replied: "What's interesting is that in the last forty years, the quality of new instruments has increased exponentially with the idea that there are no secrets between makers—it's the collapse of secrets. That's part of Carleen's legacy."

Intermezzo

Market – "Messiah" as Metaphor

Fiddles are a universe, a pretty self-contained universe.
It has gods and lesser gods and people who dirty the universe.
— Robert Bein, violin dealer

The most famous violin in the world has never been heard. What's more, it gained its reputation by being invisible. "The Messiah" sits in its glass display case just outside the Print Room of the Ashmolean Museum of Art and Archaeology in Oxford. Measuring just less than 23 inches, with a 13³⁄16-inch body, the famous fiddle soon grew gargantuan in stature not because of its sound but because of its story. In fact, the conundrum is that nobody knows how the old fiddle actually sounds. A big part of its mystique lies in the fact that, as the only Stradivari in existence still preserved in pristine condition, it has virtually never been played!

The Messiah is not unlike clockmaker John Harrison's H-4, the last of the four famous clocks that reside in the Old Royal Observatory at Greenwich, England, in the place where east meets west on the prime meridian — zero degrees longitude. All four Harrison clocks — H-1, H-2, H-3, and H-4—keep accurate time and so made the determination of longitude possible. But H-4 is the only celebrated clock of the four that never runs. As Dava Sobel explains in *Longitude*: "It *could* run, if curators would allow it to, but they demur, on the grounds that H-4 enjoys something of the status of a sacred relic or a priceless work of art that must be preserved for posterity. To run it would be to ruin it."[1]

"Le Messie" became an icon without anyone ever putting a bow to its bridge. Its story is much larger than air, wood, and strings. Sitting in its display case, or on an examining table in the Prints Room, the "Messiah" encapsulates the entire violin world, an exquisitely Italian icon inextricably linked to Oxford and the collecting legacy of W. E. Hill & Sons. One begets the other — the fiddle and the collector intertwined in a way that magnifies the legacy and esteem of both maker and collector.

The violin world is a world based on lineage, secrecy, and the "war" between authenticity and deception inside an elite group. It consists of a cloister of craftspeople, dealers, and "experts" passing very specific knowledge down to the very few willing to take the time to learn this time-intensive skill that for centuries has been based on copying old fiddles. It is a world in which even the player—especially the player—has been left in the dark without access to insider knowledge. The maker, expert, and dealer own the knowledge that each parcels out judiciously, less he or she dispel the mystique of violinmaking "secrets," for there is power and money in marketing secrecy. It is a world in which a maverick questioning sacred tradition sticks out like a sore thumb or a diamond in the rough, depending on who stands to win or lose by the knowledge the maverick uncovers.

In a very real sense, one virtuoso may have inadvertently created the violin market. In 1782, when the violin virtuoso Giovanni Battista Viotti gave his Paris debut, he attributed his success to playing a Stradivarius. As a result, the French luthiers Louis Pique and Nicolas Lupot took note and began making instruments based on the "golden period" of Stradivari. By 1810, with collectors William Corbet and Count Cozio di Salabue reinforcing this preference, scarcity reversed the market, and suddenly Cremonese instruments were worth four times the price of the best contemporary instruments made in London and Paris.[2]

When Pique and Lupot died in 1822 and 1824, respectively, without successors, the path opened for a new kind of dealer, one of whom was also a luthier and one of the greatest copyists of all time, French master luthier Jean-Baptiste Vuillaume. At this incredibly auspicious time, Vuillaume met legendary violin dealer Luigi Tarisio. Vuillaume was as notorious at bidding as Tarisio was at collecting. While most dealers tended to bid conservatively at first, Vuillaume paid whatever it took to procure these old fiddles. He appears to have been the only Parisian dealer to foresee the economic link between old violins and the much wider antiquities market.[3]

Simultaneously, even as Vuillaume was promoting the "value" of Old Italian Master violins, he was also promoting his own copies—conferring status to both old fiddle and the facsimile copy, both valued as objets d'art. Timing was golden for Vuillaume—he came to prominence when the market for violins was relatively level and golden period Strads were rare. In addition, Vuillaume bet on the obsessive Tarisio—and won, thereby single-handedly inventing the violin market almost overnight. In his dissertation on the violin market, contemporary violin consultant Ben Hebbert explains the singular genius of Vuillaume: "His feat as a businessman was to invent an entirely artificial market by dovetailing the supply of rare violins into pre-existing bourgeois values. His feat as a craftsman was to sustain the market by making many of the finest copies of Cremonese work to this day."[4] In 1854, when Tarisio died, Vuillaume made the greatest purchase of his career—first, from the small farm near Fontaneto where Tarisio's body was found, the six finest violins of the collection, including the celebrated "Messiah" and no fewer than 24 Stradivaris and 120 other Italian masterpieces; and second, another 246 fiddles found in Tarisio's attic in Milan that Vuillaume purchased for the paltry sum of £3,166.[5]

The Messiah is also valuable because it has a name. Naming a violin actually enhances market value. But names of fiddles never actually appear on the instrument. Instead, the label inside a violin ostensibly acts as the maker's signature. In reality, fraudulent labels are as old as the violin itself. Documentation shows that as early as 1685, violin labels were being falsified in Italy. Early dealers got into the fraudulent label game. Count Cozio di Salabue collected not only violins, but violin labels. Vuillaume often inserted copies of Stradivari labels in his copied instruments. Evidently, Tarisio often placed a label by a premiere maker into a second-rate fiddle—it was a common practice.[6]

Issues of authenticity lead to the need to consult violin "experts." An expert is a dealer, maker, or scholar of the craft who has studied the work of at least twenty-five to thirty of the most important makers and can readily recall defining details of a fiddle to ostensibly "prove" authenticity. But when the "expert" has a vested interest as a dealer, the waters get murky. As the Boston violin dealer Christopher Reuning attests, "The very people who know enough to help often have a financial interest in the deal—or in killing the deal, or trying to ruin the reputation of another expert or dealer. . . . You really have to have your commerce and expertise separate. . . . [Y]ou have to be objective and look at those objects as they are. And if you're not, your reputation suffers."[7]

The lineage of "experts" leads to the dealers themselves—of which there have been surprisingly few over the past four centuries. American violin dealing began before the Civil War with the Rudolph Wurlitzer Company of Cincinnati, Ohio. When Rudolph Henry Wurlitzer, son of Rudolph, saw the commercial potential in the violin business, he founded a branch of the company in New York City and encouraged his son Rembert to study violinmaking and specialize in rare stringed instruments. Rembert Wurlitzer joined the firm in 1930 and became one of the world's most respected "experts" in the field. When Wurlitzer died, the baton eventually passed to two luthiers who had worked with him — Jacques Français and René Morel — both of whom came from a distinguished line of French violinmaking families trained in Mirecourt.

During their thirty-year partnership, Français and Morel were the dealers at the center of American violinmaking world.[8] Working alongside Fernando Sacconi, Stradivari expert and master luthier, Morel brought restoration to a high art, bordering on alchemy. With tools, measuring devices, powders, tiny mirrors, peroxides, and palettes of varnish, they restored each fragile hundred-year-old plate (weighing less than six ounces) by patching, grafting, soaking, and reshaping, then covering each repair meticulously.[9] Morel repeated the dealers' mantra: "Modern instruments cannot compare except in decibel levels. A musician can only really *sculpt* sound out of an instrument that is old. It is like wine, improving with age."[10]

Or not. When does repair go way beyond reason and recognition? In fact, this two-century-old fetish for violin repair and restoration created a violin world composed largely of smoke and mirrors — according to Joe Peknik, former Metropolitan Museum of Art principal technician in the Musical Instruments Department. "I hate to say it, but it's all a sham. To modernize an old violin to be played and sound well in a modern concert hall, one has to first stabilize the instrument by removing the top and in many cases, relining or doubling the edges, putting in a breast patch, and in some cases, make it thicker or thinner. Then a new, longer and thicker bass bar must be added, lengthening the neck and tilting it back a bit to put more tension on the top — all to make an instrument louder and stronger. These changes are all made to make an instrument more effective in a large concert hall, the size of which the original maker could never have imagined. The violin is the only object in the world of antiques that increases in value with this large amount of restoration. Most other objects that are restored to this extent would be devalued by half or less."[11]

Peknik explained further: "Because of the fetish to rework the Old Masters, there are very few great master violins that remain in original condition. The modern violinmakers who are making instruments to fill the modern large concert hall get a small fraction of what these souped-up Old Masters make in the marketplace." He recalled the time he saw an ultraviolet light beamed on a cello to highlight the spots where it had been repaired. "An early eighteenth century Goffriller cello was being offered to the museum by an eminent New Yorker dealer. When we opened the case, we were astounded by its magnificent varnish and condition — a beautiful dark, reddish brown with a light crackling in the varnish here and there that you would expect of an instrument of this age. When we put the UV light on it, the entire body of the instrument turned an opaque, milky white except for a perfect rectangle in the middle of the back — the only place that you could actually see the grain of the wood. The conservator remarked that this was a sign of a non-UV, penetrable over-varnish that's used by art dealers to mask restoration. The cello was going to be used in a concert that week. After rehearsal, the cellist approached us to complain that the varnish had come off on his shirt! It turned out that the entire instrument had been completely revarnished."[12]

In fact, there has always been a fine line between restoration and fraud, as forgery and fakes have been a huge part of the violin world since its inception. The most commonplace violin frauds are "trade" fakes, pretending that a common violin is a valuable "old" one. There are handmade fakes deliberately built in the style of a copied maker; modern instruments imported from foreign factories in the white, then varnished and "distressed" to look old; and genuinely old instruments, often of good quality, into which a fraudulent label is inserted.[13]

In 1894, one bold violin forger actually described his methods in copious detail, highlighting sixteen steps. The eleventh reads: "Eleventh, take off the belly, and put it on again, letting the glue be quite hardened, at least three times, using different coloured glues and letting a little encroach each time upon the linings to show how many times it has been repaired. . . . By observing these rules you can also detect when you buy a piece of violin-swindling."[14] Much more recently, the *Times* of London, May 27, 1982, reported that in 1978 Sotheby's actually offered for sale a forger's kit consisting of a collection of modern blocks engraved with good imitations of fine makers' labels. Great alarm was caused by a successful Japanese bid, and Sotheby's bought the kit back, with the collaboration of the International Society of Violin and Bow Makers. Interpol has since investigated violin dealing rackets, and a leading Tokyo instrument dealer was arrested. Later, an international ring of fraudulent dealers was uncovered.[15]

One notorious case involving two violin dealers and one obsessive collector highlights another aspect of the violin marketplace — dealers fiddling with "value" to take unfair advantage of eager but unsuspecting clients. In a large collectors' arena like art or antiques, one individual dealer or collector does not hold such all-pervasive power. But in a world as small and inbred as rare violins, powerhouse violin dealers hold all the cards, playing the roles of buyer, seller, investor, broker, appraiser, wholesaler, and retailer and are able to control both the flow and price of antique instruments. "They generally provide expert appraisals to a seller who has no other way to determine the true market value of an instrument."[16] One such dealer, Robert Bein, was not the least bit repentant: "Is it scandalous to make a profit? If this were a criminal charge, would I tell my lawyer to plead to 'first-degree violin dealing'? Fiddles are a universe, a pretty self-contained universe. It has gods and lesser gods and people who dirty the universe."[17]

In the determination of whether a violin is authentic or fake, the violin world, the violin culture, the violin market sits squarely in the camp of these violin experts. One such expert works with the Musikmuseet collection in Stockholm, brokering old violins to young players at the Royal Academy. He said of violin experts: "They are good guys mostly with morals accommodated by economic necessity." That is to say, if times are lean, an "expert" might change his or her appraisal, not because of acoustics, but because he needs the money. Though he used to know Hutchins and back in the 1960s actually collaborated with her in comparing violin and guitar plates, this dealer, in an interview in 2004, now sang a very different tune and had very little praise for Hutchins. He said: "Joseph Curtin is possibly the best violinmaker in the U.S.A. You must talk to the experts and ask what they think of Carleen. . . . They will say that Hutchins has had virtually no impact on anything in the violinmaking world. Why? Because she has had no impact."[18]

In June 2013, two events took place in Oxford that encapsulated the "smoke and mirrors" violin world, which revolves around old violins and the perceived impeccable value of a Stradivari. First, on June 12, the Ashmolean Museum hosted its pre-opening reception for *Stradivari*, an exhibition featuring the largest collection of Stradivari instruments ever gathered in one place. Two days later, the Sheldonian Theatre hosted a very special concert featuring Canadian violin virtuoso James Ehnes performing on three Stradivari violins — the first time such a thing had been done in a concert setting.

On stage with Ehnes was Sir Curtis Price, former principal of the Royal College of Music, King Edward Professor of Music, Kings College, London; owner of the "Viotti" Stradivari; former chair of the British Violin-Making Association and head of the jury for the 2006 Cremona International Triennale Violin-Making Competition; and member of the Nippon Music Foundation, knighted for his services in 2005. Also on stage was renowned British violin dealer Charles Beare. One could not have expressed "the lineage" of the violin world any better.

The evening concert turned into a tale of two virtuosos.

"How many Stradivari violins have you played?" Sir Curtis Price asked Ehnes. On the table behind them were three Stradivari violins — the 1666 "Serdet" Strad, the 1711 "Parke" Stradivari, and the 1715 "Marsick" owned by Ehnes.

"This will be the ninety-second and the ninety-third!" Ehnes exclaimed triumphantly.

There was an audible gasp in the audience. When Beare asked Ehnes to compare Guarneri and Stradivari, Ehnes waxed eloquent: "The 'del Gesù' is very different from the Strad — they respond in different ways. The Guarneri requires a dense bow. Stradivari violins create their own acoustic. A great Strad relies on its acoustics environment. I'm a Strad guy — but I adore Guarneri."[19]

After intermission, violinist Adrian Chandler led his group, La Serenissima, on stage — two violins, two violas, a giant lutelike instrument, a harpsichord, and cello — seven players for the first piece — "Sinfonia" by Navara. Chandler addressed the audience: "Needless to say, we play violins that are much less expensive." The audience laughed. Then just before he launched into the next piece, he added as an afterthought: "The cheapest instrument here cost ten quid — I'm not joking!" In the last two pieces — the Vivaldi and the Valentini — the audience discovered the virtuosity of Chandler as a soloist. Both Ehnes and Chandler received a bouquet of flowers at the close of their performance. But, given the focus of the evening on the violins made by the master, similarities between the two players stopped just short of the auction house.

On February 16, 2010, thanks to the generosity of Ashmolean Museum curator Jon Whiteley, research for the Hutchins biography took me to Oxford, where I had the good fortune to have a private audience with the most famous of fiddles — white gloves in hand. Holding the "Messiah," I thought of all the recent controversies surrounding it. Though its provenance was relatively established — from Count Cozio di Salabue to Tarisio to Vuillaume — major questions remained. Why did Vuillaume keep it a secret for fifty years? And then why did he modify it before he displayed it in 1872? In his book *The Violin World*, Norman Pickering, electrical engineer, Juilliard-trained musician, acoustics professor, and high-fidelity equipment designer, said of Vuillaume's actions: "If this was to be preserved as an original Stradivari, that amounts nearly to an act of vandalism."[20] Vuillaume further complicated matters by making copies of the Messiah — and then was thrilled when no one could tell the difference.

In 1994, while curating *The Violin Masterpieces of Guarneri del Gesù* exhibition at the Metropolitan Museum of Art in New York, Stewart Pollens, former museum instrument restoration expert, secured the services of Dr. Peter Klein of the Ordinariat fur Holzbiologie of the University of Hamburg, to date the spruce tops of twenty-five violins assembled for the exhibition. A few years later, Pollens asked Klein to use his skills to date the wood used in the "Messiah." Pollens recalled: "Though he initially determined that the last datable year-ring of that instrument was 1738 (which postdated Stradivari's death in 1737), members of the violin trade maneuvered him into temporarily retracting his findings in exchange for an opportunity to remeasure the Messiah's year-rings at the Ashmolean Museum. However, because of a dispute that developed during that session, he was unable to leave the Ashmolean with his measurements. Klein now declines to date violins. . . ."[21]

Other scholars have noted discrepancies and inconsistencies, most of which have been explained away by those who insist the instrument is authentic. Pickering wrote: "The position of the British expert, Charles Beare, seemed to be that it is a genuine Strad because he says so, with no further explanation. His attitude towards the eminent Pollens was dismissive and insulting." Pickering zeroed in on the issue at the heart of the matter. "The jury is still out, but there is one powerful force suppressing the likelihood that any serious investigation will be resumed — the power of money. As a

Strad, its value is beyond price; as a copy, it would have considerable value to a collector, but even that would be less than a tenth of what it is now as a 'certified' original. Nobody gains, either by exposure or positive affirmation, except those who want to know the truth. . . . Furthermore, not all of the several hundred existing Strads are of concert quality, although they all bring very high prices on the market."[22]

Returning to the fiddle on the table, as I looked at my white gloves, I imagined how thrilled Carleen would have been to be by my side. She would pick it up gingerly, study the thicknesses of the plates, the purfling, the tapering of the sound-holes. She would tap the four-corner "hot-spots" on the top plate, holding her ear to the fiddle, listening, trying to confirm her own suspicions spawned from hundreds of hours of experimentation.

Still, as I placed the fiddle back on the table, I thought about touching the untouchable, about timing, and about the story of a luthier whose legacy, like a starfish with its tentacles pointing in all directions, points in all directions of the violin world — but here, in this moment, to a market built on "old" fiddles and the question of authenticity. I watched Whiteley prepare the "Messiah" to go back on its throne in the glass case where thousands will mill around and study it through a glass, dimly.

"Do you think she is a real Strad? Or a fake?" I ask.

He smiles coyly: "It doesn't really matter, does it? It is still a beautiful work of art, and the fact that research cannot determine either way beyond a shadow of a doubt makes it all the more intriguing."

17 ∫ *Fiddles on Exhibit*

THE METROPOLITAN MUSEUM OF ART

On October 27, 1999, Carleen sat for a moment in her porch office staring at another group of fiddles—her own version of modern iconography staring back at her. The March 6, 1989, *New Yorker* magazine cover, all dog-eared and worn, had been pasted to the side of her office file cabinet for ten years. It was forever linked to the year Hutchins had donated an octet to the Metropolitan Museum of Art—but how exactly? Hutchins would never find out the truth, but she had her inklings. Was this image making fun of the violin octet? Or was it a figment of artist John O'Brien's imagination?

It had been the same year—nearly the same moment—that the violin octet would be featured in an exhibition of new acquisitions at the Metropolitan Museum of Art in honor of the one hundredth anniversary of the museum's Crosby Brown Musical Instrument Collection. Now, out of the blue, a decade later, a phone call had come from Joe Peknik, musical instrument technician at the Met. "Are you sitting down, Carleen?" Joe had asked.

"Yes," said Carleen, expecting nothing.

"Well, we have just had a change in curators, and we are finally going to get your violin octet out of storage. Will you come and see how they have fared all these years?"[1]

After a long moment's pause to allow the shock to fall away, Carleen had agreed, a day had been chosen, and that day had arrived—October 27, 1999.

The March 1989 *New Yorker* cover looked like a spoof of the violin octet. And the timing—the very week of the opening of the 1989 exhibition at the Met—was just too eerie to be coincidental—at least that was Carleen's first thought. "Had they gotten to me?" she wondered. Gotten to the *New Yorker*, even? Of course, here, in one of the most populated cities in the world, everyone was connected to everyone else in ways one never ever fathomed, much less understood. So much behind-the-scenes of who-knows-whom. The artist John O'Brien—whose name was scrawled whimsically in the lower right-hand corner—had drawn an exaggerated orchestral pit that looked like a sports arena banked with fiddles escalating in size. And there were exactly eight different-sized fiddles! In the first two rows—players played violins and violas "da braccio"—with outstretched arms. Then a row of cellists, behind whom stood two rows of bass players standing next to their instruments in the traditional position. But in next row, players stood on stools to play their basses. Behind them, in the last two rows of stringed basses, each row bigger than the last—tuxedoed men and women in black gowns literally "scaled" ladders to play the gargantuan instruments. It looked like a chamber orchestra on steroids! Who could make this up? Was it the octet—made fun of?—in a *New Yorker* cartoon?! Carleen thought it was entirely possible.

When she had heard of the upcoming exhibition in 1989 to celebrate the centennial of the Crosby Brown Musical Instruments Collection, Carleen had loved the idea of donating an octet to the Metropolitan Museum of Art. It would be her personal contribution to the violin world, musicology, and historical preservation. Prior to the late nineteenth century, virtually every museum collection of musical instruments resided in Europe, the historical roots of Western musical instruments. One of the most important early musical instrument collections began in Edinburgh, Scotland, with John Donaldson, who in 1858 built a museum devoted to musical acoustics. The idea for a music museum had started in 1795 in Paris, when the Conservatoire National de Musique was founded to include not just contemporary and valuable instruments but also ancient and foreign instruments. In 1861, the instrument museum was finally opened to the public when the French state purchased a collection of eighty-eight instruments from composer Louis Clapisson; today the museum is the Musée de la Musique in Parc de la Villette in Paris.[2] In 1860, Victorian tea trader Frederick John Horniman began collecting artifacts illustrating natural history and the arts, and he founded the Horniman Museum in London.[3] In 1877, in Belgium, the preservation work and collections of the Belgian musicologist Francois-Joseph Fetis formed the collection of the Musée des Instruments de Musique.

The American counterpart to this endeavor began on February 16, 1889, when Mary Elizabeth Adams Brown, wife of John Crosby Brown, a respected New York merchant banker of Brown Bros. & Co., wrote to the trustees of the Metropolitan Museum (as it was called then) to offer to donate her collection of 270 musical instruments to the museum.[4] As early as 1870, on a trip to Europe, Mrs. Brown had become enamored of an ivory pandurina

— a lutelike Italian instrument — and began collecting musical instruments to furnish her home, Brighthurst, in Orange, New Jersey. In 1884, when Mrs. Brown obtained four instruments from a friend in Italy — a Savoyard harp, a seventeenth-century Paduan ivory mandolin, an eighteenth-century Viennese piano made by Anton Vatter, and an eighteenth-century Italian serpent — she officially began her collection.[5]

Despite the fact that Mrs. Brown suffered greatly from rheumatism, she managed to develop her collection primarily by keeping up an extensive correspondence with European collectors, without whom she could not have amassed a collection of any significance. In her extensive, handwritten catalogue, Mrs. Brown thanked directors of many chief European museums and United States consuls: Rajah Sourindro Mohun Tagore, of Calcutta, India; Alfred J. Hipkins, of London; the Reverend F. W. Galpin, of Hatfield Vicarage, England; and Victor Mahillon, curator of the Museum of the Royal Conservatory of Music in Brussels.[6]

In 1889, when Mrs. Brown donated her entire collection — 276 artifacts — to the Metropolitan Museum of Art, where they joined 44 instruments already in the collection — it became the first significant musical instruments collection in the United States. According to her great-granddaughter Sally B. Brown, visiting committee co-chair, Department of Musical Instruments, Mrs. Brown named it the Crosby Brown Musical Instruments Collection of All Nations, in order "to recognize the initial and then later consistent intellectual and financial support of her husband in her work. It was indeed a very formal title and without doubt the proper protocol for a married woman in her time, whose name was never properly meant to be visible in public except when she married or died!"[7] By 1893, the collection had increased to seven hundred objects; by 1896, two thousand. By 1902, the musical instruments collection at the museum numbered 3,390. In 1900, Yale University became the first American university to begin a collection of musical instruments.[8]

For Carleen, donating an octet to the Met had seemed logical for several reasons. First, there was Carleen's fond memory of her first contact with Dr. Emanuel Winternitz, the former celebrated curator of musical instruments, who, upon seeing her second viola, had suggested she apply for a Fulbright — a pipe dream to Carleen at the time, but these memories remained with her. And second, Carleen had an indirect connection to Mrs. Crosby

Brown through her great-granddaughter Sarah "Sally" Brown, whom Carleen had taught at Brearley.[9] In 1984, nearly two decades after Winternitz had examined her first viola, Hutchins had attempted to contact him again, for help in locating the musical notebooks of Leonardo da Vinci, only to discover Winternitz had died, replaced by Laurence Libin.

In September 1985, Libin wrote to Hutchins to ask about documentation for a new acquisition, a Louis Condax vertical viola made according to Hutchins's plans. Three years later, when Hutchins learned that the May 1989 American Musical Instrument Society meeting would be held at the Metropolitan Museum, she had pitched an idea to Libin—why not use the upcoming meeting as an opportunity to present the octet violins in concert? The pitch worked better than Carleen anticipated. Within a month, Libin contacted her regarding acquiring a violin octet for the collection. Hutchins was thrilled to donate a set of her violins to the Met, and in December 1988, she traveled to the Met to deliver them personally. In the inventory list, Hutchins credited those apprentices who helped make this octet possible. It consisted of the following instruments: Treble SUS #125, 1986 (CMH and Carolyn Field); Soprano SUS #117, 1978 (CMH); Mezzo SUS #110, 1976 (CMH); Alto SUS #136, 1982 (CMH and Rafael Bernstein); Tenor SUS #146, 1971 (CMH, Louis Dunham, and Burritt Miller); Baritone SUS #199, 1985 (CMH and Rafael Bernstein); and Contrabass SUS #177, five-string, 1985 (CMH, Thomas Coleman, and Donald Blatter). No small bass was part of this group; it was scheduled to arrive later. The gift designation read: "Instruments designed and developed by Carleen M. Hutchins, Frederick A. Saunders and John C. Schelleng with the assistance of many other members of the Catgut Acoustical Society, Inc. . . . GIFT of Carleen M. and Morton A. Hutchins and the Harriet M. Bartlett Fund of the Catgut Acoustical Society, Inc."[10]

The next month, Carleen received a note from Philippe de Montebello, the director of the Metropolitan Museum of Art, thanking her for her donation of "your exquisitely crafted violins."[11] Hutchins wrote to Montebello: "My husband and I are very pleased to make this possible. . . . We are particularly anxious that these instruments be available for performance from time to time. . . . The dream of having a set at the Metropolitan Museum of Art has come true."[12] On the same day that she wrote Montebello, February 9, 1989, Hutchins also wrote to Libin to confirm the fact that the violin octet would be included in an exhibition that would run from March 10, 1989, through July 1989.[13]

The exhibit opened without a hitch. Carleen and Mort attended the grand reception on Thursday, March 9. Violin dealers Jacques Français and René Morel were in attendance, too. At the reception, Carleen vividly recalled passing by Français and his new wife, someone she had known at Brearley.[14] Carleen had not given Français a second thought until a few days later when she saw the latest issue — the March 6, 1989, issue — of the *New Yorker*, and the image on the cover had made her blood freeze. Carleen had searched the inside of the cover for some explanation — nothing. Carleen wished she could find this artist. Was it a tribute or a joke? But even more important, how did this artist even know of her violin octet? It was both curious and absurd to Carleen that any dealers bad-mouthing her work could feel threatened by a housewife carving fiddles in her kitchen and sprinkling sand in her basement. Now, quite dumbly, she found the octet on the cover of the most famous magazine in the country. Was it dumb luck, good luck — or an omen?

A few months later, Carleen would think back to this same cover when she read a comment Jacques Français had made about her in the July 30, 1989, *New York Times* article marking the closing of the special exhibition. The article, "What Makes a Violin Sing? Two Makers, Two Views," pitted traditional violinmaking against a scientific approach. The writer compared traditional luthier Sergio Peresson in his Haddonfield, New Jersey, studio with Hutchins, eighty miles north, adjusting her accelerometer in her Montclair acoustics laboratory. In addition, the piece quoted Français: "'She's trying to re-create the violin,'" Jacques Français, a dealer, said in assessing Hutchins' work. Mr. Français, who has bought and sold violins in Manhattan since 1948, added, 'and she's doing it backward!'" One can only surmise that Français meant that by making contemporary instruments rather than copying the old, Hutchins was reversing three centuries of tradition and going against the grain of most luthiers.

On September 27, 1989, two months after the exhibition closed, Libin told Hutchins: "We're ready to put your octet on display in our galleries and would like to have the bass as soon as possible. Would you please let me know when we might expect it to arrive?"[15] Then, sometime later, Libin phoned Hutchins to say that the octet violins would be removed from the exhibit and placed in the archives. No explanation was offered. From Carleen's point of view, the instruments had been in hiding in the catacombs of the museum ever since.

All those events now seemed like ancient history to Carleen as she busied herself putting tools in her little black bag. What would she need to fix the fiddles? It had been ten years. Would they be cracked? She placed four sound post–setting tools in her black doctor's bag, wrought-iron prongs with flower-shaped ends. She added four large vises used to glue together a bass. Then Carleen added the long, yellow envelope containing incorporation papers for the New Violin Family Association. Just as the taxi driver stopped at the Met's back door loading dock at 84th and Fifth, Carleen pointed to the spot where she had pulled up her car a decade ago to make a gift of the violin octet to the Met.

Inside, Joe Peknik ushered Carleen into the Instrument Conservation Department, a small workshop where Stewart Pollens, an associate conservator, worked on musical instruments in a museum collection that now numbered more than five thousand. Two minutes later, Ken Moore, the newly appointed curator of musical instruments, appeared in the doorway and shook hands with Carleen. Margaret Sachter, CAS legal counsel, was just behind him, along with Sally Brown. There was a long pause; a look of tension was written all over Carleen's face. Joe picked up on it and ushered Carleen through the winding narrow back corridors of the museum to the musical instruments storage room. Every wall was covered with shelves from floor to ceiling at least twenty feet tall, packed to the brim with as many as three thousand musical instruments. It was clear that space was at a premium. Today, it was obvious from Joe's careful attention and the great interest shown to Carleen that he had cleared the way to focus only on the octet instruments now displayed across long tables covered in green felt. Carleen felt honored and grateful.

First Carleen examined the Mezzo SUS #110. She and Joe determined the bridge needed to be lowered a bit and the sound post needed to be moved a bit closer to the bridge. Next, the Treble SUS #125 also required a tiny bit of adjustment. In the meantime, as Joe later noted, Margaret Sachter had just signed the NVFA incorporation papers in the Musical Instruments Storage Room—at the very moment that the Hutchins violin octet came out of hiding at the museum. Joe then ushered Carleen over to the largest bass,

SUS #177, a five-string instrument, lying on a table near the door. She began to tap it, to test it for consistent tones that told her that nothing had come unglued. "It sounds solid as a rock. The bridge height is great; the sound post couldn't be more perfect. Joe, you've done a marvelous job taking care of them."[16]

Joe beamed with satisfaction. "I never let an octet instrument touch the floor in this gallery, not an easy thing to do, considering how little space we have for five thousand instruments!" After Carleen examined each violin to her satisfaction, she, Joe, Margaret, Ken and Sally adjourned to the Patrons Lounge to discuss hosting a violin octet concert. "It would be so exciting to introduce the octet. For three hundred years, we have had the same kinds of things in classical music. On the cusp of the new millennium, we need to think about new music," said Sally.

"I have to be honest," began Carleen. "The New York music scene has been very hard on me. Two New York dealers have bad-mouthed me for thirty years. They told players to watch out for Hutchins violins because they have electronic synthesizers in them! I have made 168 violas, and yet I cannot sell one in the city of New York. There is the old saying about a red herring in a mound of fish. It is the only thing that keeps the fish alive! This fight has only made me more determined!" said Carleen.

"It is the worshipping of old violins that is so amazing. Why we have a Strad in our collection now that is, to my way of thinking, no longer anything but glue and plywood because it has been restored and overhauled so many times!" said Joe. After a few more moments, Carleen bid good-bye to Joe: "Joe, thanks again, for taking care of my instruments. You have done a marvelous job!" said Carleen. "Ten years is a long time," replied Joe. "Today was the perfect day! Paganini's birthday!"

Two years later, on May 10, 2002, a new exhibition, *The New Violin Family — Augmenting the String Section*, opened in the upstairs musical instrument galleries of the Metropolitan Museum of Art. Two days later, on May 12, the Hutchins Consort gave a concert in Grace Rainey Rogers Auditorium. The exhibit was set to run until March 30, 2003. Instead, it ran until October 24, 2005, making it one of the longest-running exhibits in museum history. Joe Peknik later observed in the fall of 2005, when the exhibition closed: "I really wasn't sure about the statement that the octet had been seen by more than a million people. My colleagues sat down with our figures, and I must say that now I agree with you. Even we were surprised by the big numbers!"[17]

Was the *New Yorker* magazine cover a tribute or a jibe? When later interviewed about his "cartoon" of the comical out-of-control orchestra, John O'Brien looked totally surprised. He had never heard of the violin octet or Hutchins.[18] The title O'Brien assigned to his illustration was "Symphony of Strings: Rich in Fundamental." It was rich in fundamental irony how the uncanny timing of one cartoon could have haunted Carleen for decades.

18 ∫ *Fiddles in the Palace*

RUSSIA

Bringing eight violins to St. Petersburg, Russia, was the violin octet scenario that was the most unexpected of all — at least in Carleen's mind. The Russian octet caught everyone off guard. The seeds were planted by others and then blossomed while Carleen was looking the other way. In fact, she could not have constructed a more unlikely house of cards than those of the Russian octet. How does a potluck supper in Wolfeboro, New Hampshire, bring a family of fiddles to the imperial palaces of Russia? How does a Russian film crew find its way to 112 Essex? How does an old friend come back from the dead? How does a postage stamp produce a recording?

The Russian octet — the brightest star of all the overseas octets — did not die with a whimper, but with a wail reflective of the "Russian soul" itself, at least according to Russian American Marina Markot, the person whose contacts, labor, and enthusiasm made the Russian octet possible. In an interview in September 2014, Markot, a trilingual speech acoustician and director of Cornell Abroad, the international student exchange program at Cornell University, explained: "The military march is the major key, while the Russian soul is the minor key, that key of yearning — not foolishly optimistic" — the soul that is keenly aware of the bittersweet truth that the extremes of success and failure are often intertwined.[1]

The Russian octet was a long shot from every possible perspective, yet it flourished beyond all expectation because all points of light seemed to shine on it simultaneously — the players, the venues, the audience, and the timing. The combination of all these influences formed a confluence nothing short of the perfect storm. But even the perfect storm cannot sustain itself indefinitely.

In 1986, Barbara Hobbie, a *Granite State News* arts reporter, interviewed Hutchins and became smitten with her story. In 1991, Hobbie hosted Marina Meleschkina (Markot's name at that time), who had come to Wolfeboro with a group of foreign exchange students. As Carleen's daughter, Cassie, was also hosting an exchange student, she invited her mother to join them for a potluck supper. Hutchins and Meleschkina, who had a doctorate in speech acoustics, immediately clicked. Meanwhile, everything back in Russia was topsy-turvy, with the official dissolution of the USSR in December 1991 resulting in political, economic, cultural, spiritual, and personal upheaval for everyone. In this time of total uncertainty, everyone was looking in new directions, seeking connection. It was this impetus for exploring and forging new connections that had brought Meleschkina to America. Meanwhile, Hobbie had developed an interest in screen writing and brainstormed with Meleschkina about making a film about Hutchins and her fiddles.

In January 1993, Meleschkina moved to Hamburg, Germany. One of the businesses with which her husband was involved was the SWAN/Hamburg film company that had entrepreneurial connections to filmmaking studios in St. Petersburg. In this time of economic flux, one could use German resources to make a film much less expensively in a Russian studio.[2] Meleschkina and Hobbie hatched their idea to do a film on Hutchins and her violin octet. In December 1993, a crew from Public Television in St. Petersburg, Russia, arrived at 112 Essex Avenue to film a short documentary on Hutchins. The crew included Sasha (Alexander) Dobriyanik, director; Elizaveta Tereshkina, editor; and Svetlana Shabanova, music editor. Hobbie and Meleschkina were executive producers, with Meleschkina acting as translator.

The Russians arrived in Montclair in a blizzard. The next morning, after they made their way to 112 Essex, they received a very subdued greeting from Hutchins. Carleen's reserved reaction caught the entire crew offguard. Shabanova recalled: "Dressed in his best suit, Dobriyanik was going to have a conversation with Carleen over tea, discuss the filming process, the nuances of the work ahead, and, as was customary in Russia, get on the same page with the subject of the story." Instead, the Russian crew quickly realized that Hutchins was first and foremost a person of action. Shabanova knew Carleen had accepted the film crew when Carleen approached her the next evening offering her a glass of sherry to relax—without emotion, but with a twinkle in her eye.[3] In the process of making the film, *Luthier in the Light of Science*, Meleschkina and Shabanova were struck by the dilemma that though Carleen had created remarkable violins, they were mostly hidden in museums.

In January 1994, Meleschkina and Shabanova asked the St. Petersburg Conservatory piano professor Lydia Voltchek about potential interest in the violin octet among the conservatory's students. On January 30, Meleschkina wrote to Hutchins: "Some musicians got quite excited about the octet. What are your current plans?"[4] Less than two weeks later Meleschkina asked Hutchins about obtaining an octet, as she had worked out sponsorship by SWAN to bring the octet to Russia. On July 12, 1994, a Hutchins violin octet arrived in St. Petersburg: Treble SUS #123; Soprano SUS #301; Mezzo SUS #153; Alto SUS #137; Tenor SUS #151; Baritone SUS #198; Small Bass SUS #172; and Large Bass SUS #178. To Carleen's surprise, the professors were so taken with the octet violins that they decided to play them themselves instead of turning them over to their students.

Shortly thereafter, in October 1994, back in America, an old friend seemed to come back from the dead — Virginia Apgar — through the efforts of her protégé, Dr. L. Joseph Butterfield, a Colorado physician and pioneer of modern neonatology who in 1965 had founded the Children's Hospital Newborn Center in Denver. Butterfield, a father of a child with a birth defect, had just completed a ten-year campaign to create a twenty-cent U.S. postage stamp to honor Apgar, who in 1958 had redirected the mission of the March of Dimes from infantile polio paralysis to the prevention of birth defects. On October 24, to celebrate the Virginia Apgar stamp at the annual meeting of the American Academy of Pediatrics in Dallas, a string quartet performed Apgar's favorite pieces on the Apgar String Quartet instruments.[5] Because the Apgar-Hutchins friendship had built the Apgar quartet, this concert inspired Butterfield to think about ways to promote the Apgar instruments and the Hutchins violin octet.

Meanwhile, in St. Petersburg, on October 17, rehearsals had begun in earnest. The musicians included Grigori Sedukh, treble; Vladimir Stopichev (International Contest laureate), soprano; Vladimir Ovtcharek (professor), mezzo; Alexei Massarsky (International Contest laureate), alto; Iosif Levinson (professor and artistic director), tenor; Leonid Gultchin, baritone; Alexei Ivanov, small bass; and Alexander Shilo, contrabass. Throughout the five years of the Russian octet, there was only one change in personnel — when cellist Alexei Massarsky left the group in December 1994. Igor Viktorovitch then took over the alto violin.

The Russians debuted their first violin octet concert on November 27, 1994, in the Maly Hall of the Rimsky-Korsakov St. Petersburg State Conservatory — the first of seven concerts held in six palatial venues over the next three years. Active repertoire throughout the seven concerts featured old and new works. Classical repertoire included Overture Suite #2B in B-flat Minor, by J. S. Bach; Adagio from Baryton Trio #82, Haydn; *The Children's Album*, Pyotr Tchaikovsky; and ragtime pieces by Scott Joplin. New works included "Variation on a Theme of Handel," by Lawrence Rackley; "Basse Dance," by Pierre Atteignant, arranged by Roderick Skeaping; "A Generation Gap?," by Marie Bond Riggenbach; and *Aphorisms*, by Gordon Jacob.

The first concert was sandwiched in the middle of a two-day symposium for violinmakers and acousticians, held on November 26 in the Conservatory and on November 28 in the Museum of Musical Instruments. Carleen wore a bright blue paisley silk dress, looking the most festive she had ever looked, when she addressed the hall, her words translated by Meleschkina. Carleen bowed, smiling, and averred to the audience: "You can make a violin of any size and make it sound good."[6] Thanks to efforts and contacts of Meleschkina, Shabanova, and Voltchek, the packed house of two hundred people represented a wide array of professionals from St. Petersburg's most important cultural institutions. In the audience were the staff of various orchestras, and conservatories; musical venues; composers' unions; and museums; musical instruments factories; governmental personnel, acousticians and researchers; and the German, Russian and English press — easily the most impressive audience that had ever witnessed a violin octet concert anywhere.[7] A live recording was made of this concert, covered by the *St. Petersburg Press* on November 27 and broadcast by St. Petersburg Public Radio on December 4, 1994. On December 26, the second concert took place in the State Academic Capella of St. Petersburg, recorded live and filmed on Beta cam for a promotional fifteen-minute video, sponsored by the St. Petersburg Conservatory Charity Foundation and SWAN in Germany.

On March 22, 1995, the third concert was held at one of the most magnificent ceremonial buildings in imperial St. Petersburg — the White-Column Hall of Moika Palace, also known as the Yusupov Palace, the family residence of princes that today houses the Museum of Noble Life and the St. Petersburg Palace of Culture. A month later, on April 26, the fourth concert took place in the prestigious Small Hall of the St. Petersburg Philharmonic. The fifth concert occurred on September 22 in the Theater of the Yusupov Palace, the most intimate and easily the most elaborate of the Russian venues to date — with its high-arched, frescoed ceilings and golden rococo balustrades surrounding a small theater seating between one hundred and two hundred people.

By January 1996, the Russians had given five very successful concerts to sold-out crowds. As a result, there was a need to clarify roles, because the Russian octet was becoming a viable, exciting reality.[8] Thus far, the Catgut Acoustical Society had shipped and loaned the violins free of charge to Russia and had paid for two concerts, a composers' contest, arrangements, a promotional video, storage, and insurance. The St. Petersburg Conservatory Charity Foundation had found the musicians and had organized the ensemble and the five concerts, including publicity, composers' contests, arrangements, and supervised rehearsals. On January 31, CAS, on behalf of Carleen, submitted a "Letter of Understanding" placing the bulk of responsibility on SWAN for housing, storing, and insuring the violins, in addition to giving concerts. The CAS proposal sent shock waves through Voltchek, who wrote to Hutchins in February: "CAS must have decided that Russian musicians are so excited about the American instruments . . . they will agree to not only work for free, but also invest their own money to glorify the creators and owners of the instruments."[9]

The hard fact was that the Russians did not have a budget to maintain the violin octet on a daily basis. And still, the Russians played on. The sixth concert took place on April 10, 1996, at the St. Petersburg Composers Society. On May 3, Marina Markot (her name as of March 1996) wrote to Hutchins to ask about how strongly she opposed using the octet as collateral on a loan with the insurance holding company.[10] Meanwhile, on June 21, as the Russians gave their seventh concert, returning to the Small Hall of the St. Petersburg Philharmonic, the collateral issue became the sticking point. Hutchins was adamantly against the violins being used as collateral and cautioned that unless she received her proposal signed by the Russians expediently, she would have to remove the violins from Russia.[11]

In the midst of this disagreement, a much sadder event occurred. Morton Hutchins suffered a stroke from which he would never recover. Even as she was adjusting to the shock that Mort would be in a wheelchair and would never speak again, Carleen pushed ahead with the latest idea—to bring the Russians on tour in the United States.

In February 1997, Voltchek proposed a way to solve the current customs problems regarding the violin octet by suggesting that the violins be presented as a gift to the Conservatory duty-free.[12] By April, ownership of the Russian violin octet was in question. The Russians could not devote more time to the new violins unless they would be in Russia for an extended period of time. By the summer, issues concerning ownership of the Russian octet surfaced in St. Petersburg.

Meanwhile, on the home front, Butterfield kicked his promotional campaign into high gear on behalf of the Apgar Quartet instruments and the violin octet through his extensive contacts in Colorado and New York City.[13] As a well-connected Colorado physician, Butterfield had connections to the Aspen Music Festival; Central City Opera; Denver Metro College; Lamont School of Music; the Suzuki Institute in Snowmass, Colorado; the Columbia College of Physicians and Surgeons, and Juilliard.[14] Suddenly, all the threads of the medical and musical worlds of Butterfield and Apgar seemed to magically knit together in the interest of bringing the Russians on tour to the United States. Finally, to add yet another strand to the fabric, Butterfield had heard of Robert Miller, a Colorado composer-producer who had conducted and recorded with the St. Petersburg Philharmonic Symphony and knew some of the Russian octet musicians.[15]

On November 7, 1997, Butterfield and Miller met for the first time, a meeting that sparked interest to produce a recording and promote an American tour of the St. Petersburg Hutchins Violin Octet.[16] Serendipitously, the St. Petersburg Philharmonic was already scheduled to tour in America during the fall of 1998.[17] Throughout the past year, Grigori Sedukh had been touring in Russia, giving solo concerts on the treble violin, so much so that on November 23, Hutchins decided to reward him by giving him Treble Violin SUS #123 as a gift. One week later, Miller put his hat in the ring and wrote Carleen about the inner logic of bringing the Russians to Denver, given his own connections and those of Butterfield. Then, the fact that Sedukh now owned his own octet violin sparked the idea that it would be much easier to plan a tour for just *one* player.

On January 28, 1998, Marina Markot was still centrally involved, now in helping promote a solo western tour for Grigori Sedukh. But by March, the situation had reversed itself, as Markot felt excluded by Miller's increasingly evasive communication. After all of the blood, sweat, and tears that Markot had voluntarily poured into the Russian violin octet over the past four years, she now felt that Butterfield and Miller were whisking the focus away from St. Petersburg, just when the Russians had achieved real success with the violin octet.[18] On March 13, Markot appealed to Hutchins.

On March 26, Carleen responded dispassionately, trying to distance herself from Marina's turmoil, reminding her that the Russian octet was the only octet that had received funds from CAS to the tune of $15,000.[19] Furthermore, Carleen added, the issues of "management, budgets and being shrewd" were incompatible with a volunteer organization like CAS—"a concept almost totally unknown in Europe."[20] Carleen saw every reason to grasp at the enthusiasm, professional credentials, and connections of Butterfield and Miller. But, unlike Markot, she did not see it as a threat to the Russian octet. Hutchins worked out with Miller that he and Butterfield would fund the Sedukh tour without cost to CAS, and Hutchins would personally loan $16,000 from a sale of two mezzos to meet the costs of a Sedukh compact disc.[21]

In mid-May 1998, Robert Miller produced the first CD by the St. Petersburg Hutchins Violin Octet. The original cast of musicians recorded the following pieces: Concerto in D Major, op. 10, no. 3, *Il Gardellino*, by Vivaldi; excerpts from *The Children's Album*, op. 39, by Tchaikovsky, arranged by Sophia Levkovskaya; *An English Divertimento* by Falik; *Dialogues* by Belov; *Handel Variations* by Rackley; and *Aphorisms* by Jacob. Of two thousand copies made, Miller distributed four hundred to radio stations in the United States and Canada.

The bassist and Juilliard professor David Walter wrote: "The CD is superb! The quality of the instruments, the artistry of the players . . . the fidelity of the recording, the cleverness of the programming . . . beautifully written program notes all add up to a brilliant testimony to your remarkable accomplishments. Brava! Brava! Brava!" Michael McIntyre in Cambridge commented: "Well done! Your Russian musicians have done what I once hoped we'd do here. The CD is splendid. The Vivaldi is brilliant!" More praise came from Charles Taylor in Wales: "A superb recording! Many, many congratulations!" The composer Frank Lewin called the CD "splendid. . . . The Russians have truly mastered these instruments!"[22]

Then, just three weeks later, in June 1998, on the heels of this success, Butterfield and Miller produced a very successful seven-concert tour for Sedukh performing on the treble, soprano, and mezzo violins in Colorado and New Mexico. The tour included the Colorado Springs Fine Arts

Center; the Fechin Institute, Taos, New Mexico; St. John's College, Santa Fe; Covenant Presbyterian Church, Albuquerque; The Lamont School of Music of Denver University; The Children's Hospital, Foote Hall, University of Denver; and the Suzuki Institute, Snowmass Village, Colorado.[23]

By July, Hutchins still held out hope for the Russian octet, writing to Voltchek to ask if CAS could help the Russians raise funds to purchase the octet. Voltchek replied that the idea of raising funds to "ransom the octet" seemed "absolutely unreal."[24] In the meantime, Hutchins had asked Voltchek if Sedukh could borrow the Russian soprano and mezzo to take with him on tour to Verona. But as of Christmas, 1998, Voltchek wrote to Hutchins that this was impossible because Russian customs would not allow the octet to be separated.

Hutchins took this last letter at face value. Without any signed agreement to keep the octet beyond May 1999, it was time to move the instruments out of Russia — and Germany seemed the logical choice. Meanwhile, a sudden blow came when Dr. Joseph Butterfield — the total champion for the octet in Russia and in the United States — suffered a fatal heart attack on June 4, 1999. As the Russian octet could not sustain itself, Hutchins made plans for Dr. Volkmar Tetzner, CAS vice president in Germany, to pick up the violins. But plans for a violin octet in Germany went unexpected awry. After Hutchins talked to Japan, China, and Germany to try and find a place for the Russian octet, it had to be sent back to 112 Essex — because German customs agents required a $17,000 tax![25]

19 ∫ *Fiddling with Time*

CABIN FEVER

To Carleen, life was, after all, one grand experiment, and the only predictable thing was the element of surprise. When the alpenhorn sounded its morning fanfare on Saturday, June 27, 1998, calling to order the first day of ISMA 98—the International Symposium on Musical Acoustics—at the Sleeping Lady Mountain Resort in Leavenworth, Washington—it also signaled a major milestone for Hutchins. Three days before, in downtown Seattle, Carleen Maley Hutchins had been awarded the Honorary Fellowship of the Acoustical Society of America—the highest honor bestowed by the ASA, the very same award granted to Frederick Saunders in 1954. Hutchins was the fourteenth recipient of the award first given to Thomas Edison in 1929, and the first and only woman recipient. In addition, Hutchins, the honorary chair of ISMA 98, was excited to be able to distribute one hundred copies of the octet's first CD—*The St. Petersburg Hutchins Violin Octet*—to all of her colleagues.

The plaintive, slightly melancholy tone of the alpenhorn resonated with Carleen as she looked at the Cascade Mountains and the "sleeping lady" profile outside her window. Still, although she had just celebrated a huge milestone, Carleen Hutchins, at age eighty-seven, slept only fitfully. Her world was shifting in and out of focus. She was mentally sharp, but emotionally, she felt at sixes and sevens, increasingly torn between CAS and her desire to promote the violin octet. Though she hated to admit it, it seemed that the two goals might no longer be compatible.

This morning, as she sat in the audience, her favorite black-and-white Scandinavian intarsia sweater right in style with the mountains behind her, Carleen contemplated how she would begin the meeting. But instead, to her great surprise, Maurits Hudig, CAS president, took the podium ahead of her to announce that the CAS board of directors had established a new honorary medal: "The Medal seeks to recognize individuals who relentlessly push the boundaries of knowledge within the field of musical acoustics. . . . We have a first recipient in our midst—for whom, I must say, this award will be a complete surprise—because she might have stopped this whole thing cold if she had gotten wind of it. Carleen, to your friends and colleagues, it is only proper and fitting that you should be the first recipient of what will be known as the Carleen Maley Hutchins Medal. Would you step to the podium, please?"[1] As Carleen reached the podium, a large gray cat entered the auditorium, made its way to the stage, and climbed up on the podium, where it surveyed the laughing audience — surely a cosmic sign to Carleen that she and Catgut were in the right place.[2]

That evening, the cellist-violinmaker Anne Cole from Albuquerque, New Mexico, performed on three of her own octet violins — alto, tenor and baritone — that she had made based on Hutchins' plans. Accompanied by Craig Brown, Cole performed the Dvořák Sonatina on the alto violin (vertical viola); the Franck Sonata on the tenor; and Sonata, by the twentieth-century composer Frank Bridge on the baritone. Cole had begun making octet violins in 1968, just three years after Hutchins created the first violin octet. "And maybe because of my interest in Carleen's instruments and my willingness to play them in public, I was never accepted totally in the traditional violin-making establishment," she later wrote.[3]

When Carleen phoned Cole to ask her to perform at ISMA 98, Cole had responded readily. "Her phone call came out of the blue — sort of like a command performance from the Queen." Cole had experienced firsthand the double isolation of being a female luthier and one who was carving "new" octet violins at a time when there were no violinmaking schools in the United States and no violinmakers in New Mexico. She described the irrational prejudice that innovative players face when they try something new. One of her students could easily play the baritone as a cello yet was ridiculed for doing so. She mused: "Classical musicians have become so weird that way — this antique stuff — they have problems with something not just radically new, but even with slightly different dimensions." Cole feels that the problem for the violin octet is also lack of repertoire. "If only Dvořák was alive now — he was a viola player — he would have eaten up her violas and would have written viola concertos!" But the response of virtuosos also determines the fate of new instrument. "It just crushed me when Yo-Yo Ma made a recording of the Bartók on the alto. It was tremendous and he won a Grammy — and then he never played the instrument again. He was derided for doing it. He might say there was another reason, but I can tell you the reason was social pressure."

Much changed following that evening in the mountains, and by 1999, cause for celebration had yielded to storm clouds. Overnight it seemed, CAS president Maurits Hudig had become the sharpest thorn in Carleen's side. Just one year earlier, Hudig had praised Carleen from the podium; he had even contributed $5,000 to help produce the Russian CD.[4] This turnaround made no sense to Carleen. Hudig was now leading the charge to challenge Carleen about use of CAS funds to promote the octet, seeing it as a conflict with the original mission of CAS as a primarily a research-based rather than commercial organization. At eighty-eight, Hutchins was losing ground on the personal front as well — taking care of Mort as best she could yet also resenting domestic chores. "I have been fighting with CAS for six months about accounting for every last cent of CAS money, while on the other hand, thinking huge thoughts about the phenomenal potential of the violin octet and how I should maybe even think about creating an entirely new organization — then suddenly I am down dealing with bedpans!"[5]

In just twelve months, CAS and the Violin Octet Development Group — formed informally in Russia by Marina Markot — had reversed roles. By June 1999, things were topsy-turvy with the death of Butterfield and the end of the Russian octet. Yet, the release of the first CD spurred growing interest in the violin octet from other directions. The decision had been made to create a new organization devoted to the violin octet — the New Violin Family Association. At the same time, Cassie had convinced Carleen that she and Mort had to relocate from Montclair to Wolfeboro, New Hampshire — where Cassie lived. Hutchins later reported: "In 1999, I formed the NVFA which split off from the CAS. The following year I moved to Wolfeboro-Tuftonboro, New Hampshire, and brought the central office of the NVFA with me."[6]

In reality, the transition took much longer — a few years in fact, to effect the total relocation. Nothing in the sparsely decorated, minimalistic cabin built on the shores of Lake Winnipesaukee could prepare any visitor about what to expect upon venturing into 112 Essex. The three-story stucco Dutch colonial was filled to the brim — in nearly every room — with fiddles or fiddle paraphernalia. The first clue was just inside the front door where, in museumlike fashion, a dozen violas hung dust-free behind glass, their scrolls hooked on a wire strung inside the living room's breakfront china cabinet in lieu china plates. By the mantel four violas hung on the wall, including

Stokowski's "monster," and the inlaid wooden portrait of a cat and fiddle — the logo borrowed by the Catgut Acoustical Society. A portrait hung on the opposite wall — this one of Carleen in her favorite denim shirt sitting at her workbench, with luthier's tools, three white fiddle plates, and a series of Chladni fiddle patterns in the background, a carving knife in one hand, a scroll in the other — and a reserved smile not quite her own.

This interior living room facade never changed. It was a tableau that summed up Hutchins's passion for her life's work and testament to the fact that, as a daughter of the Depression, she never discarded anything. At the far end of the living room was the porch "office" that in the early days had once been home to a bald crow named Satan, and later, another crow named Elijah, perched in their cages, for decades, keeping company with Mort's pet turtle pen that lasted almost as long. Otherwise, the porch had long since surrendered to the wave of fiddle paperwork, housed in a wall of file drawers.

Another row of fiddles hung from a clothesline strung across the side yard window, next to a tower of concert videotapes recorded over the past thirty years. The opposite wall held three shadow box frames containing Carleen's childhood collection of moths and butterflies. The *Life* magazine photograph of Carleen sitting behind a violin suspended behind a microphone dwarfed the series of family photographs collecting dust on the china buffet. A large viola, a soprano violin, and the black epoxy violin hung from the dining room molding. A visitor to the kitchen had no way of knowing that the cornerless, curving, Formica table passed by on the way to the basement was made by Carleen to actually mimic the two distinctly different curves of a Stradivari and a Guarneri violin. Then down the steep stairwell leading to the catacombs — a basement full of fiddles and testing equipment. At the bottom of the stairs was Carleen's Chladni chamber — two corner walls covered in posters of vibration patterns of fiddle plates next to a worktable, upturned fiddle plates, and lots of black glitter. To the left of this vibration table were three more experimental chambers. In one doorway a violin hung, its four corners suspended on rubber bands, next to another cascading waterfall of different-sized fiddles hanging from the rafters and a wall of shelves holding fiddle parts — ribs, models, and plates.

The organizational transition became official in November 1999. Had these two life-changing events — the move to New Hampshire and the creation of the New Violin Family Association—not coincided, Carleen might not have survived either one. As she said goodbye to CAS and to 112 Essex, her childhood home for nearly ninety years, Carleen needed to look beyond these two anchors in her life—and the New Violin Family Association became the fulcrum around which she visualized living year-round in New Hampshire. Carleen's life and that of her fiddles were inextricably entwined. And the fact that Hutchins now had a new organization to take her time and attention was yet another way for her put off or distance herself from family dynamics. At this point in her life, Carleen could not have changed even if she wanted to. Though Carleen was now in the same neighborhood with her daughter—did it really matter to Carleen? To Cassie? Carleen did not waste any time re-creating her work in her new environs. The new NVFA mission statement presented to the NVFA Executive Committee on December 11, 1999, was nothing less than gargantuan in scope.[7] Among its thematic currents were the following goals: to educate the public, encourage players, stimulate composers, educate and instruct violinmakers, sponsor the collection and preservation of documents, and make such archives available to the public.[8]

One day in the summer of 2003, Hutchins had a fleeting opportunity to visit the cabin. Standing at the bay window overlooking the Broads, she shook her head, walking around, staring up at the carved beams overhead, then down at the floorboards she had planed herself. "I just can't do this anymore. I cannot come to the cabin. Everywhere I look, I see what I can no longer do! I see all these things I made. I see the wooden panels on the floor and walls—that I planed myself. I see the porch where I spent hours carving fiddles, cellos. And now it all reminds me of all the things I can no longer do! It is too painful to know and see all the things I can no longer do," she said. After a long moment of silence, Carleen said: "The move away from 112 Essex nearly killed me. That's when I saw for the first time how attached I had been to EVERYTHING in that house, every *thing* about the house, things like the yard, the shop, the fiddles, everything. Maybe that's the biggest mistake I made—I got way too attached to things, too many things. Things you thought you knew fly together and tell you something different."[9]

Meanwhile, Bob and Deena Spear, students of Hutchins, had relocated their shop from Maryland to Ithaca, New York. By 2003, Spear had completed five octet violins, an ensemble he named for his father-in-law, Albert Mitchell Zalkind. With a treble and contrabass violin still on his workbench, Spear envisioned completing his "next generation" violin octet. On a brisk afternoon on November 30, 2003, the Albert Quintet performed Bach's *Art of the Fugue*, pieces for string quartet by Mendelssohn arranged for tenor quartet, and Vaughan Williams's *Phantasy* Quintet to a standing-room-only crowd at the Ithaca First Unitarian Church.[10]

Throughout her life, Hutchins believed passionately in sharing her knowledge of violinmaking and as early as 1969 envisioned a violinmaking school. In 1972, in partnership with the University of New Hampshire physics professor Harry Hall (a graduate student of Saunders), she founded the summer Violin Craftsmanship Institute at UNH that opened in 1974 and continues today. In 1973, Hutchins began teaching her own classes at 112 Essex Avenue and over the next decade taught at least fifty students—two of her most loyal pupils were Bob and Deena Spear. As Hutchins began feeling her way into founding the New Violin Family Association, she seized a golden opportunity to take advantage of Spear's hard work and loyalty and coerced him to become the new editor of the NVFA newsletter. In its first issue, Spear confesses with good humor: "As your new editor, I take my seat at the desk with some amazement. I am really not sure how I got myself in this position, but others who were at the Board meeting told me I volunteered! I only hope my first newsletter turns out better than my first violin!"[11]

At the end of 2003, the Catgut Acoustical Society also came to an end by merging with the Violin Society of America, a move that ostensibly resulted in the combined enrollment of more than 1,800 members. Despite the best of intentions, Hutchins never anticipated that the organization would survive the merger. The CAS board member Tom King observed: "The good news is that the traditional violin world is now far more receptive to research than ever before. In that sense, the CAS has succeeded."[12]

Officially, Hutchins maintained appearances for a short time—at least on paper. The 2004 NVFA mission had a breathtaking breadth and a goal of a million-dollar endowment to make 42 Taylor Drive in Wolfeboro the NVFA "worldwide operations center." But in reality, lectures were nonexistent, concerts a rarity—Carleen simply had no energy.

By the fall of 2004, Bob Spear had completed a feasibility study about Octet 2005, a symposium devoted to the new violin family, and then set his sights on making it happen. Meanwhile, on Thursday, October 21, 2004, Carleen suffered a mild heart attack—but then two days later proceeded to witness the NVFA board meeting held at her house.[13]

On November 8, 2004, Morton Aldrich Hutchins died at Sunbridge Care of Wolfeboro at the age of ninety-four. The NVFA newsletter's full-page obituary, written by Carleen, highlighted his education and his career. But it was Mort's character that had left a legacy. "Mort's patience was boundless—and it often needed to be. The CAS took over his sun porch to use as an office, his wife took over his garage to teach her violin-making classes, her students took over his kitchen to prepare their meals; and his cats took over the best chairs in the living room. Mort knew how to negotiate a settlement. Everyone got the space they needed." The obit concludes: "Those fortunate enough to have known Mort will always recall his quiet but slightly impish presence in the household where he took care of numerous details others considered trivial or unpleasant. Yet it was this contribution that made Mort the unsung hero of the new violin family; without his support Carleen could not have done half of what she did."[14] Even in this instance, when Carleen pays her most personal tribute to her life partner, the tone seems detached, even a bit condescending, placing the limelight on the violin family rather than her own family.

Carleen decided on an upright double-sided granite gravestone inscribed on just one side with both their names. For now, one side read: "MORTON ALDRICH HUTCHINS" on one line, followed by "May 6, 1910–Nov. 8, 2004." Carleen seemed incapable of separating Mort from her own life with the fiddles. And when it came to inscribing the other side of their joint tombstone, Carleen would harbor a bizarre plan to keep the fiddles out front—even on the gravestone itself, but that, like her life, was yet to be completed.

20 ∫ *Fiddles Live in Concert*

THE HUTCHINS CONSORT

On January 18, 2000, in the Barclay Theater in Irvine, California, Carleen settled into her chair in the second row to hear a concert she had dreamed of for half a century—the inaugural concert of the Hutchins Consort, the first American octet and the only professional ensemble in the United States to perform on Hutchins violins owned by the ensemble.

The Hutchins Consort took the stage. The family of fiddles, graduated in size, from the smallest treble violin on the left to the largest contrabass violin on the right, looked a bit like an Alice-in-Wonderland world with violins growing, increasing in size like so many Russian nesting dolls, then escalating out of control. On the far left stood Reginald Clews on the treble violin. On the far right stood Joe McNalley cradling the contrabass. Next to Clews, stood Igor Tchetchko, soprano; Kevin Connolly, mezzo. The three cellists filling out the middle of the circle included John Acosta, alto; Omar Firestone on tenor; S. Gregory Adamson on baritone; and Michael Wais on the small bass violin.

The first piece was Benjamin Britten's *Simple Symphony*, a wonderful introduction with its four distinctly different parts—"Boisterous Bourée," "Playful Pizzicato," "Sentimental Saraband," and "Frolicsome Finale." What a sound—to hear each violin voice so distinctly—each fiddle a vivid a capella voice. The dazzling pizzicato could be heard distinctly from any point in the room. Franz Liszt's *Evocation à la Chapelle Sixtine* and Gordon Jacob's *Aphorisms* followed. At intermission, Ann Conway, the *L.A. Times* society editor, who had taken a seat next to Carleen and had peppered her with questions prior to the performance, turned to Carleen and said in disbelief: "How could you make these violins? The big bass is bigger than you are!"

Joe McNalley then introduced Hutchins, who slowly rose from her seat. On stage, Hutchins stood next to Joe, looking very nearly half the size of the contrabass between them. Hutchins lingered next to Joe and addressed the audience of three hundred, saying: "This is one of the most exciting moments of my life!"[1] At the post-concert reception, Hutchins stood surrounded by tuxedoed professionals who had made her violins come to life before her eyes. Photo opportunities at every turn, Carleen basked in the limelight and savored every moment, knowing that, at age eighty-eight, she did not expect to be making any more cross-country concert trips.

Robert Miller, the composer and arranger who had recorded the Russian octet and who was now a new NVFA board member, had traveled from Denver with his wife, Heidi, to witness the Hutchins Consort debut. Miller explained why the violin octet was so exciting for a composer: "When you write for a standard violin, there are 'sweet spots.' Carleen's violins are full, round all the way up. The violin octet can stand up to a wind instrument as an equal player, and offers possibilities for special effects like pizzicato or harmonics or double-stops."[2] This evening, Miller just looked triumphantly at Carleen as she stood surrounded by the Consort and simply said, "Bravo!"

A few years later, in 2003, as Carleen stood on stage with the Hutchins Consort after they performed in Wolfeboro, New Hampshire, she spoke from the wisdom of the history she had witnessed, and commented half to the Consort and half to the audience: "Other groups in Europe and Russia have tried, but without enough support, to undertake what the Hutchins Consort is doing. The musical world, especially in other countries, is ready for you." The telltale phrase—"especially in other countries"—spoke volumes and proved prophetic about the road ahead for Joe McNalley and the Hutchins Consort as the only American Hutchins violin octet. But McNalley was a gifted and passionate bassist, a versatile musician, and, above all, an eternal optimist.

Joe McNalley was the youngest of five in a musical family much like the one that had nurtured Frederick Saunders. The intense devotion to music in the family was evidenced by the fact that even as Sharon McNalley birthed five children in eight years in five different places—North Carolina, New York, Colorado, Germany, and Kansas—owing to the upward mobility of the career of Dr. Michael McNalley—still the band played on! The McNalley children all played in high school bands and orchestras—flute, baritone saxophone, clarinet, piano, oboe, contrabass, trombone, as well as a myriad of musical instruments collected by the family. Joe began bass lessons in the sixth grade and by seventh grade knew he would become a professional bass player. He also played trombone in the marching band, but bass had his passion, even though it meant driving 150 miles each week for lessons.

He played bass in his college jazz band and the university orchestra. Besides traditional instruments, the McNalley kids also played and experimented with instruments collected by the family—a Russian balalaika, Spanish castanets, an Australian didgeridoo, Ecuadorian rain stick, bagpipes, guitars, piccolo, banjo, pump organ, Allen organ, and sousaphone. His mother, Sharon McNalley, recalled: "There was always music-making at our home. No one was ever 'required' to practice—sometimes they had to compete for the time and opportunity to do so."[3]

In college, Joe McNalley studied at the New England Conservatory and then transferred to the University of California at San Diego. Beyond musical inspiration at home, McNalley studied bass with two celebrated professional bassists—David Walter and Bert Turetzky—both gifted teachers and maverick professionals pushing the solo potential of their instrument at a time when no one else was doing it. Walter taught double bass and ensemble at the Manhattan School of Music for more than thirty years and was professor of double bass at Julliard from 1969 until he died in 2003. His volume of double bass solos, *The Melodious Bass*, has been one of the consistent best sellers in American double bass literature. Walter found his way to 112 Essex Avenue in the early 1960s and became an early member of CAS.

Over his fifty-year career, Turetzky became the most frequently recorded contrabass soloist in America, creating an impressive bass repertory, including more than three hundred new compositions for string bass that have been written for, performed by, and recorded by him. Turetzky knew of Hutchins and the violin octet, most likely through Walter. So in 1983, with the news that the University of California–San Diego would host the next ASA Symposium, Turetzky asked Hutchins to ship out a violin octet for the meeting in order to present a concert. In May 1983, Hutchins complied.[4] The concert took place on November 9, 1983, at the Town & Country Hotel, San Diego, California. The concert was a huge hit, performed to a packed house of five hundred that left people standing in the aisle cheering.

Despite the success of the concert, Turetzky found it increasingly difficult to sustain interest among players for these "new" violins. "The octet violins are quite fantastic," he said in a phone interview, "but one of the things they say in an interview of a famous player is what instrument do you play?—meaning what *Strad* do you play? That's prejudice. Carleen punched a hole in it, but it's got to be the players who say, 'Listen to this!'"[5]

That's exactly what happened to Joe McNalley. He recalled the first time he played a Hutchins contrabass in an orchestra in 1983. "I played the Hutchins big bass, and we played Brahms' First Symphony which opens up with this series of low G's on the bass, and there was a resonant frequency under the floor such that that G traveled through the stage and on [to] the other side; it lifted up the violins — it actually made their chairs bounce. I was completely smitten with the sound of it."[6]

Over the next five years while living in Hawaii, McNalley built a contrabass violin himself and began consulting with Hutchins over the phone. Upon his return from Hawaii, McNalley kept thinking about the Hutchins bass and the violin octet. When he learned that Hutchins had a complete octet at 112 Essex, McNalley began to work out a two-year plan to purchase the set. The next day he was at a recording session with two other players and found that both Igor Tchetchko and Omar Firestone were both very interested. McNalley recalled: "Within just two days, I had four of the best players in southern California interested in the octet. The stars aligned. I thought it would be two years planning, and instead it was just two months!"[7]

A few weeks later, on December 28, 1998, Joe McNalley took the plunge and wrote directly to "Dr. Hutchins." Three days later, Hutchins responded: "How serious are you in [obtaining] an octet? With the exception of the large bass, I could send you instruments from here."[8] A week later in early January 1999, McNalley wrote to Hutchins: "Things are moving along much faster (and better) than I dared imagine. I am meeting with some potential donors already this evening, with more to follow."[9] Within just three weeks, McNalley had raised $20,000 — primarily through contacts and sponsorship of his mother, Sharon McNalley — and was ready to receive an octet. McNalley wrote to Hutchins: "How soon can we get them sent? I am really amazed at how quickly this turned from an idea to a bona-fide reality."[10]

On February 8, McNalley wrote Hutchins a formal letter of intent accompanied by a $5,000 deposit toward the $80,000 purchase price with the understanding that seven violins would be sent immediately. The contrabass violin to join that octet was still on the bench and would be finished within the year.[11] The agreement was formulated in extremely simple, straightforward language — as close to a simple handshake as either could muster, a fact that directly reflected the character of Hutchins and McNalley. They had not even met in person, and yet McNalley had already committed himself to purchasing the octet, largely on the basis of his memory of the contrabass he had played a decade before. The fact that he chose to name his ensemble after Hutchins also spoke broadly about McNalley. He was a no-nonsense, passionate professional who believed in giving credit where credit was due. The whole agreement had flown together so quickly; he and Hutchins were reeling from the momentum. In late March 1999, the sale of the first Hutchins Violin Octet to a professional ensemble took place — the first performing American octet![12]

Joe McNalley immediately flew to New Jersey and picked up seven of the eight instruments at 112 Essex Avenue. The California octet instrument set consisted of Treble SUS #302, Soprano SUS #310, Mezzo SUS #107, Alto SUS #144, Tenor SUS #193, Baritone SUS #166, and Small Bass SUS #326. As big bass was not yet ready, McNalley wrote to André Larson at the National Music Museum in South Dakota to ask to borrow the big bass in its collection.[13]

On May 14, 1999, Sharon McNalley wrote to Hutchins: "Things are going well for the 'Hutchins Consort.' Lots to do . . . enthusiasm . . . is high. . . . Thank you for your confidence in Joe. We look forward to an exciting future for the Hutchins Consort."[14] A few days later, on May 28, the Hutchins Consort presented its first concert to a masters' recital audience in Erickson Hall at the University of California, San Diego. The second concert, on June 19, was a "musicale" concert held at the Center Club in Costa Mesa. Then on November 13, 1999, Dr. and Mrs. Michael McNalley, Joe's parents, presented a "Seaside Musicale" at a private home, to introduce the Hutchins Consort to its new Hutchins Consort Board members and local supporters.

The January 18, 2000, "world debut" inaugural concert at the Barclay Theater, in Irvine, was actually the fourth concert for the Hutchins Consort but the first one that Hutchins would witness. At the closing performance of Samuel Barber's Adagio for Strings, the audience gave a standing ovation. To mark its debut year, between June 11 and 23, the Hutchins Consort toured Italy, where it presented concerts in the Villa Toronia in Rome, the Vatican's Aula Magna Pontificale; and the Oratorio dei Vanchetoni and the Convento di San Jacopo Soprarno, both in Florence.

One highlight of the 2002 season was an April concert at the Lied Center in Lawrence, Kansas. Then on May 12, the Hutchins Consort performed an afternoon concert in the Grace Rainey Rogers Auditorium at the Metropolitan Museum of Art, to coincide with the opening of new exhibit featuring the octet in the André Mertens Galleries for Musical Instruments.

On September 20, 2003, the Hutchins Consort traveled to Wolfeboro, New Hampshire, to perform a concert in Carleen's hometown. It was a blisteringly hot and humid Indian summer afternoon in the All Saints Episcopal Church on Main Street, but the Hutchins Consort did not seem to mind the ninety-degree heat. At least five hundred people had packed the house for the sold-out concert. People were seated in the aisles, choir loft, and lobby and on the lawn outside, where another one hundred were listening through open windows. The concert was so packed that when eight violinmaking students from Boston's North Bennett Street School arrived, McNalley seated them on the stage behind the performers. Carleen and Morton Hutchins were seated in the front row.

Dr. Paul R. Laird of the University of Kansas — who had written a biographical monograph on Hutchins — spoke on the history of the new family of violins. McNalley recalled: "Paul Laird gave a really impassioned speech on how the Consort was the future of the NVFA; I had no idea how prescient he really was at that point. He offended a lot of the luthiers by saying that the NVFA should throw all of its backing behind the Consort — but he was entirely right."[15]

Coda

Concluding segment of the entire fugue

Timothy A. Smith, "Anatomy of a Fugue"

21 *Fiddles on the Marquee*

RETURNING TO ITHACA

Carleen had come full circle since her days at Cornell. The marquee above the entrance to the State Theater in downtown Ithaca read: "New Violin Family Association Nov. 2." It had been seventy-five years since she ventured to Ithaca as a Cornell freshman and later began helping Dr. Allen record birdsong in Sapsucker Woods, and sixty years since she carved her first viola. Now her violin octet was up on the marquee. It announced "Octet 2005: October 31 to November 2," the three-day symposium sponsored by the ASA and the NVFA held at the Ithaca Holiday Inn, paying tribute to Carleen Hutchins and her violin octet. Carleen would have loved to see the marquee and witness the workshops, technical sessions, and concerts. But owing to a fall just days before the event, she was unable to attend.

The musical highlights of the symposium included concerts performed by various members of the Hutchins Consort and other musicians who, through the patronage of Hutchins, had been performing on Hutchins instruments for some years, instruments that were either on loan, purchased, or given as gifts. On Sunday evening, October 30, the Hutchins Consort bass violinist and composer-in-residence Frederick Charlton and pianist Irena Tchetchko performed a recital featuring some of Charlton's own compositions. Monday evening performances included a world premiere treble violin duet of a movement from Bach's Concerto for Two Violins in D Minor, featuring Grigori Sedukh and Chien Tan, the Portland Symphony principal second violin, who had purchased a treble violin from Hutchins in 2003.[1] Sera Jane Smolen performed on the tenor violin with pianist Diane Birr, followed by the celebrated improvisational violinist Stephen Nachmanovitch, who performed on the mezzo violin. Nachmanovitch, who plays both acoustic and electric violin and viola, said that the Hutchins mezzo violin has "a throatier, richer, and more powerful sound than a conventional violin. Listeners remark that the sound source seems to be not the instrument, but the entire room."[2]

Tuesday night concerts featured Diana Gannett, a University of Michigan professor in bass, performing on the original Hutchins/Blatter small bass; Chien Tan, treble violin; Carrie Hummel, soprano violin. The baritone violinist Akua Dixon and her husband, the well-known jazz trombonist Steve Turre, longtime neighbors of the Hutchinses in Montclair, performed a duet. Dixon said of the baritone loaned to her by Hutchins: "It was not until I acquired the baritone that I could perform with my husband without amplification, since it would be nearly impossible for a standard cello to hold its own in a duet with a brass instrument."[3] In and around these three concerts, more than one hundred NVFA enthusiasts attended Octet 2005.

Five technical papers were presented in the general session: Tom King, on the Cremonese method for f-hole placement; Steve Sirr presented John Waddle's paper on CT-scanned instruments; Edwin Fitzgerald on the effects of coumarin on the aging process of spruce; Duane Voskuil on harmonic reinforcement in the octet violins; and Steve Nachmanovitch presented a session about improvisation.

The greatest surprise at the noon NVFA board meeting was the extensive "pie-in-the-sky" list of ideas offered by Carleen, in absentia. Even at age ninety-six, Carleen was pitching ideas for the future—no matter how far-fetched they might seem: (1) Violinmaking at Taylor Road—a school? Training? (2) Shrine to Music Museum—its role? (3) Queen Elizabeth Competition in two years? (4) Brussels Museum in 2008. (5) Violin Octet centers—in Europe? (6) Send an octet back to St. Petersburg.[4]

The culminating concert for Octet 2005 took place on November 2—a double-violin-octet-plus-fiddles concert featuring an ensemble that Bob Spear named the "Tallis Orchestra." For the past year, Bob Spear had devoted his entire life to organizing and pulling off Octet 2005. And he had done so against all odds. Within the past year, though the New Violin Family Association was essentially a brand new organization, it had just lost its second chief operating officer in R. J. Miller as a result of a freak accident resulting in extended hospitalization. Miller had been instrumental in helping the New Violin Family Association through its difficult transition period from 2001 to 2004. Now he was gone.

Nevertheless, Spear held to his plan—and managed to stick his neck out artistically as well. In addition to all of his other tasks related to Octet 2005, Spear orchestrated Vaughan Williams's *Fantasia on a Theme of Thomas Tallis,* scored in twenty-one parts so that it could feature a small orchestra of violin octet players in three groups—large orchestra (Hutchins Consort plus octet violin players); a smaller "echo" orchestra (Albert Consort); and a quintet composed of octet violin soloists.[5] It had all seemed like a great idea—until the morning of November 2, when Spear witnessed the rehearsal of the Tallis Orchestra—the largest violin octet group ever to gather together. Spear recalled: "It just hit me all at once that all the elements for a disaster were firmly in place."[6] Spear had twenty-three players who had never played together before, more than a few musicians who were new to their instruments, unusual seating, a new conductor, a complex piece, and only two ninety-minute rehearsals to get it ready. Spear recalled: "It occurred to me that the quality of our playing for one hour might define octet instruments for the next ten years. We were betting the New Violin Family Association on this single piece of music. What had I been thinking?"[7]

Just before the finale concert, all the musicians and audience gathered together on stage to pay a video tribute to Hutchins. In that moment on screen, as she thanked Bob Spear and all the performers, Carleen was more emotional than anyone who knew her had ever seen. Minutes later, the finale concert took place in the State Theater in Ithaca. As conductor Ubaldo Valli gave the downbeat for the standing-room-only turnout, the concert began with the first few tranquil measures of the piece that seemed to "float into the hall." The alto violinist Jamie Kibelsbeck said: "I had the most amazing experience. . . . The chords in the first two measures of the piece were so beautiful that I felt as if I were floating out of my chair."[8] One of the most telling comments came from Alfred B. Grunwell, a recording engineer who witnessed the concert: "I've been a recording engineer my entire adult life and never heard strings with such power. I kept going to the front . . . to check microphones. I was sure I'd put them in the wrong place. The sound I heard in my headphones was what I heard myself when I got closer. The intensity was unbelievable."[9]

Two days after the conference, on November 4, Grigori Sedukh gave a special solo performance of the his Octet 2005 repertoire in the André Mertens Galleries for Musical Instruments of the Metropolitan Museum of Art to an enthusiastic audience of more than one hundred people. Joe Peknik recalled this concert: "I particularly remember when Grisha picked up the mezzo violin and played 'Kamarinskaya' only using pizzicato, the pizzicato filled the galleries. I was standing in the back of the audience and fifty or sixty feet away from Grisha and I heard the pizzicato as if it were right in front of me. . . . The De Beriot violin concerto, with its trick bowing and double and triple stops, ended on a high note that, had I been sitting closer, would have shattered my glasses. It was so high, just within audible range — absolutely astounding. To hear all that music coming out of that violin was just phenomenal."[10]

A year later, the Hutchins Consort brought down the house in the first concert it presented to the Guild of American Luthiers, at Pacific Lutheran University in Tacoma, Washington, June 21–25, 2006.[11] What had Tim Olsen, the founder of the Guild of American Luthiers, an organization of 3,500 guitar makers, been thinking by inviting eight violinists to his convention? Olsen remarked: "What was I thinking? I was thinking this was a great opportunity!" The crowd at Lagerquist Recital Hall gave a standing ovation to the Hutchins Consort, followed by an encore performance of *Ozark Swamp Gas*, composed and performed by the bassist Fred Charlton. One audience member said: "Any time a group of violinists gets a standing ovation from over 300 guitar makers, it's a real accomplishment."[12] Olsen continued: "I think that the standing ovation meant a lot of things: respect for Carleen and the NVFA, honoring the sheer lutherie achievement of one person building a complete octet . . . the skill and intensity of the musicians, the success of the arrangements in demonstrating the unique voice of the octet, and the success of the octet in extending the voice of the violin across the entire musical range."[13]

On May 31, 2007, a small birthday party was held a few days late to celebrate Carleen's ninety-sixth birthday. The newsletter reported optimistically that Hutchins had taken on teaching violinmaking and plate-tuning to a few students on Monday afternoons. In reality, things were not as rosy as Bob Spear was kind enough to make it sound. Carleen was increasingly in pain, spent more time in her chair, and was less connected to the world around her — except for her cloistered world of fiddles. Obsessed with her own legacy, Carleen failed to see how isolated she was and how blind she had become to the needs of others. By November 2007, her health was so uncertain that the NVFA Board meeting moved its meeting at the last moment down the street to the Wolfeboro Inn. As of 2007, NVFA had just 109 paid members. No projects could be planned because there was no money.

Despite interest in the violin octet from the likes of the Peabody Quartet, NVFA had no finished instruments to loan.

On numerous occasions during the last decade of Carleen's life, Joris Wouters, Carleen's last student, who also made the first Belgian violin octet, made the trip from Belgium to visit her at 112 Essex and over the last seven years, at 42 Taylor Drive. On September 18, 2007, Wouters drove Hutchins out to see the cabin.[14] They sat in the sun outside and enjoyed a toast of the scotch that Carleen kept in the wooden silverware drawer by the back door. Afterward, she asked Joris to drive her to the Tuftonboro Town Hall cemetery, as she wanted to show him something on the Hutchins headstone. To the great surprise of Joris, a new one-line inscription (in capital letters) had been added on the back of the gravestone, below Carleen's name: "SHE DEVELOPED THE NEW VIOLIN OCTET WITH HER HUSBAND'S SUPPORT."

Even in honoring her husband, Carleen had placed her own stamp on a stone that was meant to honor them both — as husband and wife. What's more, the fact that she wanted one of her closest companions at that point — her last student — to see the stone of which she was evidently so proud — made the moment even more awkward. But that was not the half of it. Carleen then got out of the car to walk around the stone to show Wouters the other (front) side of the stone on which was carved the family name in massive letters: HUTCHINS. Below those letters was a life-size, carved-in-granite relief of a treble violin! Wouters was spellbound, silent. As they got back in the car and pulled away, Carleen made her parting comment — not to Joris or to Mort but to the stonecutters: "The pegs are too close — you can't turn them!"

Carleen Maley Hutchins died on Friday morning, August 7, 2009.

Finale ∫ *Counterpoint*

One human being in a thousand . . . is passionately interested in his job for the job's sake. The difference is that if that person in a thousand is a man, we say, simply, that he is passionately keen on his job; if she is a woman, we say she is a freak.

—Dorothy Sayers, *Gaudy Night*, 1935

The most impressive and yet least known monument of national significance sits on a hillside in Rindge, New Hampshire. This special place is the Cathedral of the Pines, and most everyone knows it because it is the site of the Altar of the Nation, a fieldstone and medal-encrusted altar that overlooks Mount Monadnock, paying tribute to all American war dead. But most everyone—male or female—cannot tell you about the other monument on the same site—a fifty-five-foot bell tower that is the only monument dedicated to all women who gave their lives for their country.

The bell tower is ten times bigger than the Altar of the Nation, and visitors have to walk right by it in order to see the altar—yet most people do not know what they are passing by. On each face of the fieldstone tower, halfway to the sky, hang four different bronze relief portraits designed by Norman Rockwell. Each is dedicated to a different population of women—the pioneer woman, a rifle in her hand and a child at her knee; Clara Barton and the nurses; the women in uniform; and all of the "other" women—a journalist, a Sister of Charity nun, a USO entertainer, and Rosie the Riveter. The bell tower is the most hidden of national monuments—yet it is invisible in plain sight. It is also a symbol for the anonymity and invisibility of women since the beginning of time.

Anonymity takes many forms. On the evening of February 23, 2008, in a concert held in Carlsbad, California, at the National Association of Music Merchants headquarters, three violinists, three cellists, and two bassists upstaged the renowned virtuoso Anne Akiko Meyers. This concert celebrated the opening of a special NAMM exhibition, *The Violin in America: Old World Tradition, New World Sound*, that examined "the immigration and innovation of the violin." The voluminous and variegated sounds emanating from each violin in this new kind of chamber music caused listeners to marvel. That night, the impression left by the Hutchins Consort hovered in the room — and all throughout the performance of Anne Akiko Meyers that followed. There was nothing Meyers — or any virtuoso soloist — could do about it. This was the last word, the word left by the players and the fiddles themselves, despite the glaring, blatant omissions all around them.

The major portion of the special exhibition was housed in the Henry Z. Steinway Gallery. An opening statement listed members of the "new generation" of American luthiers on the "leading edge" of their craft: Carl Becker, David Burgess, David Gusset, and more recently, Joseph Curtin, Greg Alf, Guy Rabut, and Samuel Zygmuntowicz. Another portion of the exhibition featured the theme of "American Ingenuity." Within this field, another roster of names appeared under the category "Top U.S. Makers." This list, according to the Amati Foundation, included Greg Alf, David Burgess, Joseph Curtin, Christopher Germain, Joe Grubaugh, and Philip Injeian.

Most curious was the fact that in both exhibits, the name of Carleen Hutchins appeared nowhere on these two rosters even though her new violin family was being featured in a concert in the same setting, and her experimental graphite-epoxy and "Swiss Cheese" fiddles were included in the exhibit. Was she not on the leading edge of nearly everything in violin acoustics for fifty years? Did she not publish the two *Scientific American* articles that have influenced the field more than any other? Did she not edit the two voluminous two-volume sets of papers devoted to violin acoustics? Did she not teach her own plate-tuning methods to Joseph Curtin and Greg Alf?

The afternoon pre-concert panel discussion accompanying this exhibition was perhaps most surprising of all. Moderator David Lusterman, the publisher of *Acoustic Guitar* and *Strings*, introduced three men sitting on stage: Bill Townsend, the founder of the Amati Foundation; the bow maker Benoît Rolland; and Joseph Curtin, the violinmaker who had been awarded a 2005 MacArthur "Genius" fellowship. Curtin, the first luthier ever to win a MacArthur fellowship would seem to be a good choice for a panelist charged to speak about innovation in violinmaking. MacArthur Fellows are generally awarded to talented individuals who have shown extraordinary originality and dedication in their creative pursuits. But the facts beg to differ. Curtin did not begin making violins until 1977, and for two decades he copied Cremonese instruments almost exclusively. By his own admission, he did not begin to explore innovations in violinmaking until 1985.

What was most strange was that even though Curtin was charged to speak on the topic of innovation in violinmaking in connection with this special exhibition, he seemed to dance around the subject. Curtin talked about aesthetics, corners, art deco and minimalistic styles, carving a scroll in the shape of an angel's head, how one could create a violin from six hundred different pieces of wood, and then pointed out the different-sized sound holes in one of his violins. He discussed everything under the sun *except* Carleen Hutchins. Curtin did not bring up violin acoustics, the Catgut Acoustical Society, the violin octet, the "Swiss Cheese" or the graphite fiddle. Though he had been given the podium to talk about American innovation in violinmaking, the fact that Joseph Curtin chose to omit Hutchins, speaks volumes.

The point is that if Hutchins had been a man, she most likely would have been included in these rosters. None of the above-mentioned makers did anything except make violins. Not only did Hutchins do more than any other luthier to develop her field, she single-handedly changed the paradigm from one of secrecy to one of an open forum — thereby revolutionizing the entire international violinmaking world. At the close of this NAMM concert featuring the Hutchins Consort, Sharon McNalley revealed the elephant in the room when she asked: "Why did no one talk about Carleen?" In summing up his own experience thus far with the Hutchins Consort, founder Joe McNalley is philosophical and forever optimistic: "First they ignore you, then they fight you, then they hate you — then you win!"

Carleen Maley Hutchins devoted her life to exploring the riddle of the fiddle. But she also lived the riddle of woman's life, the life of a woman interested in more than the invisible women's work of "dishes, diapers, and spinach," as her husband said to her before she made her first viola. Why does a woman seek to escape the tedium? Women's work has traditionally been, by its very nature, repetitive and monotonous. Though it was as necessary and crucial for the survival of the culture as that of the male hunter or gatherer, still, it was invisible — not valued in the same way as men's work. But unlike her male counterparts who have access to visible paths reinforced by traditional roles publicly valued by society, mentors to emulate, and a community to reinforce belonging, women have historically been overlooked or excluded in so many realms of society. This was and is especially true of women interested in science, but most notoriously, the discipline of physics —where women have had no paths to follow, no predecessors, and no mentors. And instead of paths, women have faced walls to climb, and confining boxes from which they are perpetually trying to escape.

The violin world—with its makers, dealers, and collectors—has been a male-dominated world since Amati perfected the form in the late 1500s. The fact that Carleen Hutchins was awarded the highest honor of the Acoustical Society of America should be viewed in light of the fact that physics is the branch of Western science that has, since its very inception, consistently denied women access, credit, and privilege. The practice continues to this day, according to female physicists who gathered in Waterloo, Canada, for the 2014 International Conference on Women in Physics. In her article "Female Physicists Worldwide Fight Sexist Stereotypes," in the September 3, 2014, issue of *Scientific American*, Clara Moskowitz writes: "Despite cultural and geographic divides separating the home countries of many of the women, their stories are remarkably similar. A woman from Burkina Faso used nearly the same words as another from Peru to describe the cultural perception that 'physics is not the domain of women—it's for men,' as University of Ouagadougou physicist Petronille Kafando put it."[1]

Violinmaking and the violin world are based on a very similar male-dominated lineage. In my travels researching this craft, I kept coming across a reference to a female violinmaker in a book by Cyprien Desmarais titled *Archéologie du violon*, published in Paris in 1836. But every time I found it listed in a card catalogue and I went to the shelves to pick it up, the book was always missing. I was beginning to feel as if someone did not want me to find this book. I finally found it at the Library of Congress, where I gained access only through the surreptitious good graces of an unnamed female librarian who, upon hearing my tale of woe, broke all the rules about a book of this age and photocopied it for me. Cyprien Desmarais wrote of her:

> Florentine Demoliens, wife of Georges Chanot, is the author of two other violins, equally extraordinarily beautiful. The first one she ever made represented one of the products of French industry in 1827. This violin was greatly admired by both musicians and amateurs; however, the exhibition jury was not enthusiastic. One must conclude, in order to be fair

> to everyone, that the jury's admiration was paralyzed by the strangeness of the fact, and that they preferred not to believe, that this masterpiece of violinmaking was the work of a woman rather than award her the prize. A distinguished stringed instrument maker from Paris bought it from Mrs. Chanot for a great deal of money.
>
> The second violin made by Mrs. Chanot was created at the request of an Englishman, M. Carleton, distinguished amateur player of the cello and whose sons were pupils of M. Cartier.
>
> She presented her third violin in tribute to the very same M.J.B. Cartier, a pupil of Viotti, author of *The Art of the Violin*, as well as a history of this instrument. This same violin is the one on which M. Cartier engraved the historic drawing, designed by him, and which he thus named "the historic and monumental violin."[2]

The violin continues to be its own conundrum — for many reasons, beginning with its enigmatic and rather mysterious anatomy. Unlike the guitar, with its clear-cut borders; unambiguous planes for top, back, and sides; and long straight, essentially flat neck, the violin is nothing of the sort. There are neither straight lines nor flat surfaces anywhere in the fiddle — it consists instead of archings, protruding C-bouts, serpentine curves of the f-holes, overlapping edges, flutings, the curve of the neck, and the spirals of the scroll.[3] Likewise, there is nothing logical, linear, predictable, or straightforward about life, especially the life of a woman balancing a passion or a career with mothering. However good or bad she was at that balance, throughout most of history, she has been held to a different standard than her male peers — or simply held back.

Hutchins was a most contradictory figure. Open to discussing violins with any stranger who might knock on her door, she was closed about her own life, her family, and her feelings. She applied an essentially feminine, noncompetitive paradigm to a largely secretive, competitive world, encouraging communication and the sharing of ideas, yet had trouble applying the same openness outside the realm of her work and its community. She kept her eyes on her violins and the violin world, while turning away from the realization that the fiddles had overtaken the house, forever alienating two children who never knew life without violins hanging in every nook and cranny of their home at 112 Essex Avenue.

First and foremost, Hutchins was drawn to the music, to the immediate experience of chamber music. Catherine Bowen wrote of the mysterious power of music: "Music has been called the most abstract, the 'purest' of the arts. And yet, of all the arts music is, in a sense, the quickest to reach the centre; its very purity, its disinterestedness, its brave quality of belonging to no man, give to it this privilege. A Beethoven sonata has no axe to grind. Like lightning, music strikes through to the heart, having no delay of words, no slow intermediary of language or of those pictorial symbols that travel home through the eye. Impudent futility, to endeavor to translate music into color or poetry or any dimension but its own!"[4]

In his book *Music of Silence*, the Catholic Benedictine monk David Steindl-Rast describes vespers, the hour when day is turning into night, as the hour that "invites peace of heart, which is the reconciling of contradictions within ourselves and around us." Paraphrasing a poem from Rilke in *The Book of Hours*, Steindl-Rast writes: "Whoever gathers his life's many contradictions into one, gratefully makes of them a single symbol, expels all the noisy ones from his palace and becomes in a new way festive."[5]

In the vespers of our lives, how do we make sense of our own contradictions? In a park in Martigny, Switzerland, there is an outdoor sculpture by Arman (born Armand Fernandez, 1928–2005) called *Contrepoint pour violoncelles* that looks like a totem pole of violin parts—a visual synecdoche for the life and work of Carleen Hutchins. For Hutchins, the fiddle was totem, talisman, and temple. As does Arman's tower of fiddle parts, Carleen took apart the violin and the violin world, one assumption at a time. In the process, she improvised how to make the parts fit, reassembling the personal parts in a way that would allow her to fit her passion into her life and bring life to her passion.

If the violin itself might be likened to represent the violin world, then of its eighty-one individual parts, Carleen Hutchins might best be likened to the sound post.

The sound post is a piece of wood inserted inside the cavity of the finished violin.

An outsider, Hutchins inserted herself into the violin world because she was curious, forging ahead with the unpredictable genius of the untrained mind.

The sound post spans the inside of the fiddle, touching top and back plates.

Hutchins touched the entire, interior box of the violin world—from making a better fiddle and building an international community to inventing a new family of violins.

The sound post is not glued, but stays in place through friction.

Hutchins faced the tensions of the violin world, firmly wedged between luthiers and players who resented science and scientists who applauded her drive and dedication.

The sound post needs very little room to move from side to side.

Hutchins required very little wiggle room. She started carving fiddles in her kitchen, created an acoustical laboratory in her basement, taught students in her garage, and made contrabasses—with the help of colleagues and students—that were bigger than she was.

The sound post sits to one side, creating an essential imbalance inside the fiddle.

Ever the outsider in three male-dominated fields, Hutchins entered only through the doors that were open to her. She caught the violin world off guard, and forever kept it off-balance.

The sound post reduces locally the canceling motion of the top plate.

Through experimentation and sharing knowledge, Hutchins reduced the canceling motion—the paralysis—rampant in a world that had ossified around repetition and copying.

The sound post transfers vibrations from the top plate to the back plate.

Hutchins was the conduit between the art and science of how to make a better fiddle, merging the worlds of acoustical physics with violinmaking.

The sound post is the smallest, most significant, most invisible part of the fiddle.

Carleen Hutchins is as visible or invisible as those who know her want to acknowledge. Some luthiers who know of her choose to write her out of the violin story. She remains invisible to most outside the violin world.

To add to the enigma, the sound post and the violin are both made from a non-uniform material. There is nothing logical, linear, predictable, or straightforward about wood—each piece is different, even if two adjacent pieces are cut from the very same log. In a world in which the latest technology can "print" a violin three-dimensionally using a EOS laser-sintering 3D printer ("and it plays beautifully"), according to the cover article of a 2009 issue of the *Economist*, the idea of a violin still made of wood may seem romantic indeed. The spruce for the top is selected for its audible ring; the maple for the back for its curl and density. Niccolò Paganini once said that Stradivari "used only the wood of trees in which nightingales sang."[6]

How to plant the "fiddle tree"? On July 15, 1900, the *Violin Times* reported: "About fifty years ago, a man in Newport, NH, planted the cones of a fiddle spruce in a nursery, hoping, as he said, 'to raise his own fiddles.' They grew well, but out of over 200 seedlings, there was not a single tree fit to make into violins."[7]

In April 2013, the BBC reporter John Laurenson told the story of the Swiss "master tree picker" Lorenzo Pellegrini, who has the ability to find the one spruce in ten thousand that is just right. "He will find you the 'Stradivarius tree.' Slowly, slowly, slowly—that's how violin trees should grow," he says. "Up in these mountains, they grow so slowly sometimes they stop growing altogether. They just gather strength. There are trees here that are a thousand years old." Laurenson reports the rest of the story:

> Pellegrini has been working in the forest since he was nine. Growing up in Italy's Abruzzo mountains, he and his family would go deep into the woods each year, hours and hours from the nearest village, build a cabin to live in and stay there for eight months, cutting down trees, chopping up logs. . . . Now 83, he still climbs trees like a squirrel, and tends the forest as if it were his garden—weeding out the beech trees that would smother his precious spruces.
>
> "For the trees to grow slowly and regularly, you have to let them grow close together like the hair on your head," he says. "And there should not be too much water. The tree's heart should stay dry. That gives the best wood. Solid. Enormous resonance."
>
> Pellegrini "gardens" the forest, as he puts it. But he gardens for people who will not be born for hundreds of years. So that there will be fine resonance spruce in the 24th century. Once you have found the perfect tree, he says, you have to wait for the perfect day to cut it down. The day comes at the end of autumn when the sap has sunk back into the ground. When the moon is lowest on the horizon, and furthest from the Earth. Because, apparently, the gravitational pull of the moon does not only tug the waters of the sea and make tides, it tugs up the sap. . . .
>
> "Put your finger on one ring—that is the British army going over the

top at Ypres. On another, that is Louis XIV building Versailles; this one takes you back to the Pilgrim Fathers."

To demonstrate the wood's acoustic qualities, he takes out a little musical box. He winds it up and it tinkles. He places the tinkling box on that strip of wood and the tune suddenly fills the room. Not only much, much louder, but warm and full. . . .

We walk through the village to meet one of the many musicians of the Risoud Forest . . . David Guignard takes out his cello and plays a bit of Bach. . . . Guignard's music teacher taught him that wood is never quite dead. It is always reacting to changes in temperature and humidity, always evolving.

I listen to the crackle of the fire and the sound of the cello strings making the wood sing. And I think I will never quite hear this music in the same way again.

Because around here, when you hear an instrument like this, you think of the snow and the wind and the cuckoos and the bees in those tall violin trees.[8]

Soundpost

Just a small, sturdy, dense column of wood
that does little more than hold up the world.
Unlikely conduit wedged to edges
of carved spruce and maple, this upright post
holds the space between as if sacred.
Wedged not glued in place, a channel for sound
between opposites, top and back held at bay,
connecting nothingness to form a whole,
allowing air currents to swirl inside,
maintaining the ribs of separation.
A conduit, a short circuit between
rocking bridge and box, it amplifies sound
of bow on string, thus keeping the fiddle
from caving in on itself, air snuffed out
from the sheer force of the bow on the strings.
A minute, invisible inch of wood,
the part of the fiddle hidden from view,
except for those who know to look for it—
maker, player, dealer, or collector—
seeking to adjust the sound with the key,
a vertical post, tall talisman held still
by friction. Without it, the violin
mimics a guitar. The space between
matters most for the conduit across
time and space, between science and art,
linking the two across the great divide,
building a bridge where there had been a wall.
Wedged between two worlds, yet glued to neither,
still able to move, to change position,
jockey for space or make an adjustment.
One tiny move can make the most difference,
the space between a hush or rush of wind,
a single post poised in the space between,
finding the perfect resting place somewhere
inside the crevice that cradles the sound.

QUINCY WHITNEY

Acknowledgments

If it takes a village to raise a child, it takes a city or country to raise a biography.

First, I thank John Burke and Janet Insolia of the *Boston Globe New Hampshire Weekly* for the challenge of the blank page and for hiring me as a cultural news reporter, and then I express gratitude to Barbara Hobbie for giving me a lead about a violinmaker in a cabin on Lake Winnipesaukee.

This book would never have reached completion—or even have gotten off the ground—if not for the Musical Instruments Department of the Metropolitan Museum of Art, where I had the incredible good fortune to be a research fellow from 2004 to 2006. I am especially grateful to Marcie Karp, director of the Fellowships Program, for inviting me to apply when I was a most unlikely candidate. I am forever indebted to and grateful for my friends at the Met—J. Kenneth Moore, Frederick P. Rose curator in charge; Jayson Kerr Dobney, associate curator and administrator; E. Bradley Strauchen-Scherer, associate curator; Marian Eines, associate for administration; Joseph Peknik III, principal departmental technician; musical instruments conservator Stewart Pollens; Sally B. Brown, great-granddaughter of Mary Elizabeth Adams Brown, founder of the Crosby Brown Collection of Musical Instruments; and musicologist Alicja Knast—for encouraging me in times of doubt.

During August 2004, I traveled to Europe and interviewed twenty-five people in nine countries. In England, I thank Roderick Skeaping, a composer and musician; Michael McIntrye, a physicist-musician; the physicist-luthier James Woodhouse; the sound engineer Peter Fellgett; and the luthiers Julian Emery and Juliet Barker. At Pigotts Music Camp, I thank Nick Robinson for sharing his memories of his father Bernard Robinson.

In Oxford, I thank Jon Whiteley, honorary curator at the Ashmolean Museum; and in the English countryside, the Robert Frost scholar Linda Hart. In the tiny hamlet of Clifford Chambers, outside of Stratford-upon-Avon, I thank Sarah Hosking, the founder of Hosking Houses Trust, a unique and splendid trust dedicated to offering paid residency fellowships for accomplished women writers and artists. In Scotland, I thank Arnold Myers, director of the Edinburgh University Collection of Historic Musical Instruments.

In Belgium, I thank the luthier Joris Wouters; in Paris, Thierry Maniguet, Musée de la Musique; in Nancy, France, the forester and ultrasonic wood expert Voichita Bucur; in Lausanne, Switzerland, friends Anne-Tillie and Jean Sahli; in Genoa, Italy, the luthier Pio Montanari and his wife, Annatello, for her kind translations; in Cremona, Italy, the luthiers Lorenzo and Kathryn Cassi; and Francesco Bissolotti.

In Germany I would like to thank Frieder Eggers in Göttingen; in Munich, Helmut Müller and Paul Geissler; in Braunschweig, Jürgen and Ingeborg Meyer; and in Wolfenbüttel, Theodore Thiel. In Sweden, at KTH, I thank the physicists Eric Jansson, Johann Sundberg, and Anders Askenfeld; Hans Astrand at the Royal Swedish Academy; Hans Riben at Musikmuseet; the violin expert John Huber; and the Stockholm Symphony players Semmy and Kristine Lazaroff.

At the National Music Museum, Vermillion, South Dakota, I thank André Larson, the former museum director; Margaret Downie Banks, associate director; and Arian Sheets, curator of stringed instruments. At the Center for Computer Research in Musical Acoustics at Stanford University, I thank Max Matthews.

I am most grateful to Robert and Carolyn Schumacher, whose early interviews allowed me access to those people close to Carleen who had already died—Harriet Bartlett, Bernard Robinson, Helen Rice, Robert Fryxell. At Brearley, I thank former headmistress Evelyn Halpert and violist Kitty Benton. I give very special thanks to the Montclair artist Edith Munro for her careful diligence in the digitization of the Hutchins photograph archives.

Among the associates in Montclair and in the Catgut Acoustical Society, I thank CAS Secretary Elizabeth McGilvray; Joan Miller ; Virginia Benade; luthier Carolyn Field; Norman Pickering; cellist Akua Dixon; bassist Diana Gannett; composer Lawrence Rackley Smith; cellist Barbara Hendrian; cellists Michael Finckel, Chris Finckel, David Finckel, and Anne Cole; bassist Ronald Naspo; Dr. Victor Parsonnet; neighbors and friends Edith Munro and Charlie Rooney; Lowell Creitz; Leon Hoffman; Joseph Curtin; Portland Symphony violist Jean Alvord; luthiers Tom Knatt and Alan Carruth; and Syoko Erle at Yale.

In California, with the Hutchins Consort, I am most grateful to Joe McNalley, Sharon McNalley, and Alma Vanasse; to Geoff Gartner, baritone; Omar Firestone, tenor; Beth Folsom, soprano; Fred Charlton, small bass; Nathan Schmidt, mezzo; Carolyn Lechusza Aquallo, alto; Andrea Altona, treble; Grigori Sedukh, treble; Steve Nachmanovitch, mezzo; and Carolyn Grant, executive director of the Museum of Making Music in Carlsbad, California.

At Octet 2005, I was fortunate to interview Paul Laird; Oliver Rogers; Duane Voskuil and Joe Conrad, and later celebrated bassist Bert Turetzky.

In October 2006, I attended the Salzburg seminar "The Telling of Lives: Biography as a Mirror on Society." I thank the stellar cast of presenters, a virtual who's who in biography, led by Marc Pachter, former director of the Smithsonian's National Portrait Gallery; James Atlas; Anthony Palliser; Renée Poussaint; Claire Tomalin; and Vikram Seth.

I am deeply grateful to Marina Markot for illuminating the Russian octet story. I thank Bob Spear for his dedication and details in the NVFA newsletters. I also thank Richard Eckberg for sharing his story.

Thanks also go to a quartet of cellists who recalled Hutchins crashing Piatigorsky's master class — Paul Tobias, Jeffrey Solow, Nathaniel Rosen, and Terry King.

Thanks also to my wonderful ongoing community at Wake Forest University — my mentors and friends Pat Johansson and Ed Wilson; and my classmate and friend Tom Phillips — and my dear friends Nancy Piner and Mary Duffie, who made a silent retreat by the North Carolina coast possible in the depths of a New England winter.

I am so grateful for the original Boston Biographers writing group — Margery Heffron, Melissa Nathanson, and Elizabeth Harris — for sharing in the very personal marathon of writing biography, especially Margery Heffron for her fearless spirit in spearheading the founding of the group. And I thank BIO — Biographers International Organization — for the myriad of ways in which it nurtures the long writing journey. I also thank fellow biographers Pam Blevins and Karen Shaffer for their friendship, understanding, and encouragement.

I thank Yeou-Cheng Ma and Yo-Yo Ma, and the Academy Award–winning filmmaker and cinematographer Cynthia Wade, who is currently creating a documentary on Carleen Hutchins titled *Second Fiddle*.

All research depends on the work of other writers to whom I owe so much — thanks to Thomas Levenson, Victoria Finlay, Catherine Drinker Bowen, Dava Sobel and John Laurenson, among many others and the *New York Times* obituary writer Margalit Fox. Finally, a boatload of thanks to Beth Gianfagna, my copy editor, without whom this book would not have been born.

Above all, I thank my husband, Eli, and Gabe and Meranne who cheered me on every step of the way.

Notes

As biographer, I was fortunate enough to know Carleen Hutchins for twelve years. In that time, and during the huge transition from 112 Essex Avenue, Montclair, NJ, to 42 Taylor Drive, Wolfeboro, NH, Hutchins gave me total access to all the documentation that she had collected — many excerpts of which I copied for my files as reference and here cite as the "Hutchins archives." As such, the Hutchins files refer to a vast collection of documentation, parts of which went to Stanford University, but most of which went to her official archives in the National Music Museum at the University of South Dakota — but not completely and not entirely. That said, because I did not witness this transfer, I do not know exactly what parts of what files in that collection reside in each archives. I welcome the opportunity to pass along my files on Hutchins to the National Music Museum — should that work for the museum.

The definitions of movements of a fugue are reprinted here courtesy of Timothy A. Smith, "Anatomy of a Fugue," http://www2.nau.edu/tas3/fugueanatomy.html.

PRELUDE

1. Thomas Levenson, *Measure for Measure: A Musical History of Science* (New York: Touchstone, 1994), 116–17.

2. Acoustical Society of America, Honorary Fellowship Citation, June 24, 1998 (Melville, NY: American Institute of Physics Publishing, 1998). Used courtesy of the Acoustical Society of America.

1. NATURALIST

1. Carleen Maley Hutchins (CMH), interview by Quincy Whitney (QW), August 15, 2003. All subsequent quotations of Hutchins in this chapter are from this source and numerous other interviews with Hutchins over a period of a decade.

2. Thomas Maley to Board of Directors, Evergreen Cemetery, Hillside, NJ, September 16, 1955, in the records of Evergreen Cemetery.

3. John C. Pallister, *In the Steps of the Great American Entomologist, Frank Eugene Lutz* (Plymouth, UK: M. Evans, 1966; Lanham, MD: Rowman and Littlefield, 2014), 2.

4. *Cornell University Women's Resource Center Handbook*, http://wrc.dos.cornell.edu/aboutus/handbook/chapter_01.html.

5. Quoted in Randolph Scott Little, *For the Birds: Cornell Lab of Ornithology at Sapsucker Woods* (N.p.: Randolph S. Little, 2003), 26, 37.

2. TEACHER

1. I was allowed to view this book just once, when it was in CMH's possession, which is when I copied it. Its current location is unknown.

2. CMH, interview by QW, June 12, 2005. Unless otherwise noted, all subsequent quotations of CMH are from this source.

3. Carleen Maley, journal, August 6, 1939, 37. All subsequent quotations of CMH are from this source. The current location of this personal journal is unknown. My references are from a copy I made, with CMH's permission.

INTERMEZZO: MUSIC

1. Joel DeLisa and Walter C. Stolov, "Significant Body Systems," in *Handbook of Severe Disability*, U.S. Dept. of Education, Rehabilitation Services, 1981, 51–54, http://www.webschoolsolutions.com/patts/ear.htm.

2. Diana Deutsch, "Paradoxes of Musical Pitch," *Scientific American*, August 1992, 88–89.

3. Ibid., 88.

4. Carleen Maley Hutchins, "What Is Sound?," unpublished manuscript, September 1970, 4. My reference is from a copy I made, with CMH's permission.

5. Ibid., 15.

6. Metropolitan Museum of Art, accession number 47.100.1.

7. Liliana Osses Adams, "Sumerian Harps from Ur," *Zwoje* [The scrolls] 2, no. 35 (April–May 2003): http://www.zwoje-scrolls.com/zwoje35/text11p.htm.

8. Thomas Levenson, *Measure for Measure: A Musical History of Science* (New York: Touchstone, 1995), 22–24.

9. Jeffrey S. Cottrel, *A Brief History of the Monochord*, http://www.lowbrassnmore.com/Monochord.htm.

10. A. N. Marlow, "Orpheus in Ancient Literature," *Music and Letters* 35, no. 4 (October 1954): 362–63.

11. James McKinnon, "Jubal ve. Pythagoras, quis sit inventor musicae?," *Musical Quarterly*, 64, no. 1 (January 1978): 9–10.

12. Levenson, *Measure for Measure*, 32–33.

13. Ibid., 33–34.

14. Ibid., 34.

15. Ibid., 34–36.

16. Rev. David Swan, "The Monks of Cluny," Maybole.org, http://www.maybole.org/history/crossraguel/monks.htm.

17. Marie-France Hilgar, "Cluny," *Angelus* 25, no. 12 (December 2002): http://www.sspx.ca/Angelus/2002_december/Cluny.htm.

18. Richard Stapper, "Ecclesiastical Chant and Music," from *Catholic Liturgics*, trans. David Baier (Paterson, NJ: St. Anthony Guild Press, 1935), accessed at The Religious Congregation of Mary Immaculate Queen, http://www.cmri.org/08-ecc_chant_music.html.

19. "The Figure of David in Medieval and Renaissance Art," Jewish Heritage Online Magazine, http://www.jhom.com/topics/david/art.html.

20. Christopher Page, "The Medieval Organistrum and Symphonia, I: Legacy from the East?," *Galpin Society Journal* 35 (March 1982): 39, 41.

21. Franz Montgomery, "The Etymology of the Phrase by Rote," *Modern Language Notes* 46, no. 1 (January 1931): 20.

22. Hilgar, "Cluny."

23. Levenson, *Measure for Measure*, 35–36.

24. Ibid.

25. Meg Bodin, *The Women Troubadours* (New York: W. W. Norton, 1976), 9.

3. VIOLIST

1. *Brearley Bulletin* 14, no. 1 (December 1938): 19.

2. Evelyn Halpert, untitled essay in *The First 125 Years: The Brearley School* (New York: Brearley History Book Committee, 2010), 68.

3. CMH, interview by QW, September 22, 1998. Unless otherwise noted, all subsequent quotations of CMH are from this source.

4. Carleen Maley, journal, July 9, 1939. All subsequent journal quotations are from this source.

5. CMH, interview by QW, September 22, 1998.

6. Millicent Carey McIntosh, quoted in untitled Halpert essay, 64.

7. CMH, interview by QW, June 13, 2005. Unless otherwise noted, all subsequent quotations of CMH are from this source.

8. CMH, interview by Robert T. Schumacher, 1979, tape A, transcription p. 11. These tapes were given to Hutchins after the interviews were conducted, and she shared them with me when I met her in 1997.

9. CMH, interview by QW, June 13, 2005.

10. Carleen Maley, March 1943, 70–71. (The 1938–39 journal contains an additional separate entry for March 1943.)

11. CMH, interview by QW, June 12, 2005.

12. Carleen Maley, journal, March 1943, 72–73.

13. CMH, interview by QW, June 12, 2005.

14. Ibid.

15. Ibid.

16. Carleen Maley Hutchins, “P.S. 33 Man,” *Brearley Bulletin* 19, no. 2 (April 1944): 7–8.

17. CMH, interview by Schumacher, tape A, transcription p. 11.

18. CMH, interview by QW, June 12, 2005.

INTERMEZZO: HISTORY

1. Metropolitan Museum of Art Accession number 53.6a, b, http://www.metmuseum.org/collection/the-collection-online/search/503043, 1.

2. *Maria V. Coldwell, “Jougleresses and Trobairitza: Secular Musicians in Medieval France,” in Women Making Music: The Western Art Tradition, 1150–1950*, ed. Jane Bowers and Judith Tick (Urbana: University of Illinois Press, 1986), 41.

3. Pierre-F. Roberge, “Alfonso X ‘el Sabio’ (1221–1284): A Discography of Attributed Works,” Medieval Music and Arts Foundation, http://www.medieval.org/emfaq/composers/cantigas.html.

4. Roger Edward Blumberg, “Blumberg’s Music Theory: Cipher for Guitar and Other Stringed Instruments,” TheCipher.com, 2002, http://thecipher.com/viola_da_gamba_cipher.html.

5. Thomas Levenson, *Measure for Measure: A Musical History of Science* (New York: Touchstone, 1995), 64–65.

6. Quoted in ibid., 67.

7. Levenson, *Measure for Measure*, 67–68.

8. William Prizer, “Una ‘Virtù Molto Conveniente a Madonne’: Isabella D’Este as a Musician,” *Journal of Musicology* 17, no. 1 (Winter 1999): 113–14.

9. Ibid., 115–16.

10. Ibid., 111.

11. Emanuel Winternitz, *Leonardo da Vinci as a Musician* (New Haven, CT: Yale University Press, 1982), 38.

4. LUTHIER

1. CMH, interview by Robert T. Schumacher, 1979, tape B, transcription p. 8. Unless otherwise noted, all subsequent quotations of CMH are from this source.

2. CMH, interview by QW, June 13, 2005. Unless otherwise noted, all subsequent quotations of CMH are from this source.

3. CMH, interview by QW, August 31, 1998.

4. CMH, interview by QW, June 13, 2005. Unless otherwise noted, all subsequent quotations of CMH are from this source.

5. Audrey Brown, "Home Is the Workshop," *Montclair Times*, February 7, 1952.

6. Frank Eakin Jr., "Violas the Product of This Montclair Woman's Hobby," *Newark Sunday News*, November 8, 1953.

7. CMH, interview by Schumacher, tape A, transcription p. 22.

INTERMEZZO: ANATOMY

1. Carleen Maley Hutchins, "The Physics of Violins," *Scientific American*, November 1962, 79–83.

2. Peter D'Epiro and Mary Desmond Pinkowish, *Sprezzatura: 50 Ways Italian Genius Shaped the World* (New York: Random House, 2001), 255.

3. Ibid., 256.

4. Ibid., 250–51.

5. Aristotle, *Poetics*, 1459a4. The European Graduate School, Graduate and Postgraduate Studies, "Aristotle — Quotes," http://www.egs.edu/library/aristotle/quotes.

6. Antonio Pace, "Violin Making as an Exercise in Creative Anachronism," *Catgut Acoustical Society Newsletter* 38 (November 1982): 11.

5. SCIENTIST

1. Frederick A. Saunders (FAS) to CMH, May 12, 1949. My references are from copies I made of these letters, with CMH's permission.

2. D. Quincy Whitney, "True Pioneer — Octogenarian Turned the Ears of the World to Her Stringed Boxes," *Boston Sunday Globe, NH Weekly*, August 24, 1997, 13.

3. Ibid.

4. Carleen Maley Hutchins, "Acoustics and the Violin — Past, Present, and Future," lecture, H. J. Reid Center, NASA Langley Research Center colloquium "What Is Music?," Langley Research Center, Hampton, Virginia, March 2, 1999, tape 13.10.

5. Frederick A. Saunders and Carleen Hutchins, "On Improving Violins," *Violins and Violinists* 13, nos. 7–8 (November–December 1952): 2.

6. Ibid.

7. Ibid.

8. Frederick A. Saunders, "Violins Old and New — An Experimental Study," *Sound* 1, no. 4 (July–August 1962): 10.

9. Ibid.

10. Ibid., 4.

11. Family log, February 18, 1958, vol. 4, p. 93. The family log consisted of many volumes — at least thirty, meticulously kept for more than thirty years by Mort,

primarily, with occasional entries from Carleen. I made copies of interesting excerpts with CMH's permission. Its current location is unknown.

12. Saunders, "Violins Old and New," 4.

13. Carleen Hutchins, "The Physics of Violins," *Scientific American*, November 1962, 8; and Sarah Freiberg, "How to Tame Annoying Howling Wolf Tones," All Things Strings, http://www.allthingsstrings.com/layout/set/pring/Instruments/CARE-MAINTENANCE/How-to-Tame-Annoying-Howling-Wolf-Tones.

14. Saunders, "Violins Old and New," 5.

15. Ibid.

16. Ibid., 5–6.

17. Ibid., 6.

18. FAS to CMH, February 8, 1952.

19. FAS to CMH, April 10, 1952.

20. FAS to CMH, July 1952.

21. FAS to CMH, September 11, 1952.

22. FAS to CMH, November 6, 1952.

23. FAS to CMH, January 26, 1953.

24. FAS to CMH, January 16, 1953.

INTERMEZZO: SCIENCE

1. Thomas Levenson, *Measure for Measure: A Musical History of Science* (New York: Touchstone, 1995), 28–29.

2. Ibid., 29–32.

3. Ibid., 32.

4. Ibid., 50.

5. Ibid.

6. Ibid., 53.

7. Ibid., 54.

8. Ibid.

9. Ibid., 56–57.

10. Ibid., 57.

11. Ibid., 68.

12. Ibid., 58.

13. Carleen Maley Hutchins, "Part I. 350 Years of Violin Research: Violin Development from the 16th through the 19th Centuries," introductory essay in *Research Papers in Violin Acoustics, 1975–1993*, ed. Carleen Hutchins and Virginia Benade (New York: Acoustical Society of America through the American Institute of Physics, 1996), 1:4.

14. Melvyn Bragg, "Observations of an Amateur on the History of the Royal Society 1660–2010," Wilkins Medawar Bernal Lecture 2010, *Notes and Records of the Royal Society* 64, no. 3 (September 2010 [published April 9, 2010]): 12.

15. Ibid.

16. Hutchins, "350 Years of Violin Research," 7.

6. APPRENTICE

1. FAS to CMH, March 9, 1953.
2. Ray Carbone, "Violin Lesson," *Foster's Sunday Citizen* (Dover, NH), August 6, 2000, 2.
3. FAS to CMH, June 21, 1953.
4. FAS to CMH, October 16, 1953.
5. "Violas Product of Montclair," *Newark News*, November 8, 1953.
6. CMH, interview by Robert T. Schumacher, 1979, tape B, transcription p. 3.
7. Ibid.
8. Frederick A. Saunders, "Violins Old and New—An Experimental Study," *Sound* 1, no. 4 (July–August 1962): 6–10.
9. Ibid., 12.
10. Ibid., 13.
11. Ibid.
12. Ibid., 13.
13. Ibid., 14.
14. CMH, interview by QW, fall 1997.
15. CMH, interview by Schumacher, tape B, transcription pp. 3–4.
16. FAS to CMH, June 24, 1954.
17. FAS to CMH, May 10, 1955.
18. FAS to CMH, August 1, 1955.
19. FAS to CMH, September 23, 1955.
20. FAS to CMH, November 9, 1955.
21. FAS to CMH, April 13, 1956.
22. FAS to CMH, April 24, 1956.
23. FAS to CMH, May 15, 1956.
24. FAS to CMH, October 15, 1956.
25. FAS to CMH, October 15, 1956.
26. FAS to CMH, late October 1956.
27. Family log, October 19, 1956, vol. 2, p. 76.
28. PBS, *Nova*, "The Great Violin Mystery," October 11, 1981, videotape.
29. Family log, March 13, 1959, vol. 5, p. 123.

INTERMEZZO: ACOUSTICS

1. Thomas Birch, *The History of the Royal Society of London for Improving of Natural Knowledge, from Its First Rise (1756–1757)* (London: A. Millar in the Strand, 1757), 2:46.

2. *A Dictionary of Scientists* (Oxford: Oxford University Press, 1999), s.v. Chladni, Ernst Florens Friedrich.

3. Sylvette Milliot, *Histoire de la lutherie parisienne du XVIIIe siècle à 1960*, vol. 3, *Jean-Baptiste Vuillaume et sa famille: Nicolas, Nicolas-François et Sébastien Vuillaume* (Spa, Belgium: Les Amis de la Musique, 2006), 46–47. (This work includes English summaries of each section of the main text.)

4. V. A. McKusick and H. K. Wiskind, "Felix Savart (1791–1841), Physician-Physicist," *Journal of the History of Medicine and Allied Sciences* 14 (October 1959): 411–23.

5. Milliot, *Jean-Baptiste Vuillaume et sa famille*, 3:303.

6. Quoted in ibid.

7. Carleen Maley Hutchins, "Part I. 350 Years of Violin Research: Violin Development from the 16th through the 19th Centuries," introductory essay in *Research Papers in Violin Acoustics, 1975–1993*, ed. Carleen Hutchins and Virginia Benade (New York: Acoustical Society of America through the American Institute of Physics, 1996), 1:7.

8. Milliot, *Jean-Baptiste Vuillaume et sa famille*, 3:93.

9. Violinist.com, Violin blogs, "The Secret of the Strad: It's in Scientific American, 1981," March 3, 2012, www.violinist.com/blog.

10. Ibid.

11. Ibid.

12. Ibid., March 4, 2012.

7. MUSICMONGER

1. CMH, interview by Robert T. Schumacher, 1979, tape B, transcription p. 17.

2. Family log, November 28, 1956, vol. 2, pp. 101–2.

3. CMH, interview by Schumacher, tape B, transcription p. 17.

4. FAS to CMH, November 29, 1956.

5. CMH, interview by QW, June 13, 2005.

6. FAS to CMH, November 29, 1956.

7. Family log, November 5, 1956, vol. 2, p. 87.

8. CMH, interview by Schumacher, tape B, transcription p. 18.

9. Ibid.

10. Family log, December 9, 1956, vol. 2, p. 113.

11. Family log, December 10, 1956, vol. 2, p. 114.
12. Family log, December 11, vol. 2, p. 115; December 13, vol. 2, p. 116.
13. Family log, December 22, 1956, vol. 2, p. 126–27.
14. Family log, December 22, 1956, vol. 2, p. 126.
15. Family log, December 22, vol. 2, p. 127.
16. Family log, January 6, 1957, vol. 2, p. 137.
17. Family log, January 8, 1957, vol. 2, p. 137.
18. Family log, January 10, 1957, vol. 2, p. 138.
19. Family log, March 2, 1957, vol. 3, p. 22.
20. Family log, March 12, 1957, vol. 3, p. 28.
21. Family log, March 14, 1957, vol. 3, p. 29.
22. Family log, March 17, 1957, vol. 3, p. 32.
23. CMH, interview by Schumacher, tape B, transcription p. 18.
24. Ibid.
25. Ibid., tape B, transcription p. 20.
26. Family log, March 31, 1957, vol. 3, pp. 39–40.
27. Family log, April 10, 1958, vol. 4, p. 123.
28. Family log, May 17, 1958, vol. 4, p. 144.
29. Family log, May 24, 1958, vol. 4, p. 149.
30. Family log, June 4, 1958, vol. 5, pp. 1–2.
31. Family log, March 10, 1958, vol. 4, p. 105.

INTERMEZZO: LUTHERIE

1. Joseph Wechsberg, *The Glory of the Violin* (New York: Viking Press, 1973), 23.
2. "The Glorious Violins — The Cremona School," Digital Taiwan — Culture and Nature, http://culture.teldap.tw/culture/index.php?option=com_content&view=article&id=344.
3. Rebecca Weiner, "Judaism: Sephardim," section on "Christian Rule, Inquisition and Expulsion of 1492." Jewish Virtual Library, http:www.jewishvirtuallibrary.org/jsource/Judaism/Sephardim.html.
4. Victoria Finlay, *Color: A Natural History of the Palette* (New York: Random House, 2004), 174–75.
5. Laurence Vittes, posted at All Things Strings, September 2009, "Yehudi Menuhin's Legacy," quoting from Menuhin's *The Violin: An Illustrated History* (Paris: Flammarion, 1996), 3.
6. Wechsberg, *The Glory of the Violin*, 20.
7. Ibid., 19.
8. Lorenzo Cassi, interview by QW, September 13, 2004.

8. INVENTOR

1. CMH, interview by Robert T. Schumacher, 1979, tape D, transcription p. 1.

2. Carleen Hutchins, "In Her Own Words," unpublished, undated essay; and CMH, interview by QW, May 23, 1999, in which she explains development of the octet.

3. Family log, May 15, 1959 (mentions going to Torrington the next day), vol. 5, p. 149.

4. Jean Dautrich to CMH, February 20, 1960.

5. CMH to Dautrich, March 18, 1960. The bulk of CMH's letters are archived at the National Music Museum, University of South Dakota, Vermillion, SD, the primary CAS archives.

6. CMH to Fryxell, April 1, 1965. In the same letter, Hutchins detailed how she used and modified the Dautrich instruments, as follows:

> *Vilonia* (alto): Air resonance originally at E164 cps and I moved it up to G 196 by slicing about an inch off the rib height. Original plate peaks matched and were unnecessarily thick. I thinned the plate from 6.0 mm in the center and 3.5 mm on the edges to 3.0 mm all over. 216 grams to 177 grams. Back plate tuned to this by going from original 349 grams to 283 grams.
>
> *Vilon* (tenor): Original air resonance OK at D 155 cps. Original wood resonance was at B247 and I moved it down to A220 by removing 20 grams of wood from the top plate (280 to 260) making it 3.5 mm to 4.0 thick. Back plate regraduated and tuned to top—went from 570 grams to 498.5 grams.
>
> *Vilonio* (original small bass tuning—now cello tuning). Resonances—main wood and air—were found to be just right for the projected large cello. I removed plates and found them to be properly tuned—the back weighing 1101 g. and the top plate 768 g. Reassembled without change. Put extra long cello strings on and it sounded very well. George Finckel played it at our first concert in 1961. Finckel: "Delighted with its formidable tone—can even talk back to the piano in the Brahms 'Sonata.'"

7. CMH, interview by Schumacher, tape D, transcription p. 13. Unless otherwise noted, all subsequent quotations are from this source.

8. Carleen Maley Hutchins, "Acoustical Parameters of Violin Design Applied to the Development of a Graduated Series of Violin-Type Instruments," lecture delivered at the annual ASA Meeting, New York City, New Yorker Hotel, May 15, 1963, my copy of the typescript, p. 11. The location of the original is unknown.

9. Carleen Maley Hutchins, "The New Contrabass Violin," *American String Teacher*, March 4, 1966, 5.

10. Ibid.

11. CMH, interview by Schumacher, tape D, transcription pp. 13–14.

12. Ibid., tape D, transcription p. 14.

13. CMH, interview by QW, September 13, 1999.

14. Ibid.

15. CMH, interview by QW, August 16, 1999.

16. Hutchins, "Acoustical Parameters," 4.

17. Carleen Maley Hutchins, my transcription of a taped NASA lecture, March 2, 1999.

18. Family log, February 16, 1961, vol. 7, p. 111.

INTERMEZZO: CONSORTS

1. Emanuel Winternitz, *Leonardo da Vinci as a Musician* (New Haven, CT: Yale University Press, 1982), 72.

2. Ibid., 138.

3. Ibid., 164.

4. "Leonardo da Vinci's Wacky Piano Heard for the First Time after 500 Years," The Age, November 18, 2013, http://www.theage.com.au/entertainment/music/leonardo-da-vincis-wacky-piano-is-heard-for-the-first-time-after-500-years.

5. Quoted in Winternitz, *Leonardo da Vinci as a Musician*, 166.

6. Michael Praetorius, *The Syntagma Musicum of Michael Praetorius,* vol. 2, *De Organographia, First and Second Parts*, trans. Harold Blumenfeld (New York: Barenreiter, 1962), 44.

7. Ibid., 49.

8. Peter Holman, "*Terpsichore* at 400: Michael Praetorius as a Collector of Dance Music," *Viola da Gamba Society Journal* 6 (2012): 43.

9. Leo Sir, "Can the Violin and Cello Be Modified? History of the Double-Quintette 'Leo Sir,'" *Le Violoncelle* (Paris) (July–October 1924): 462–63.

10. Fred L. Dautrich, *Bridging the Gaps in the Violin Family: Inventor of the Vilonia, Vilon and the Vilono*, rev. ed. (Torrington, CT: Fred L. Dautrich, 1935). This brochure is in the Hutchins archives.

11. Catherine Drinker Bowen, *Friends and Fiddlers* (Boston: Little, Brown and Co., 1934), 123.

12. Ibid.

13. Ibid., 40–41.

9. AUTHOR

1. Family log, January 7, 1959, vol. 5, p. 97.

2. CMH, interview by Robert T. Schumacher, 1979, tape B, transcription pp. 13–14.

3. Christopher Germain, "Wurlitzer Shop History," October 2007, All Things Strings, http://www.allthingsstrings.com/layout/set/print/Instruments/HISTORY2/Wurlitzer-Shop-History, 1–2.

4. CMH, interview by QW, August 31, 1998.

5. Carleen Maley Hutchins, "Carleen M. Hutchins, Violinmaker and Scholar," essay in Simone Fernando Sacconi, *The Secrets of Stradivar: With the Catalogue of the Stradivarian Relics Contained in the Civic Museum Ala Ponzone of Cremona* (Cremona: Libreria del Convegno, 1979), 147.

6. CMH, interview by Schumacher, tape C, transcription p. 1.

7. Family log, July 24, 1960, vol. 7, p. 30.

8. Family log, May 14, 1961, vol. 7, p. 143.

9. Family log, September 30, 1961, vol. 8, p. 50.

10. Family log, February 28, 1962, vol. 8, p. 95, includes a clipping: Mary T. Arne, *Montclair Times*, February 21, 1962.

11. Family log, April 18, 1962, vol. 8, p. 120.

12. Family log, May 25, 1962, vol. 8, p. 112.

13. CMH, interview by Schumacher, tape B, transcription pp. 14–15.

14. F. A. Saunders, "Violins Old and New: An Experimental Study," *Sound*, July–August 1962.

15. CMH, interview by Schumacher, tape D, transcription p. 20.

10. CATALYST

1. "Leopold Stokowski Biography—a Brief Biography of the Eventful Career of Leopold Stokowski," The Stokowski Legacy, http://www.stokowski.org.

2. Robert Fryxell, interview by Robert T. Schumacher, May 16, 1978, tape 6. This tape was given to Hutchins after the interview was conducted, and she shared it with me when I met her in 1997.

3. Ibid., tape 9.

4. Ibid., tape, 4.

5. Transcript, *Science in Action* (San Francisco: California Academy of Sciences, 1964), 1.

6. *CAS Newsletter*, May 1964, 2–3.

7. Stokowski to Hutchins, October 6, 1965.

8. Hutchins to Stokowski, October 8, 1965.

9. Stokowski quoted by Jay Nelson Tuck, "New Designs for Old Instruments," *BRAVO* 5, no. 3 (1965): 23–24.

10. *CAS Newsletter*, November 1966, 3.

11. Samuel L. Singer, "New Family of Fiddles: '16 Concerto Soloists' Concert," *Philadelphia Inquirer*, January 15, 1967, 2.

12. *CAS Newsletter*, May 1967, 6.

13. Ibid.

14. CMH to Fryxell, March 9, 1967.

15. CMH, interview by QW, January 22, 2002.

16. Hutchins to Stokowski, October 20, 1967.

17. *CAS Newsletter*, November 1967, 1.

18. Hutchins to Stokowski, April 11, 1968.

19. Stokowski to Hutchins, April 15, 1968.

20. CMH, interview by QW, January 22, 2002.

21. Hutchins to Stokowski, January 24, 1969; and Stokowski to Hutchins, January 27, 1969.

22. CMH, interview by QW, January 22, 2002.

23. Larry Livingston, "ARTS: Conducting Philosophies," YouTube, www.youtube.com/watch?v=pRJKcxcVC7g, uploaded September 12, 2007.

INTERMEZZO: COLLECTIONS

1. Emanuel Winternitz, "The Golden Harpsichord and Todini's Galleria Armonica," *Metropolitan Museum of Art Bulletin*, February 1956, 154–56.

2. Ibid.

3. Dr. Jörn Günther Rare Books, "The Famous Munich Wedding of 1568," www.guenther-rarebooks.com.

4. Frank Harrison and Joan Rimmer, *European Musical Instruments*, chap. 5, "Consorts and Contrasts 1500–1610" (Tiptree, Essex: Anchor Press), 25.

5. Emanuel Winternitz, "The Evolution of the Baroque Orchestra," *Metropolitan Museum of Art Bulletin*, new ser., 12, no. 9 (May 1954): 258–59.

6. Lowell Creitz, "The New and the Old Violin Families: An Organological Comparison," *CAS Newsletter*, 19.

7. Quoted in Thomas Levenson, *Measure for Measure: A Musical History of Science* (New York: Touchstone, 1995), 43.

8. Dayton Clarence Miller, *The Science of Sound* (New York: Macmillan, 1916), 9.

9. Ibid., 22.

10. Ibid., 24–26.

11. Levenson, *Measure for Measure*, 116–17.

12. Ibid.

13. Ibid.

14. Ibid.

15. Wendy Powers, "The Golden Harpsichord of Michele Todini (1616–1690): Thematic Essay," Heilbrunn Timeline of Art, http://www.metmuseum.org/toah/hd/todi/hd_todi.htm.

11. EDITOR

1. Mary Harbold, "Summary of Current Developments in Musical Acoustics," paper presented at the Music Educators National Conference, Philadelphia, March 15, 1964, Hutchins archives.

2. Ibid.

3. Ibid.

4. CMH, interview by Robert T. Schumacher, 1979, tape C, transcription p. 7.

5. *CAS Newsletter*, November 1967, 3–4.

6. CMH, interview by QW, September 15, 1998.

7. *CAS Newsletter*, November 1970, 1.

8. CMH, interview by Schumacher, tape C, transcription p. 12.

9. CMH, interview by QW, September 15, 1998

10. David Brownell, review of *Research Papers in Violin Acoustics, 1975–1993*, edited by C. M. Hutchins and V. Benade, *Journal of the Catgut Acoustical Society*, n.s., 3, no. 4 (November 1997): 59.

12. LECTURER

1. Program, *The 1969 Fine Arts Festival, University of North Carolina at Chapel Hill*, Hutchins archives.

2. Richard Eckberg to D. Quincy Whitney, e-mail message, November 17, 2011.

3. Ibid.

4. *CAS Newsletter*, May 1, 1971, 3.

5. Paul Tobias to D. Quincy Whitney, e-mail message, March 29, 2006.

6. Frank Lewin, "New Violins Exhibited at Leipzig Messe," *CAS Newsletter*, November 1980, 7.

7. John McLennan, "Catgut Conference in Australia 1980," *CAS Newsletter*, November 1980, 1.

8. Unsigned and untitled article, *CAS Newsletter*, November 1980, 25.

9. Carleen Maley Hutchins, "Orient Adventure with the Fiddles," *CAS Newsletter*, May 1983, 5.

10. Ibid.

11. Ibid.

12. Ibid.

13. Ibid.

14. Ibid.

15. George Brooks, introductory remarks to lecture by CMH, "Acoustics and the Violin—Past, Present, and Future," NASA Langley Research Center, Hampton, VA, March 2, 1999 (my transcription; I was in the audience).

16. Carleen Hutchins, on the occasion of being interviewed by David Nicholson, *Daily Press*, Hampton, Virginia, March 2, 1999.

13. FIDDLES AND GUITARS

1. Carleen Maley Hutchins, "Examples of the Way the Catgut Acoustical Society Functions," report, April 1971, Hutchins archives.
2. John Huber, interview by QW, September 23, 2004.
3. Ibid.
4. C. F. Martin to CMH, April 23, 1971. Courtesy of C. F. Martin Archives.
5. Family log, January 28, 1975, vol. 13, p. 56.
6. Family log, March 11, 1975, vol. 13, p. 77.
7. D. W. Haines, C. M. Hutchins, M. A. Hutchins, and D. A. Thompson, "A Violin and a Guitar with Graphite-Epoxy Composite Soundboards," *CAS Newsletter*, November 1975, 27 and 28.
8. "Three Important Experimental Instruments," *Violin Octet: New Voices for the 21st Century* 2 (Winter 2004): 13. This publication was routinely referred to as the "NVFA (New Violin Family Association) newsletter" rather than its actual title on the masthead.
9. *CAS Newsletter*, May 1976, 1.
10. Ibid., 3.
11. Carleen Maley Hutchins, "Acoustics of Violins," *Scientific American*, October 1981, p. 8 of reprinted article.
12. "Three Important Experimental Instruments," 13.
13. Untitled item, *CAS Newsletter*, May 1973, 1, last item.
14. Family log, May 26, 1977, vol. 16, p. 119.

14. FIDDLES IN THE CONSERVATORY

1. Family log, April 13, 1960, vol. 6, p. 141.
2. Bernard Robinson to CMH, October 26, 1961.
3. Charles Taylor to CMH, September 26, 1972.
4. Michael McIntyre to CMH, July 12, 1973.
5. Unsigned article, *CAS Newsletter*, May 1, 1974, 1.
6. Bernard Robinson to CMH, March 11, 1974.
7. Anthony Woollen, "New Instruments Unveiled in Britain," *Strad*, September 1974, reprint, n.p.
8. McIntyre to CMH, December 6, 1974.
9. CMH to McIntyre, May 1, 1975.
10. CMH to Taylor, April 4, 1975.

11. Family log, July 2, 1976, vol. 15, p. 56.

12. Roderick Skeaping, interview by QW, August 8, 2004.

13. Taylor to CMH, December 7, 1976.

14. Jon Darius, "Catgut in Cambridge," *New Scientist*, July 21, 1977.

15. C. A. Taylor, "Notes on the visit of Mr. Yehudi Menuhin to the R.C.M. to see the N.V.F. April 12, 1978," Hutchins archives.

16. McIntyre to CMH, October 8, 1978.

17. CMH to Skeaping, October 23, 1978.

18. CMH to Skeaping, October 23, 1978.

19. Taylor to Tress, November 13, 1978, Hutchins archives.

20. Tress to Taylor, November 21, 1978.

21. Roderick Skeaping, informal summary, May 12, 2012, Hutchins archives.

22. Myers to Hancock, February 21, 1987, Hutchins archives.

23. Robinson to CMH, July 21, 1987.

24. Christopher Field to CMH, October 28, 1988.

25. Fellgett to CMH, April 17, 1993.

26. Skeaping to CMH, fax, May 11, 1995.

15. FIDDLES IN THE BAKERY

1. Hans Olof Hansson, "Constructional Principles for the Five-Stringed Violino Grande," *CAS Newsletter*, November 1972, 25.

2. CMH to Olof Hansson, August 24, 1968.

3. CMH to Hansson, October 31, 1969.

4. Untitled article, *CAS Newsletter*, May 1, 1973, 7.

5. Hansson, "Constructional Principles for the Five-Stringed Violino Grande," 23–32.

6. Carleen Maley Hutchins, "Six Weeks Abroad with the Fiddles," *CAS Newsletter*, November 1974, 1.

7. Ibid., 3.

8. Semmy Lazaroff, interview by QW, September 23, 2004.

9. CMH to Roderick Skeaping, October 5, 1978.

10. Hans Astrand, interview by QW, September 23, 2004.

11. Johan Sundberg, interview by QW, September 22, 2004.

12. "Stockholm Music Museum," http://en.wikipedia.org/wili/Stockholm_music_museum, 1.

13. CMH to Hans Astrand, November 29, 1979.

14. Gunnar Larsson to CMH, July 1, 1981.

15. Family log, March 18, 1982, vol. 24, p. 73.

16. Untitled article, *CAS Newsletter*, November 1983, 3.

17. Ibid., 2.

18. Family log, May 20, 1990, vol. 33, p. 90.

19. Karp to CMH, September 4, 1990.

20. "News and Correspondence," *Journal of the Catgut Acoustical Society*, ser. II, 1, no. 6 (November 1990): 42.

21. Lazaroff to CMH, October 30, 1994.

22. Hans Riben, interview by QW, September 23, 2004.

23. Hans Astrand, interview by QW, September 23, 2004.

INTERMEZZO: INNOVATION

1. Andy Fein and Angie Newgren, "Paganini's Violin: Il Cannone," August 10, 2011, blog by violinmaker Andy Fein, http://blog.feinviolins.com/2011/08/paganinis-violin-il-cannone.html, 1.

2. Max Wade-Matthews and Wendy Thompson, eds., "Niccolò Paganini," *The Encyclopedia of Music: Instruments of the Orchestra and the Great Composers* (Wigston, UK: Hermes House, Anness Publishing, 2003), 355.

3. Ibid.

4. Ibid., 171.

5. "Arcangelo Corelli: A Concise Biography," Baroquemusic.org, http://www.baroquemusic.org/bqxcorelli.html.

6. "Francesco Geminiani: A Detailed Informative Biography," Baroquemusic.org, http://www.baroquemusic.org/bqxgem.htm1,1.

7. "Francesco Geminiani: A Detailed Informative Biography," Baroquemusic.org, http://www.baroquemusic.org/bqxgem.htm1,1.

8. Encyclopedia Britannica online, http://www.britannica.com/Ebchecked/topic/143328/Bartolomeo-Cristofori, s.v. Bartolomeo Cristofori.

9. "Famous Piano Players — The Greatest Classical Pianists," Favorite Classical Composers, http://www.favorite-classical-composers.com/famous-piano-players.htm1.

10. Miles Hoffman, "Franz Liszt at 200: An Important, but Not Great, Composer," NPR, http://www.npr.org/blogs/deceptivecadence/2011/10/21/141562068/franz-liszt-at-200-an-important-but-not-great-composer."

11. Ibid.

12. Ibid.

13. "John Coltrane Biography Discography," John Coltrane.com, http://www.johncoltrane.com/biography.htm1.

14. Teresa Santoski, "Adolphe Sax, Accident-Prone Child and Inventor of the Saxophone, Dies Today in 1894," *Telegraph*, February 4, 2010, 1–2, http://www.nashuatelegraph.com/print/?sid=1835514.

15. Rachel Barton Pine, "Maud Powell: Lifetime Achievement Award" citation, awarded January 25, 2014, at the 56th annual Recording Academy's Special Merit Awards ceremony, held at the Ebell Theater, Los Angeles, Grammy.com, http://www.grammy.com/news/lifetime-achievement-award-maud-powell.

16. Andy Fein and Angie Newgren, "Paganini's Violin: Il Cannone," Wednesday, August 10, 2011, blog by violinmaker Andy Fein, http://blog.feinviolins.com/2011/08/paganinis-violin-il-cannone.html, 2.

17. Alberto Giordano, "Paganini's Violin 'Il Cannone,' Giordanoviolins de Alberto Giordano&C, http://www.giordanoviolins.com/en/paganini%e2%80%99s-violin-%e2%80%9Cil-cannone%e2%80%9D, 1.

18. Fein and Newgren, "Paganini's Violin: Il Cannone," 2.

19. Pio Montanari, interview by QW, September 12, 2004.

16. FIDDLES IN THE LIMELIGHT

1. David Finckel, interview by QW, October 26, 2009.

2. Ibid.

3. Diana Gannett, interview by QW, November 2, 2005.

4. Ibid.

5. Tom Knatt, untitled article, *National Capital Cello Club Newsletter*, Winter 1993.

6. Tamara Bernstein, "Yo-Yo Ma's Performance a Musical Disaster," *Toronto Globe and Mail*, January 16, 1993.

7. Heidi Waleson, "The Yo-Yola: Mr. Ma's Experiment," *Wall Street Journal*, February 17, 1993.

8. Stephen Wigler, "The Cello Master & The Cello Maker—Yo-Yo Ma's Latest Challenge: An Onstage Experiment with an Overgrown Viola," *Baltimore Sun*, February 28, 1993, 1; http://articles.baltimoresun.com/1993–02–28/features/1993059247_1_viola-concerto-yo-yo-ma-play-the-viola.

9. Stephen Wigler, "Ma Plays Cello Concerto by Albert with Nobility," *Baltimore Sun*, March 11, 1993.

10. Sara Stackhouse to CMH, April 5, 1995.

11. Yo-Yo Ma, phone interview by QW, December 2, 2014. All subsequent quotations of Ma are from this interview.

INTERMEZZO: MARKET

1. Dava Sobel, *Longitude: The True Story of a Lone Genius Who Solved the Greatest Scientific Problem of His Time* (New York: Penguin, 1995), 108.

2. Benjamin Hebbert, "The Invention of Tradition: The Price of Stradivari Vi-

olins," in Tom Wilder, ed., *The Conservation, Restoration, and Repair of Stringed Instruments and Their Bows*, 3 vols. (Montreal: International Pernambuco Conservation Initiative; London: Archetype Publications, 2010), 1:186.

3. Ibid., 13.

4. Ibid, 19.

5. Hugh Reginald Haweis, *Old Violins* (Edinburgh: John Grant, 1910), 180–81.

6. Joseph Wechsberg, *The Glory of the Violin* (New York: Viking Press, 1972), 164.

7. Erin Shrader, "Exactly What Makes a Violin Expert an Expert?" *Strings*, July 2011, 63.

8. Erin Shader and Greg Olwell, "Remembering Master Restorer René Morel, 1932–2011," *Strings*, February 2012, 49.

9. Caroline Seebohm, "Strads for Sale: Jacques Français Keeps the World's Greatest Stringed Instruments in the Hands of the World's Greatest Players," "The Dealer's Eye," *House and Garden*, June 1985, 92.

10. Morel quoted in ibid.

11. Joe Peknik phone interview by QW, April 21, 2015.

12. Ibid.

13. Brian W. Harvey and Carla J. Shapreau, *Violin Fraud: Deception, Forgery, Theft, and Lawsuits in England and America*, 2nd ed. (Oxford: Clarendon Press, 1997), 58.

14. Quoted in ibid., 63.

15. Harvey and Shapreau, *Violin Fraud*, 66.

16. Howard Reich and William Gaines, "Dealers Gain Collector's Trust, Score Multimillion Bonanza: London, Chicago Experts Finagle Holy Grail Cache of Violins," *Chicago Tribune*, June 17, 2001, 1.

17. Bein quoted in ibid.

18. John Huber, interview by QW, August 2004.

19. Author witnessed the concert.

20. Norman C. Pickering, *The Violin World* (East Hampton, NY: Keener's East End Litho, 2003), 20–24.

21. Stewart Pollens, "Dendrochronology and the Dating of Violins," http://www.stewartpollens.com/papers.htm, 1.

22. Pickering, *The Violin World*, 20–24.

17. FIDDLES ON EXHIBIT

1. I happened to be visiting CMH when this telephone call took place.

2. "History of the Musée de la Musique Museum in Paris: The Beginnings of a Music Museum." EUtouring.com, http://www.eutouring.com/history_musee_de_la_musique.html.

3. "Bring the World to Forest Hill," Horniman Museum and Gardens, http://www.horniman.ac.uk/about/museum-library.

4. Sally B. Brown, visiting committee co-chair, Department of Musical Instruments, "Mary Elizabeth Adams Brown's Collection Celebrates 125 Years at the Met," February 18, 2014, http:www.metmuseum.org.

5. Emanuel Winternitz, "The Crosby Brown Collection of Musical Instruments: Its Origins and Development," *Metropolitan Museum Journal* 3 (1970): 338.

6. Ibid., 338.

7. Sally B. Brown to Quincy Whitney, e-mail message, July 22, 2015.

8. "History," Yale University Collection of Musical Instruments, http://www.yale.edu/musicalinstruments/history.htm.

9. CMH to Winternitz, April 20, 1972.

10. Susan Snyder, administrative assistant, Department of Musical Instruments, Metropolitan Museum of Art, to CMH, January 23, 1989.

11. Philippe de Montebello to CMH, January 23, 1989.

12. CMH to Montebello, February 9, 1989.

13. CMH to Libin, February 9, 1989.

14. QW journal, October 27, 1999, 129.

15. Libin to CMH, September 27, 1989.

16. The following conversation has been reconstructed from my personal journal (hereafter "QW journal") and recollections of October 27, 1999, the day I accompanied Hutchins to visit the Metropolitan Museum of Art, at which time we met with Ken Brown, Joseph Peknik, Margaret Sachter, and Sally Brown.

17. *Violin Octet* 2, no. 4 (Fall 2005): 13.

18. John O'Brien, interview by QW, May 15, 2001.

18. FIDDLES IN THE PALACE

1. Marina Markot, interview by QW, September 13, 2014.

2. Ibid.

3. Svetlana Shabanova recollections, translated by Markot, October 2014.

4. Meleschkina to CMH, January 30, 1994.

5. "News and Correspondence," *Journal of the Catgut Acoustical Society*, n.s., 2, no. 6 (November 1994): 37.

6. Barbara Hendrian, "St. Petersburg, Russia, November 24–December 2, 1994. 'What would I write of my week-long visit to St. Petersburg?,'" an essay written by the Montclair amateur cellist and neighbor of CMH who accompanied Hutchins to Russia and later wrote an informal recollection. She passed it along to me when I interviewed her on October 26, 2009.

7. Markot, interview by QW, September 13, 2014.
8. Meleschkina to CMH, January 12, 1996.
9. Lydia Voltchek to CMH, February 7, 1996.
10. Markot to CMH, May 3, 1996.
11. CMH to Voltchek, Summer 1996, no date.
12. Voltchek to CMH, February 5, 1997.
13. L. Joseph Butterfield to CMH, July 26, 1997.
14. Ibid.
15. Ibid.
16. Butterfield to Hutchins and Markot, November 15, 1997.
17. Markot to Miller, November 17, 1997.
18. Markot to CMH, March 13, 1998.
19. CMH to Markot, March 26, 1998.
20. Ibid.
21. Ibid.
22. All of these encomiums appeared in "Octet CDs," *Journal of the Catgut Acoustical Society*, n.s., 3, no. 7 (May 1999): 45.
23. "Octet News," *Journal of the Catgut Acoustical Society*, n.s., 3, no. 5 (May 1998): 48.
24. Voltchek to CMH, September 21, 1998.
25. CMH to QW, phone call, June 18, 1999.

19. FIDDLING WITH TIME

1. "Carleen Maley Hutchins Medal," *Journal of the Catgut Acoustical Society*, n.s., 3, no. 6 (November 1998): 49.
2. Ibid., photo caption, 50.
3. This and the subsequent quotations of Anne Cole are from an e-mail message to QW, August 30, 2014.
4. QW journal (author's notes on informal conversations with CMH), May 24, 1999.
5. Ibid., May 26, 1999.
6. *Violin Octet* 2, no. 1 (Winter 2004): 4.
7. Unsigned, "If the New Violin Family were a river . . . ," draft of NVFA mission statement, December 7, 1999, Hutchins Consort files, with NVFA literature, Hutchins archives.
8. QW journal, May 30, 1999.
9. QW journal, July 14, 2003.
10. "Albert Consort Forms," *Violin Octet* 2, no. 1 (Winter 2004): 7.

11. "Letter from the Editor," *Violin Octet* 2, no. 1 (Winter 2004): 2.

12. "Catgut Acoustical Society, Violin Society of America Agree to Merge," *Violin Octet* 2, no. 1 (Winter 2004): 14.

13. QW journal, October 25, 2004.

14. Carleen Maley Hutchins, "Morton Aldrich Hutchins, May 6, 1910–November 8, 2004," *Violin Octet* 2, no. 3 (Spring 2005): 14.

20. FIDDLES LIVE IN CONCERT

1. These events have been reconstructed from my personal journal and recollections of the day I accompanied CMH to this concert.

2. D. Quincy Whitney, "A True Pioneer: Octogenarian Turned the Ears of the World to Her Stringed Boxes," *Boston Globe NH Weekly*, August 24, 1997, 13.

3. Sharon McNalley to QW, e-mail messages, October 10, 2014, and July 23, 2015.

4. Unsigned article, *CAS Newsletter*, November 1983, 1.

5. Bert Turetzky, interview by QW, August 11, 2014.

6. Joseph McNalley interview by QW, August 6, 2014.

7. J. McNalley, interview by QW, February 22, 2008.

8. CMH to Joseph McNalley, January 7, 1999.

9. J. McNalley to CMH, January 15, 1999.

10. J. McNalley to CMH, February 4, 1999.

11. J. McNalley to CMH, February 8, 1999.

12. "Highlights of the Past Year," *Journal of the Catgut Acoustical Society*, n.s., 3, no. 8 (November 1999): 44.

13. J. McNalley to André Larson, May 5, 1999.

14. Sharon McNalley to CMH, May 14, 1999.

15. J. McNalley, interview by QW, August 6, 2014.

21. FIDDLES ON THE MARQUEE

1. "Treble Delights," *Violin Octet* 2, no. 2 (Fall 2004): 5.

2. "People in the News," *Violin Octet* 2, no. 3 (Spring 2005): 10.

3. "The New Violin Family's Premiere Convention a Success," *Violin Octet* 2, no. 4 (Fall 2005): 3.

4. QW journal, October 31, 2005 (eyewitness account; I attended the meeting, and took notes).

5. "The New Violin Family's Premiere Convention a Success," *Violin Octet* 2, no. 4 (Fall 2005): 3.

6. "Totally Tallis," *Violin Octet* 2, no. 4 (Fall 2005): 4–5.

7. "The New Violin Family's Premiere Convention a Success," *Violin Octet* 2, no. 4 (Fall 2005): 3.

8. Ibid.

9. "Heard in the Hall," *Violin Octet* 2, no. 4 (Fall 2005): 7.

10. "Treble Trials," *Violin Octet* 2, no. 4 (Fall 2005): 8.

11. "Hutchins Consort Brings Down the House at 2006 GAL Convention," *Violin Octet* 2, no. 5 (Fall 2006): 1.

12. Ibid., 2.

13. Ibid.

14. What follows is an eyewitness account. QW journal, September 18, 2007.

FINALE

1. Clara Moskowitz, "Female Physicists Worldwide Fight Sexist Stereotypes," *Scientific American*, September 3, 2014, http://www.scientificamerican.com/blog/post/women-in-physics-fight-sexist-stereotypes.

2. Cyprien Desmarais, *Archéologie du violon* (Paris, 1836), 20.

3. Antonio Pace, "Bee in a Foxglove Bell: Historical and Cultural Perspectives on the Stylistic Quandary of the Present-Day Violin-Maker," *Journal of the Catgut Acoustical Society*, n.s., 1, no. 8 (November 1991): 4.

4. Catherine Bowen, *Friends and Fiddlers* (Boston: Little, Brown and Co., 1934), 79–80.

5. David Steindl-Rast, *Music of Silence* (New York: HarperCollins, 1998), 95–96.

6. "Older and Richer, Violinmaking Is Flourishing, but the 450-Year Ones Are Still the Best," *Economist*, December 17, 2009, 88. Paganini is quoted in the *Violin Times* (London), July 15, 1900.

7. *Violin Times* (London), July 15, 1900.

8. John Laurenson, "Stradivarius Trees: Searching for Perfect Musical Wood," *BBC News Magazine*, April 13, 2013.

Index

Acoustical Society of America (ASA), xvii, 77, 80, 85, 136, 150, 154–55, 159–60, 168, 180, 223, 232, 239, 248
acoustics: history of research in, 44, 85–90; Hutchins's early interest in, 10; Hutchins seminar on, 154; modes and, 22. *See also* violinmaking experiments
"Acoustics of Violin Plates" (Hutchins), 89
Allen, Arthur A., 14, 239
Amati, Andea, xiv, 105–7, 151
Amati family, xiv, 104–6, 119
Apgar, Virginia, 95–102, 112, 127, 137–38, 171–72, 217, 220
Arnaut, Henri, 42–43, 73
Ashmolean Museum, 74, 80, 198, 203–6
Astrand, Hans, 182–85
Australia, Hutchins in, 159

Bach, Johann S., 148, 180
Backhaus, Hermann, 88–89
Bartlett, Harriet, 35–36, 94
Beare, Charles, 124–25, 204–5
Beethoven, Ludgwig van, 189, 197
Belgium, Hutchins Octet in, 243
Benade, Arthur, 166, 168–69, 182
Benchmark Papers in Acoustics, 150, 154–55
Berger, Karl, 50–51, 53, 61–63, 76, 126
Bessaraboff, Nicholas, 152–54
Bissolotti, Francesco, xiii–xiv, 107
Blatter, Donald, 114, 116, 210
Bowen, Catherine D., 123, 250
Brant, Henry, 111, 113–15, 138–39, 141
Brearley School, Hutchins at, 31–34, 36–39, 45–49, 51–52, 94, 210
Bridging the Gaps in the Violin Family (Dautrich), 112, 122
Brooklyn Botanic Garden, 16–17
Brown, Mary E. A., 208–10
Brown, Sandy, 172
Brown, Sarah "Sally," 209–10, 212–13
Budapest Quartet, 128–29, 151–52
Butterfield, L. Joseph, 217, 220–22, 225

Cannone, 186–87, 190–91
Cassi, Lorenzo, xiv, 107–8
Catgut Acoustical Society (CAS), 90, 130, 135–41, 143, 151–52, 154, 159, 165–70, 172–75, 178, 180–83, 192, 210, 219, 221–22, 225, 227–28, 247
Cathedral of the Pines, 245
cello, components of, 55
C. F. Martin Co., 165–66, 168
chamber music, Hutchins and, 32–33, 39, 46, 48, 63, 78, 97–100, 123, 145, 250
Chandler, Adrian, 204
Chanot, François, 85–86
Charlton, Frederick, 239, 242
China, Hutchins in, 159–61
Chladni, Ernst, 85–86, 89, 178
Chladni patterns, xviii, 85–86, 89–90, 127, 159, 168, 181, 226
Chopin, Frédéric, 189
Christianity, and music, 25–27, 73
classical music world, and change, 197, 224, 232
Conant, Billy, 34–35

Conant, Edith, 11–12, 16, 19, 33–35, 94, 98
Conant Inn (Wolfeboro, NH), 16, 18–19, 31, 33–35
Corelli, Arcangelo, 187–88
Cornell University, Hutchins at, 12–15, 239
Corresponding Society for Musical Sciences, 148
Creitz, Lowell, 145
Cremona, Italy, xiii–xv, 56, 103–8
Cristofori, Bartolomeo, 188–89
Curtin, Joseph, 203, 246–47

Dautrich, Fred, 112, 114, 121–22
Dautrich, Jean, 112, 137–38
Demoliens, Florentine, 248–49
Desmarais, Cyprien, 248–49
D'Este, Isabella, 41, 43–44
Donaldson, John, 178, 208

ear, anatomy of, 20
Eckberg, Richard, 156–57
Edel, Oliver, 77, 81
Ehnes, James, 204
Erle, Broadus, 50, 69, 169
Esty, Mary Lee, 168
Evans, Petie, 48, 94, 99–100, 152

families of violins, history of concept, 43, 119–23, 130, 144–45. *See also* Hutchins violin octet
Fellgett, Peter, 171, 178–79
Finckel, David, 192–93
Finckel family, 114, 192
Finlay, Victoria, 105
"Founding a Family of Fiddles" (Hutchins), 140
Français, Jacques, 201, 211
France, violin octet in, 169
frequency, 21, 73
Fryxell, Robert, 68–69, 114, 135–38, 141
Fulbright Scholarship, 53

Gaffurius, Franchinus, 44, 146
Galilei, Galileo, 73, 147
Galilei, Vincenzo, 73, 119
Gannett, Diana, 192–94, 239–40
Gasparo da Salò, 51, 62, 82, 106
Geminiani, Francesco, 187–88
Genoa, Italy, 186, 190–91
Germany, violin octet in, 172–73, 222
Girl Scouts, Hutchins and, 8–12, 17, 93, 124
Gist, Irving, 129–30
graphite-epoxy violin, 167–68, 247
Great Britain, violin octet in, 171–79
Guarneri, Andrea, 104, 106
Guarneri, Bartolomeo Giuseppe (Giuseppe del Gesù), xiv, 104, 106, 186, 204
Gubbio Studiolo, 103
Guggenheim Fellowships, 111, 128
Guild of American Luthiers (GAL), 165, 169, 242
guitars, Hutchins's work with, 165–68
Gusnasco, Lorenzo, 43

Haines, Daniel, 167
Hansson, Hans Olaf, 180–81
Harbold, Mary, 70, 151–52
Harrison, Lulu, 93, 96, 100
Haydn, Joseph, 121–22
Hegeman, Stuart, 116, 137, 154, 166
Heifetz, Jascha, 124, 190
Helmholtz mode, 111, 113
Heron-Allen, Edward, 48, 54
Hobbie, Barbara, 215–16
holographic interferometry, 166

Hopping, A. S., 78, 100, 126
Hudig, Maurits, 223–25
Hunkins, Sterling, 111, 114, 141–42
hurdy-gurdy, 26
Hutchins, Carleen Maley: birth of, 4; childhood of, 3–13, 17; death of, xix, 243; education, 7, 9–15, 17; emotional life, 19, 33–35, 227, 249; gravestone of, 229, 243; health issues of, 93–98, 127, 155, 229, 242; honors received by, xvii, 223–24, 248; legacy of, 245–48; life, overview of, xv–xix, 250–51; scientific mind of, xviii; and sports, love of, 10, 13, 15. *See also* marriage and family life; *entries under* violinmaking; *other specific topics*
Hutchins, Carolyn "Cassie" (daughter), 52, 63, 93, 96–98, 100–102, 128, 140, 215–16, 225, 227, 249
Hutchins, Morton "Mort" (husband): Apgar and, 97–98, 100; career of, 35–36; death of, 229; decision to live with in-laws, 52; decision to marry, 36–37; family responsibilities borne by, 96–97, 100–102; gravestone of, 229, 243; Hutchins on, 127; and Hutchins's health problems, 96–97, 127; meeting and courtship, 35–36; and music, inability to enjoy, 39; stroke suffered by, 219; summers at New Hampshire cabin, 39; support for Hutchins, 48–50, 76–77, 126, 174–75, 211, 235; and Susie the Pig, 46–47; travel with Hutchins, 156, 159–60, 167, 173–74, 181–82; wedding, 37. *See also* marriage and family life
Hutchins, William "Bill" (son), 49, 82, 93, 96–97, 99–100, 102, 140, 249
Hutchins Consort, xvi, 230–35, 239, 242, 245–47
Hutchins violin octet, 111–17; acoustical problems discovered in, 176–77; associates helping with, 112–16; attracting players to, 192–97; CD of, 221, 223, 225; commission for, xv, 111; on cover of *Research Papers in Violin Acoustics*, 150–51; Dautrich's earlier work on, 112, 114; demonstration concerts for, 114–15, 136–39, 141–42, 152–54, 156–58, 161, 169, 182–83, 210, 213, 217–19, 232, 240–41; donation to National Music Museum, 169; in Europe, 171–79, 181–85, 243; as first scientifically scaled family, xviii; influence of, 184–85; media interest in, xviii, 129–31, 172, 176, 218; at Metropolitan Museum of Art, 207–14; new possibilities for composers in, 231; patent for, as issue, 117; problem addressed by, 122; as product of amateur's love of music, 123; repertoire for, 193, 197, 217–18, 224; research necessary for, 117; resistance to, 141–42, 174, 177, 193–95, 211, 213, 232; in Russia, 179, 216–22; Stokowski's interest in, 135, 139, 141–43, 151, 153
hydraulis, 70

Inquisition, 27, 104–5
International Congress on Acoustics, 172, 174
International Symposium on Musical Acoustics, 223–24

Japan, Hutchins in, 159
Jews, expulsion from Spain (1492), 104–5

Kimball, Maxwell, 116, 137
Kircher, Athanasius, 147
Knatt, Tom, 194
Kreisler, Fritz, 124, 190
Kroll, William "Fritz," 52, 78, 114–15, 126, 137, 151, 154
Ktesibios, 70

Larson, André, 169–70, 234
Laurenson, John, 252–53
Lazaroff, Semmy, 181–84
Lehner, Eugene, 77, 81, 84
Leman, Anatoly I., 88
Leonardo da Vinci, 44, 85, 117–18, 210
Levenson, Thomas, xvi–xvii, 72–73, 147–49
Leverhulme Trust grant, 174, 177–78
Lewin, Frank, 154, 158–59, 169, 221
Libin, Laurence, 210–12
Library of Congress, 128–29, 248
Life magazine, 138, 151, 193
lira da braccio, 24, 41, 43–44, 54, 104, 117
Liszt, Franz, 189, 197
Lorenzo da Pavia, 43
Lupot, Nicolas, 199
Luthier in the Light of Science (film), 216
luthiers: challenges of, 58; defined, ix; disdain for scientific approach, 83–84, 89, 131, 162, 251; early, trial and error by, 74; prominent modern figures, 246; secrecy of, xvi, 67, 74–75, 125, 197–99, 247, 249. *See also entries under* violinmaking
Lutz, Frank, 12–13

Ma, Yo-Yo, 107, 194–97, 224
Maley, Grace Isabel Fletcher (mother), 3–11, 16, 33, 36–37, 47, 52, 63, 98–100, 127
Maley, Nellie Reeves (father's first wife), 3
Maley, Thomas William, Jr. (father), 3–8, 10–12, 16, 33, 36, 52, 63, 81–82
Markot, Marina Meleschkina, 215–21, 225
marriage and family life: balancing of work and family, 51–52, 76, 93–94, 150, 249; early frustrations of, 39–40, 94; first apartment, 37; Hutchins's limited participation in, 100–102; late-life move to Wolfeboro, 225–27; media interest in, 139–40; Mort's stroke and, 225; move to West 69th Street, 49; pets and animals, 127–28, 226; pregnancies, xv, 48–49, 52, 62–63; return to Maley family home, 52, 63; sacrifices necessitated by, 40, 53, 63, 94; violinmaking as escape from, 63–64, 67–68, 76, 94–95, 227, 249
Martha Baird Rockefeller Fund for Music, 152
Martin, C. F., 165–66
Martin, C. F. III, 165–67
Martinengo, Giovanni Leonardo da, 105
McIntosh, Millicent Carey, 31–32, 34, 39, 46–47, 51
McIntyre, Michael, 171–76, 221
McNalley, Joe, 230–35, 247
McNalley, Michael, 231, 234
McNalley, Sharon, 233–34, 247
mean-tone tuning, 73
Measure for Measure (Levenson), 72–73, 147–48
media interest in Hutchins, xviii, xix, 53,

129–31, 135–37, 139–41, 154, 159, 167, 172, 176, 183
Meinel, Hermann, 80, 88–89
Meisel Violinmaking, 48
Menuhin, Yehudi, 106, 124, 176, 190
Mersenne, Marin, 73, 121, 147
Messiah violin, 80, 198–200, 205
Methot, Arthur, 127
Metropolitan Museum of Art (New York), 23, 41, 53, 103, 149, 154, 188, 205, 207–14, 235, 241–42
Miller, Robert, 220–21, 231, 240
modes, 22
monochords, 24
Montanari, Pio, 191
Monteverdi, Claudio, 56–57
Morel, René, 124, 201, 211
Mozart, Wolfgang A., 197
Murch, Walter Tandy, 129–31
museums of musical instruments, 208–9
music: in ancient cultures, 23–25; concepts embedded in, 24; Hutchins's childhood involvement in, 7–8, 10; of Middle Ages, 25–27, 41–44; modes and, 22; of prehistoric peoples, 22–23; secular versus sacred, 23–24
musical instruments: by Hutchins, numbering system for, 50; of Middle Ages, 41–44; tone color of, 22
musical notation, 42, 146
musical scale, 24
musicology, 145
music perception, 20–21
music theory, early research in, 70–73
Musikmuseet (Stockholm), 182–84, 203
Mussolini, Benito, 107
NASA lecture, 161–62
Naspo, Ronald, 115–16, 138
National Association of Music Merchants, 245–46
National Music Museum (University of South Dakota), 165, 169, 234
"New Designs for Old Instruments" (Tuck), 139
"New Family of Fiddles" (Singer), 139–40
Newton, Isaac, 147–48
New Violin Family Association, 212, 225–29, 231, 239–42
The New York Album (Ma), 196
New Yorker magazine, 207–8, 211, 214
New York Public School 33, Hutchins at, 37–40, 47
New York Times, xix, 140, 211
nodal points (nodes), 22
Norway, violin octet in, 182

O'Brien, John, 207–8, 214
Octet 2005, 229, 239–41
Odo of Cluny, 25–26
Olsen, Tim, 165, 242
"On Improving Violins" (Hutchins and Saunders), 77
orchestra, modern: development of, 57; violins in, 57, 114
organ: as church instrument, 26, 71; and early music theory, 70–72; introduction to Europe, 25; invention of, 70; medieval, 71; portable, development of, 42–43, 73
Orpheus, 24–25
overtones, 22

Paganini, Niccolò, 186–87, 190–91, 252
Peknik, Joe, 201–2, 207, 212–14, 241–42
Pellegrini, Lorenzo, 252–53

"The Physics of Violins" (Hutchins), 56, 89, 129–31
Physics Today, xviii, 140
piano: invention of, 188–89; masters of, 189
Piatigorsky, Gregor, 124, 157–58
Pickering, Norman, 205
Pique, Louis, 199
pitch, 24, 88
Plato, 25, 44
Pollens, Stewart, 205, 212
polyphony, and early music theory, 71–73
Powell, Maud, 190
Praetorius, Michael, 119–21, 130, 146–47
publications by Hutchins, 124, 129–31, 135–36, 140, 150–51, 154–55, 159, 168, 172, 246
purfling, 55
Pythagoras, 24, 147
Pythagorean comma, 72–73

rebec, 54, 104
Research Papers in Violin Acoustics, 1975–1993 (Hutchins, ed.), xiv, 150–51, 155
restoration of violins, 201–2, 213
Rice, Helen: and Amateur Chamber Music Players, 52; background of, 45–46; as center of social network, 47–48, 50–53, 61, 63, 68–69, 78, 112–13, 123, 135, 171, 192; friendship with Hutchins, 45, 49, 53, 61, 97, 126–27; as role model for Hutchins, 94; and Susie the Pig, 46; and violin octet test concerts, 114
Robinson, Bernard, 171–75, 178
Rood, Louise, 50, 61, 81, 94, 111–12, 114, 137–38
Royal Society, 74
Ruggieri, Francesco, 104
Russia: Hutchins violin octet in, 179, 216–22, 225; U.S. tours of octet players from, 220–22

Sacconi, Simone, 52–53, 124–26
Sachter, Margaret, 94, 212–13
Saunders, Frederick A.: and CAS, 137; death of, 137, 139, 169; experiments with Hutchins, xviii, 62–69, 78–82, 94–95, 100, 151, 210; first meeting with Hutchins, 61–62; friendship with Hutchins, 63, 76, 80, 93; and group surrounding Hutchins, 135; honors received by, xvii, 80; on Hutchins, 76–77, 82; Hutchins's fame and, 136; and Hutchins's professionalization, 63, 94; and Hutchins violin octet, 112–13, 123, 171; papers of, 154; as pioneer in acoustical research, 89; publications by, 77, 129
Savart, Félix, 65, 85–88, 115, 155
Sax, Antoine-Joseph, 189–90
Schelleng, John, 113, 115–16, 135–36, 138, 155, 166, 176, 210
Schneider, Mischa, 128–29, 151–52
school of violinmaking established by Hutchins, 228
Schumann, Robert, 186
science: Hutchins as teacher of, 17–19, 31–34, 36, 45–48; Hutchins's early interest in, 10, 12–13; Hutchins's study of at Cornell, 13–14; music and, 70, 147
Science in Action (film), 138
science of violinmaking: Hutchins as pioneer in, 89, 96, 108, 143, 151–52, 177, 193, 251; Hutchins on primitive

state of, 176; Hutchins's emphasis on, xvii, xviii, 131, 211; Hutchins's test lab, 152; luthier's disdain for, 83–84, 89, 131, 162, 251; media interest in, 129–31, 135–36. *See also* violinmaking experiments
Scientific American: articles by Hutchins in, xviii, 56, 89, 129–31, 135–36, 158–59, 165, 167, 168, 172, 191, 246; Hutchins's research and, 116; Moskowitz article on sexist stereotypes in physics, 248
The Secrets of Stradivari (Sacconi), 124–25
Sedukh, Grigori, 220–22, 241–42
Shabanova, Svetlana, 216–18
Shepard, Roger N., 20–21
Sir, Leo, 121, 155
Skeaping, Roderick, 171, 175–77, 179
sound perception, 20–21
"Soundpost" (Whitney), 254
sound waves, 21–22
Spear, Bob, 89–90, 227–29, 240–42
Stokowski, Leopold, 135, 139, 141–43, 151, 153
Stradivari, Antonio, xiii, xiv, 52–54, 103–4, 106–8, 121, 124, 128, 130, 151, 187, 198–99, 252
Stradivarius violins, xiv, xviii, 78, 83, 87, 107–8, 114–15, 125–26, 128, 200; copies of, 200; market for, 203–6. *See also* Messiah violin
"The Strads of Montclair" (*Time* magazine), 129
stringed instruments: bowed, origin of, 42, 118; history of, 23–27, 41–44, 103–8
string quartet: and gaps in string family, 122; viola as backbone of, 122–23
Sundberg, Johan, 181–82
Susie the Pig, 46–47, 50
Sweden, violin octet in, 181–85
"Swiss Cheese" violin (Le Gruyère), 168–70, 246–47

Tallis Orchestra, 240–41
Tarisio, Luigi, xvi, 199–200
Taylor, Charles, 171–72, 174–75, 177–78, 221
Tertis, Lionel, 83–84
Todini, Michele, 144, 149
tone color, 22, 64–67, 94
treatises on music, history of, 146–49
troubadours, 26–27, 41–42
tuning, mean-tone, 73
Turetzky, Bert, 232

vielle, 41, 54–55, 104
viola: as backbone of string quartet, 122; components of, 55; Hutchins's experiments with, 62–69; Hutchins's learning to play, 32–33, 101
viola organista, 118–19
violin(s): ancestors of, 44, 54–55, 104, 118; birthplace of, 56; creation of, 105–6; market for, 198–206; prominence in classical music, 57
violin(s), by Hutchins: Carnegie Hall debut of, 117; demonstration concerts for, 159; Hutchins's faith in sound quality of, 161–62; power and volume of, 114–15, 157, 240–42; sales of, 53, 77–78, 81–84, 126, 174, 183, 193, 233–34; view of as radically new, 158. *See also* Hutchins violin octet
Violin Craftsmanship Institute, 228
violinmaking: nineteenth-century design changes, 88; traditionversus creativity in, 58; wood for, 55, 84, 251–53

Violin-Making (Heron-Allen), 48, 54
violinmaking by Hutchins: competition for, 83; cooperations with other luthiers, 83–84; decision to begin, xv, 48; early positive feedback, 76–78, 81–82; early ramping up of production, 68; first instrument, 48–51; and fresh insights of outsider, 65; Hutchins's lack of secrecy in, xvi, xvii, 197, 247, 249; mentors in, 48–53, 76, 124–26; obsession with, 135, 250; production levels, 53, 77–78, 111; renown in, xiv–xv; second instrument, 51–53, 62; students of, 100, 194, 251; wood, sources of, 98–100, 125. *See also* Hutchins violin octet
violinmaking experiments: accolades from violinists, 69; on age effects, 80; on air tone, 65–67; on carrying power, 79; with Chladni patterns, xviii, 89–90, 127, 159, 168, 181, 226; controversy surrounding, 89–90; on ditching, 67–68, 77; on ease of playing, 79; on loudness curves, 64–65; with "pancake" cellos, 81; plate thickness, 80–81; and plate tuning, xviii, 78–80, 89–90, 94, 126–27, 159, 168, 181, 226; potential impact on violin market, 67–68; publications on, 68, 77; on quickness of response, 79–80; with Saunders, xviii, 62–69, 78–82, 94–95, 100, 151, 210; "Swiss Cheese" (Le Gruyère) violin, 168–70, 246–47; tap tone testing, 78–80, 89, 94, 126–27; in tone color, 64–67, 94; unusual instruments resulting from, 78; on varnishes, 80. *See also* science of violinmaking
Violin Society of America, 228
"Violins Old and New" (Saunders), 129
violin structure: bass bar, 56; bridge, 55–56; components of, 54–56; lack of flat surfaces in, 249; mysteries surrounding, 54–57, 84; sound post, 56, 250–51; and sound production, 55–56, 62–69, 93; S-shapes in, 57; wood types in, 55, 252
violin world: Hutchins's efforts to negotiate, 76; Hutchins's influence on, xvii, 184–85, 191, 203, 246–48, 251; as male-dominated, 248, 251. *See also* luthiers
virtuosos: influence of, 186–87, 224; and violin octet, 192–97
Vivaldi, Antonio, 187–88
Voltchek, Lydia, 216–20, 222
Vuillaume, Jean-Baptiste, xvi, 85–89, 155, 190–91, 199–200, 205

Wagener, Alice, 11–12, 17
Walter, David, 221, 232
Winternitz, Emanuel, 53, 119, 209–10
Wolfeboro, New Hampshire: Hutchins Consort in, 235; Hutchins's cabin at, 35–36, 39, 227, 243; Hutchins's late-life move to, 225–27; purchase of land in, 35. *See also* Conant Inn (Wolfeboro, NH)
wolf tones, 66–67, 73
Woodward School, Hutchins at, 17–19, 31
woodworking, Hutchins's interest in, 7, 9–10, 17–18, 38, 48
Wouters, Joris, 243
Wurlitzer, Rembert, 124–25, 137–38, 169, 201
Wurlitzer Company, 33, 48–49, 52, 67, 124–26, 200–201